Frommer's™

D0455670

Cape Town
day BY day™

1st Edition

by Lizzie Williams

Please return to
The Butlers

WILEY

A John Wiley and Sons, Ltd, Publication

Contents

15 Favorite Moments   1

1 The Best Full-Day Tours   7
The Best in One Day   8
The Best in Two Days   14
The Best in Three Days   20

2 The Best Special-Interest Tours   23
Cape Town's Apartheid History   24
Cape Town for Kids   26
Cape Town for Shopaholics   30
Gourmet Cape Town   34

3 The Best Neighborhood Walks   37
City Center   38
Government Avenue   44
Bo-Kaap to Green Point   50

4 The Best Shopping   55
Shopping Best Bets   56
Cape Town Shopping A to Z   60

5 Cape Town Outdoors   67
Cape Town Beaches   68
Cape Town Adventures   72
Cape Town Parks & Reserves   76

6 The Best Dining   79
Dining Best Bets   84
Cape Town Dining A to Z   85

7 The Best Nightlife   95
Nightlife Best Bets   98
Cape Town Nightlife A to Z   99

8 The Best Arts & Entertainment 105
Arts & Entertainment Best Bets 106
Arts & Entertainment A to Z 110

9 The Best Lodging 115
Lodging Best Bets 120
Cape Town Lodging A to Z 121

10 The Best Day Trips & Excursions 131
The Whale Coast 132
The Winelands 136
West Coast 142
Route 62 146
Where to Stay—Winelands 151
Where to Stay—West Coast 152
Where to Stay—Route 62 152

The Savvy Traveler 153
Before You Go 154
Getting There 157
Getting Around 158
Fast Facts 160
Cape Town: A Brief History 164
Tips on Dining 167
South African Words & Phrases 168
Recommended Books 170
Recommended South African Wines 171
Airline Numbers & Websites 173

Index 174

Copyright © 2009 John Wiley & Sons Ltd,
The Atrium, Southern Gate, Chichester,
West Sussex PO19 8SQ, England
Telephone (+44) 1243 779777

Email (for orders and customer service enquiries): cs-books@wiley.co.uk.
Visit our Home Page on www.wiley.com

UK Publisher: Sally Smith
Executive Project Editor: Daniel Mersey
Commissioning Editor: Fiona Quinn
Development Editor: Claire Baranowski
Content Editor: Erica Peters
Photo Research: Jill Emeny
Cartography: Jeremy Norton

Wiley also publishes its books in a variety of electronic formats. Some
content that appears in print may not be available in electronic books.

British Library Cataloguing in Publication Data

A catalogue record for this book is available from the British Library

ISBN: 978-0-470-72121-6

Typeset by Wiley Indianapolis Composition Services

Printed and bound in China by RR Donnelley

5 4 3 2 1

A Note from the Editorial Director

Organizing your time. That's what this guide is all about.

Other guides give you long lists of things to see and do and then expect you to fit the pieces together. The Day by Day guides are different. These guides tell you the best of everything, and then they show you how to see it *in the smartest, most time-efficient way*. Our authors have designed detailed itineraries organized by time, neighborhood, or special interest. And each tour comes with a bulleted map that takes you from stop to stop.

Hoping to enjoy the spectacular views from Table Mountain, tour the scenic Cape Peninsula, or visit the attractions at the famous V&A Waterfront? Are you looking forward to touring the historic winelands or spot whales or penguins around the coast? Whatever your interest or schedule, the Day by Days give you the smartest routes to follow. Not only do we take you to the top attractions, hotels, and restaurants, but we also help you access those special moments that locals get to experience—those "finds" that turn tourists into travelers.

The Day by Days are also your top choice if you're looking for one complete guide for all your travel needs. The best hotels and restaurants for every budget, the greatest shopping values, the wildest nightlife—it's all here.

Why should you trust our judgment? Because our authors personally visit each place they write about. They're an independent lot who say what they think and would never include places they wouldn't recommend to their best friends. They're also open to suggestions from readers. If you'd like to contact them, please send your comments our way at feedback@frommers.com, and we'll pass them on.

Enjoy your Day by Day guide—the most helpful travel companion you can buy. And have the trip of a lifetime.

Warm regards,

Kelly Regan

Kelly Regan, Editorial Director
Frommer's Travel Guides

About the Author

Lizzie Williams is a freelance travel writer based in Cape Town. Originally from London she was first introduced to Africa 15 years ago on an overland truck trip across the continent, and as a result became a tour leader for five years. Now a full-time author, she's written more than 20 guide books to countries in Africa and the Middle East, regularly contributes to travel magazines, and has written destination content for several websites including Kenya and Tanzania for Frommer's. When not on the road she enjoys the fabulousness of the 'Mother City' and is constantly reminded what a beautiful place it is to live.

An Additional Note

Please be advised that travel information is subject to change at any time—and this is especially true of prices. We therefore suggest that you write or call ahead for confirmation when making your travel plans. The authors, editors, and publisher cannot be held responsible for the experiences of readers while traveling. Your safety is important to us, however, so we encourage you to stay alert and be aware of your surroundings.

Star Ratings, Icons & Abbreviations

Every hotel, restaurant, and attraction listing in this guide has been ranked for quality, value, service, amenities, and special features using a **star-rating system.** Hotels, restaurants, attractions, shopping, and nightlife are rated on a scale of zero stars (recommended) to three stars (exceptional). In addition to the star-rating system, we also use a **kids icon** to point out the best bets for families. Within each tour, we recommend cafes, bars, or restaurants where you can take a break. Each of these stops appears in a shaded box marked with a coffee-cup-shaped bullet ☕.

The following **abbreviations** are used for credit cards:

AE	American Express	DISC	Discover	V	Visa
DC	Diners Club	MC	MasterCard		

Frommers.com

Now that you have this guidebook to help you plan a great trip, visit our website at **www.frommers.com** for additional travel information on more than 4,000 destinations. We update features regularly to give you instant access to the most current trip-planning information available. At Frommers.com, you'll find scoops on the best airfares, lodging rates, and car rental bargains. You can even book your travel online through our reliable travel booking partners.

A Note on Prices

In the 'Take a Break' and 'Best Bets' sections of this book, we have used a system of dollar signs to show a range of costs for 1 night in a hotel (the price of a double-occupancy room) or the cost of an entree at a restaurant. Use the following table to decipher the dollar signs:

Cost	Hotels	Restaurants
$	under $100	under $10
$$	$100–$200	$10–$20
$$$	$200–$300	$20–$30
$$$$	$300–$400	$30–$40
$$$$$	over $400	over $40

An Invitation to the Reader

In researching this book, we discovered many wonderful places—hotels, restaurants, shops, and more. We're sure you'll find others. Please tell us about them, so we can share the information with your fellow travelers in upcoming editions. If you were disappointed with a recommendation, we'd love to know that, too. Please write to:

Frommer's Cape Town Day by Day, 1st Edition
Wiley Publishing, Inc. • 111 River St. • Hoboken, NJ 07030-5774

15 Favorite
Moments

15 Favorite **Moments**

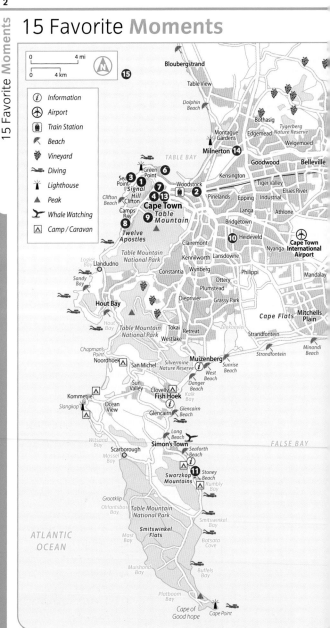

0 — 4 mi	
0 — 4 km	

⑮

Legend

- ⓘ Information
- ✈ Airport
- 🚇 Train Station
- 🏖 Beach
- 🍇 Vineyard
- 🤿 Diving
- 🗼 Lighthouse
- ▲ Peak
- 🐋 Whale Watching
- 🏕 Camp / Caravan

Bloubergstrand
Table View
Dolphin Beach
Montague Gardens
Edgemead
Bothasig
Tygerberg Nature Reserve
Welgemoed
Milnerton ⑭
Goodwood **Belleville**
TABLE BAY
Woodstock
Kensington
Tiger Valley
Elsies River
Sea Point ③ ①
Signal Hill
Green Point ⑥
⑦
Pinelands Epping Industrial
Clifton Beach Clifton
④ ⑬
Cape Town
② 🚇
Langa
Athlone
Camps Bay
⑨ **Table Mountain**
Bridgetown
Twelve Apostles ⑧
Clairemont
Kennilworth Lansdowne
⑩ Heideveld
Nyanga
Cape Town International Airport
Logies Bay Llandudno
Table Mountain National Park
Constantia Wynberg
Philippi
Mandalay
Sandy Bay
Ottery
Plumstead
Diepivier Grassy Park
Cape Flats
Hout Bay
Hout Bay **Table Mountain National Park** Tokai Retreat Westlake
Zeekoevlei
Strandfontein
Mitchells Plain
Chapman's Point
Noordhoek ⚑ San Michel
Silvermine Nature Reserve
Muizenberg ⓘ
West Beach
Sunrise Beach
Strandfontein
Minandi Beach
Kommetjie
Slangkop 🗼
Ocean View
Sun Valley
Clovelly ⚑ Danger Beach
Fish Hook ⓘ
Kalk Bay
Glencairn ⚑ Glencairn Beach
Witsand Bay
Scarborough
Mossel Bay
Long Beach
Simon's Town
Seaforth Beach ⚑
FALSE BAY
ⓘ
Swarzkop Mountains
⑪ Stoney Beach ⚑
Rumbly Bay
Grootklip
Olifantsbos Bay
Table Mountain National Park
Smitswinkel Flats
Smitswinkel Bay
Batsata Cove
ATLANTIC OCEAN
Mast Bay
Muishond Bay
Buffels Bay
Platboom Bay
Cape of Good hope
Cape Point 🗼

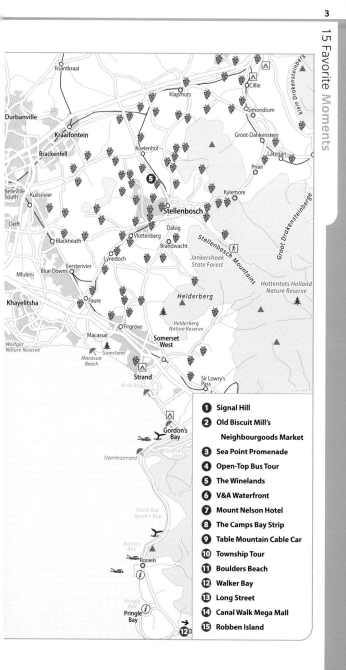

1 Signal Hill

2 Old Biscuit Mill's
   Neighbourgoods Market

3 Sea Point Promenade

4 Open-Top Bus Tour

5 The Winelands

6 V&A Waterfront

7 Mount Nelson Hotel

8 The Camps Bay Strip

9 Table Mountain Cable Car

10 Township Tour

11 Boulders Beach

12 Walker Bay

13 Long Street

14 Canal Walk Mega Mall

15 Robben Island

Cape Town is a city that's worth crossing the world for. Outdoor types head for mountains and beaches, food lovers to fabulous restaurants, history buffs to museums, shopaholics to malls, and night owls to fashionable bars and clubs. With its blend of influences and cultures and a beautiful setting under Table Mountain, you'll soon realize why it's known as South Africa's 'Mother City'.

① Watching the sunset from Signal Hill. Drive up Signal Hill, the highest place adjacent to Table Mountain. The grassy hillside at the top is a perfect place to spread out a picnic blanket. Enjoy a sundowner and watch Sea Point below come alive at night in a profusion of neon lights. See p 78.

② Nibbling at the Old Biscuit Mill's Neighbourgoods Market. The *in* place to be seen on a Saturday morning, this weekly market in Woodstock—where you can shop for organic food—serves a deliciously varied selection of homemade food. See p 35.

③ Strolling along the Sea Point Promenade. Mingle with the dog walkers, joggers, and rollerbladers on the promenade that stretches around Mouille Point and along Sea Point, and enjoy the crashing ocean and ever-present views of Robben Island and Table Mountain. See p 28.

④ Exploring Cape Town on an open-top bus. The fleet of City Sightseeing hop-on and hop-off open-top buses are the ideal way to see the sights if you don't want to drive. See p 12.

⑤ Tasting fine wines under oak trees in the winelands. Allocate a designated driver and spend the day visiting the beautiful vineyards around the historical towns of Stellenbosch, Paarl, and Franschhoek. See p 136.

⑥ Dining on South African seafood at the V&A Waterfront. With more than 70 top class restaurants, you'll be spoilt for choice for dining at the V&A. Although just about every global cuisine is represented, don't miss South Africa's delicious seafood. See p 10.

City Sightseeing bus on the road up to the Lower Cableway Station.

Vines on the Simonsig estate.

7 Indulging in afternoon tea at the Mount Nelson Hotel. Sit in the beautiful drawing room full of antiques, mirrors, and paintings or outside on the shady terrace for an all-you-can-eat high tea at this luxury hotel. *See p 127.*

8 Sipping a sundowner with the beautiful people. The Camps Bay strip opposite the beach is Cape Town's trendiest place to be seen. The long line of restaurants, bars, and clubs are filled with beach babes and surf rats during the day and glow in cool neon in the evening. *See p 69,* **2**.

9 Riding the dizzying cable car to the top of Table Mountain. A Cape Town must- do is to stand on top of Table Mountain, which rises more than 1,000m (3,000ft) above the city, and take in the awe-inspiring views. The cable car takes just a few minutes and rotates on its way to the top. *See p 10.*

10 Learning about South Africa's past on a township tour. To capture all the facets of Cape Town, take a half-day guided tour to the lively townships on the Cape Flats—the guides will explain what it was like living under apartheid rule. *See p 25.*

11 Staring a penguin in the eye on Boulders Beach. This colony, some 3,000 strong, *owns* this beach, but they do allow visitors along a boardwalk to watch them splash around in the waves, waddle along the sand, and snooze among the boulders. *See p 18.*

12 Watching whales breach and blow in Walker Bay. Hermanus is often

Stare a penguin in the eye at Boulders Beach.

Long Street nightlife.

cited as the best place in the world for land-based whale watching. In the season (July to November) the sheltered Walker Bay in front of town is full of Southern Right whales that have come to breed and calve. *See p 132*.

⑬ **Wandering the length of Long Street.** Cape Town's quirkiest and most lively street has some wonderful Victorian architecture, but the real reason to go is to experience its urban energy; the trendy boutiques, secondhand bookshops, quaint cafés, and in the evening, raucous nightlife. *See p 43*.

⑭ **Shopping 'til you drop in a mega mall.** Spend a day at Canal Walk, one of the country's largest malls. Giant shopping malls are big business in South Africa, and like all other malls, they have restaurants, cinemas, and other entertainment. 'Shoppertainment' is the best way to describe them. *See p 32*.

⑮ **Reflecting on Robben Island.** This is one of Cape Town's most popular excursions. Learn about the prison home of Nelson Mandela. From here, look back to Cape Town for one of the most incredible views of the city. *See p 12*. ●

The Best **in One Day**

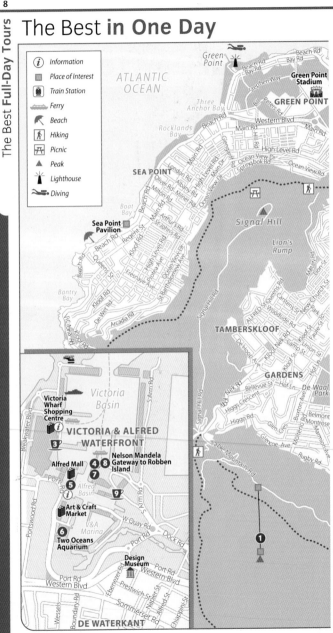

- (i) Information
- ▢ Place of Interest
- 🚋 Train Station
- ⟷ Ferry
- 🏄 Beach
- 🚶 Hiking
- 🏕 Picnic
- ▲ Peak
- 💡 Lighthouse
- 🤿 Diving

ATLANTIC OCEAN

Green Point

Beach Rd
Bay Rd

Beach Rd
Bay Rd

Stephen Way

Green Point Stadium

Bill Peters Dr

GREEN POINT

Three Anchor Bay

Western Blvd

Main Rd

Main Rd

Rocklands Bay

Beach Rd

Main Rd

High Level Rd

Glengariff Rd

High Level Rd

Springbok Rd

Ocean View Rd

SEA POINT

London Rd

Albany Rd

High Level Rd

Ocean View Rd

Oliver Rd

Milner Rd

Boat Bay

Beach Rd

Milton Rd

Main Rd

St Arthur's Rd

St John's Rd

Signal Hill

Sea Point Pavilion

Regent St

Kloof Rd

High Level Rd

Ocean View Dr

St Bartholomew Ave

Lion's Rump

Queens St

Fresnaye Ave

Victoria Rd

M'Kenzie St

Lions St

Beach Rd

Kloof Rd

De Wet Rd

Arcadia Rd

Signal Hill Rd

ALFRED

Queens Rd

Cartens Rd

New Church St

Park St

Bantry Bay

Kloof Rd

Woodside Rd

Victoria Rd

De Hoop Ave

Kloof Nek Rd

Camp St

Union St

Haste St

TAMBERSKLOOF

Signal Hill Rd

GARDENS

Bellevue St

Hof Ln

De Waal Park

Higgs Crescent

Buxton Ave

Belmont

Higge Rd

Glen Cres

Glencoe Ave

Montero Ave

Montrose

Marmion Ave

Table Mountain Rd

Rugby Rd

🚶

🚶

▲①
▢

Victoria Basin

🚢

Victoria Wharf Shopping Centre (i)

VICTORIA & ALFRED WATERFRONT

S Arm Rd

▢③

Alfred Mall ④⑧ **Nelson Mandela Gateway to Robben Island**

⑤⑦

(i) Alfred Basin

Art & Craft Market ⑨

S Arm Rd

Portswood Rd

Port Rd

Breakwater Rd

V&A Marina

⑥ **Two Oceans Aquarium**

W Quay Rd

Dock Rd

Port Rd

Design Museum 🏛

Port Rd
Western Blvd

Port Rd
Western Blvd

Prestwich St

Ebenezer Rd

Napier St

Sommerset Rd

Chiappini St

Wessels

Boundary Rd

Alfred St

DE WATERKANT

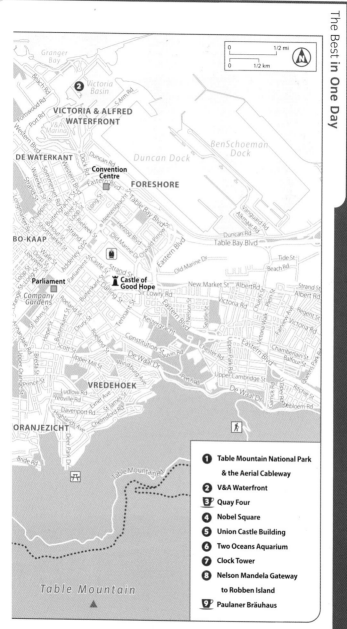

1 Table Mountain National Park
  & the Aerial Cableway
2 V&A Waterfront
3 Quay Four
4 Nobel Square
5 Union Castle Building
6 Two Oceans Aquarium
7 Clock Tower
8 Nelson Mandela Gateway
  to Robben Island
9 Paulaner Bräuhaus

This 'greatest hits' tour takes in Cape Town's most popular attractions. Begin with a dizzying cableway ride up to the top of Table Mountain, followed by a glimpse of South Africa's fascinating marine life in the aquarium. After a stroll around the historic V&A Waterfront, take the ferry to Robben Island for a look at South Africa's somber past. START: **Lower Cableway Station.**

① ★★★ kids Table Mountain National Park & the Aerial Cableway. Although the Table Mountain National Park covers the whole Cape Peninsula to Cape Point, in the city center it includes the top of Table Mountain. Rising a sheer 1,073m (3,520ft) above the coastal plain, with a perfectly flat top and occasional 'tablecloth' of swirling white cloud, this is perhaps the most evocative backdrop of any city in the world, and a beautiful wilderness bang in the middle of a bustling city. The cable car takes 10 minutes to ascend. Once at the top allow some time to follow the network of paths to the viewpoints. The vegetation is mostly *fynbos* ('fine bush' in Afrikaans), a sort of heath-like plant, and in summer there's a profusion of wild flowers. You may see *dassies* (rock hyrax), creatures that look like large guinea pigs. ⏱ *2 hrs. Take a taxi or a City Sightseeing bus (see p 12) to the Lower*

Cableway Station, Tafelberg Rd. ☎ 021-424-8181. www.table mountain.net. Return/single R145/74 adults, R76/38 (under-18s), R370 family ticket, 2 adults, 2 kids. Daily, times change monthly depending on times of sunrise and sunset. The first car up is usually at 8–8.30am, the last car down is as late as 9pm in summer and as early as 6pm in winter. Closed 2 weeks in July/August for maintenance.

Take a taxi back to the V&A.

② ★★★ kids V&A Waterfront. Named after Queen Victoria and her son Alfred, this harbor was originally built in 1860, after Alfred ceremoniously poured the first load of rubble into the sea. In 1992 it was completely refurbished and is now South Africa's top leisure, shopping, and dining attraction, receiving in excess of 10 million visitors a year. Many of the Victorian warehouses and dock buildings have

Victoria Wharf shopping mall at the V&A Waterfront.

Table Mountain Facts & Figures

The Aerial Cableway, originally opened in 1929, takes less than 10 minutes to ascend Table Mountain and has taken some 18 million people to the top to date. Today's cableway, installed in 1997, has floors that rotate allowing a 360° view, so it doesn't matter where you are standing. Always phone ahead or check the website to see if it's running, because it can close in misty or windy weather without notice. As such, you can't pre-book, which can mean lengthy queues in summer.

Check the website because there are often specials; for example in summer it's half-price after 6pm, or in winter two children under 18 can travel free with one adult.

To walk up to the top from the Lower Cableway Station, allow at least 3 hours and you need to be fit and prepared for rapid changes in weather.

been wonderfully restored and the modern Victoria Wharf is the city's premier shopping mall. *2–3 hrs to take in the attractions listed. Alfred and Victoria Basins.* ☎ *021-408-7600. www.waterfront.co.za. Shops daily 9am–9pm.*

3 ★★ **Quay Four.** This is a sociable family pub with a large outdoor deck and great V&A Waterfront views. Grab a good value seafood combo lunch served in a cast iron frying pan or a pot of creamy mussels, and look out for seals swimming in the water below. *Quay 4.* ☎ *021-419-2008. www.quay4.co.za. $$.*

4 ★ **Nobel Square.** Stop here to admire the four life-size statues of South Africa's Nobel Peace Prize laureates: **Albert Luthuli** (1960), **Desmond Tutu** (1984), and **FW De Klerk** and **Nelson Mandela**, who jointly won in 1993. Stand back and take a photo of the four of them with Table Mountain in the background. *5 min. Alfred Basin. www.nobelsquare.com.*

5 **Union Castle Building.** This imposing structure was built in 1919 by the acclaimed architect Herbert Baker (1862–1946) as the HQ for Union Castle, the company that ran mail ships between South Africa and Britain between 1900 and 1977. Upstairs, it now houses a (free) small, mildly distracting **Maritime Centre** museum with some model ships, photographs, and memorabilia from the mail ship era. *20 min.*

Quay Four restaurant.

Statue of Archbishop Desmond Tutu at Nobel Square.

Alfred Wharf. ☎ *021-405-2880. www.iziko.org.za. Daily 10am–5pm.*

❻ ★★★ kids Two Oceans Aquarium. This critically acclaimed aquarium is home to more than 3,000 marine species, with the focus on the unique underwater environment created by the meeting of the Atlantic and Indian oceans in the Cape. Look for wild seals in the bay through a glass panel, and take youngsters to the touch pool where they can pick up starfish and sea slugs. The highlight is the massive predator tank where you can watch ragged-tooth sharks, manta rays, and barracudas glide past in the neon-lit blue water. Qualified divers can dive in the tank (see p 75, ⓯). Also look out for the giant kelp tank—watching the slithery kelp swing drunkenly among the colored lights is quite mesmerizing. ⏱ *1 hr. Dock Rd, V&A Waterfront.* ☎ *021-418-3823. www.aquarium. co.za. R82 adults, R65 kids (aged 14–17), R38 (aged 4–13), free for under 4s. Daily 9.30am–6pm.*

❼ Clock Tower. This bright red, octagonal clock tower is reached by crossing the swing bridge that links with Alfred Basin and opens to allow yachts out to sea. It was built in 1882 as the port captain's office. Adjacent is the Clock Tower Centre (see p 31), with its many shops and restaurants, a VAT Refund desk (see p 66), and a helpful branch of Cape Town Tourism (see p 42). ⏱ *15 min. Alfred Basin.*

❽ ★★★ Nelson Mandela Gateway to Robben Island. Robben Island is today a World Heritage Site, but from the 17th century, when it was a leper colony, to 1966, when the last prisoner left the notorious maximum-security prison later located here, it was a place of banishment. It's best known for being the place where political prisoners

City Sightseeing

City Sightseeing (☎ 021-511-6000; www.citysightseeing.co.za) runs a fleet of smart, red, hop-on hop-off open top buses that operate on set routes around the city and is one of the best ways to get between key tourist sites. Buses come by every 30 minutes on the Red Route and every 60 minutes on the longer Blue Route. One-day tickets are R120/60 for adults/kids (under-15s), two-day tickets are R200/120. The booking office is outside the Two Oceans Aquarium at the V&A Waterfront.

Nelson Mandela

As leader of the banned African National Congress (ANC), Nelson Mandela was arrested in 1963 and sentenced to life imprisonment on Robben Island. He was transferred to other prisons on the mainland from 1982 until he was finally released in 1990. With then President FW De Klerk, he negotiated the dismantling of apartheid, for which they jointly earned the Nobel Peace Prize in 1993. Democratic elections were held in 1994 and Mandela became the country's first black president. Affectionately known as Madiba (his clan name) and adored by all South Africans, he stepped down as President in 1999 but continued as an activist for many causes, namely the fight against HIV/AIDS. He retired from public life on his 90th birthday in 2008.

were jailed during the apartheid era, the most famous of whom is Nelson Mandela. Ferries take 30 minutes and leave from the Nelson Mandela Gateway at the Clock Tower. Take a look around the small museum while waiting to embark. Once out to sea enjoy magnificent views of the city and Table Mountain. The excursion includes a guided bus

Two Oceans Aquarium at the V&A Waterfront.

tour around the island, which visits the leper graveyard, the limestone quarry where Mandela and other prisoners crushed rocks all day, and the village where the wardens lived. Inside the prison, you can peek into Mandela's tiny cell and try and imagine how one of the world's greatest statesmen lived here for the majority of his 27 years of incarceration. Book this excursion well in advance in high season and always phone ahead first because this is an activity that is weather-dependent.
🕐 *3½ hrs. Clock Tower.* 📞 *021-419-1300. www.robben-island.org. R180 adults, R90 kids (under-18s). Ferries depart daily at 9am, 11am, 1pm, and 3pm.*

🍺 ★★ **Paulaner Bräuhaus**. This popular German beerhouse is a hop, skip, and a jump away from the Nelson Mandela Gateway. Drink a cold one here while reflecting on your Robben Island experience. Beers are home brewed—try the yeasty Weissbier—and food is all things sausagey. *Clock Tower.* 📞 *021-418-9999. $$.*

The Best **in Two Days**

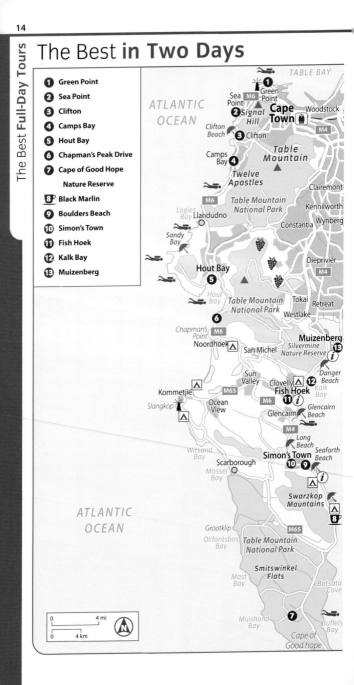

1 Green Point
2 Sea Point
3 Clifton
4 Camps Bay
5 Hout Bay
6 Chapman's Peak Drive
7 Cape of Good Hope
   Nature Reserve
8 Black Marlin
9 Boulders Beach
10 Simon's Town
11 Fish Hoek
12 Kalk Bay
13 Muizenberg

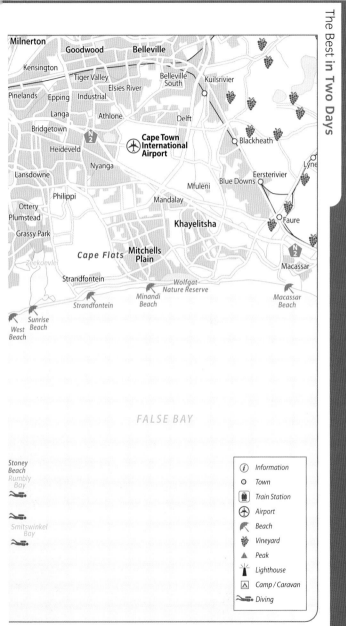

Milnerton
Goodwood
Belleville
Kensington
Tiger Valley
Belleville South
Kuilsrivier
Pinelands
Epping
Elsies River
Industrial
Langa
Athlone
Delft
Bridgetown
Heideveld
Cape Town International Airport
Blackheath
Lyne
Lansdowne
Nyanga
Eersterivier
Philippi
Mfuleni
Blue Downs
Ottery
Plumstead
Mandalay
Faure
Grassy Park
Khayelitsha
Zeekoevlei
Cape Flats
Mitchells Plain
Macassar
Strandfontein
Wolfgat Nature Reserve
Minandi Beach
Macassar Beach
Strandfontein
Sunrise Beach
West Beach

FALSE BAY

Stoney Beach
Rumbly Bay
Smitswinkel Bay

ⓘ	Information
○	Town
🚉	Train Station
✈	Airport
🏖	Beach
🍇	Vineyard
▲	Peak
🗼	Lighthouse
△	Camp / Caravan
🤿	Diving

The Cape Peninsula stretches from Table Mountain down to the tips of Cape Point and the Cape of Good Hope. A day's driving tour will take in all the beauty of this area, from the ritzy Atlantic Seaboard suburbs, to quaint False Bay fishing towns, gorgeous beaches, and the penguins at Boulders Beach. This is an easy self-drive tour, or book with a tour operator. START: **M61 Somerset Road.**

❶ kids Green Point. The main attraction here is Green Point Stadium (see walking tour on p 50 for more details). As Somerset Road leaves the city, you first pass through **De Waterkant**, a picturesque quarter with historical, characterful artisan houses that are for the most part smart holiday cottages. As you drive down the main road, the stadium is to your right and high-rise apartment blocks on the lower slopes of **Lions Head** are on your left. ⏱ *20 min to drive through.*

❷ kids Sea Point. Main Road (M61) continues through Sea Point, again a crop of high rises and one of the most densely populated areas in the city. Many hotels and guesthouses are located here and it has a holiday atmosphere. ⏱ *15 min to drive through.*

❸ kids ★★★ Clifton. Now you've reached the stomping ground of the rich and famous where the most expensive real estate in Cape Town is found. The beaches here are spectacular and there are sweeping ocean views. To your right as you drive along are the four Clifton Beaches (p 70): **First Beach** is the largest, and popular for games of soccer or volleyball; **Second Beach** is where the beautiful people pose in their Prada sunglasses; **Third Beach** is a gay venue; while **Fourth Beach** is favored by families. ⏱ *10 min to drive past.*

Now take the M6 to:

❹ kids ★★★ Camps Bay. After you've passed Clifton, the stunning half-moon beach at Camps Bay comes into view. With its line of restaurants and bars along Victoria

The beautiful beaches at Clifton.

Cape Peninsula Practicalities

After a full first day in Cape Town, this is an easy one-day self-drive tour, but I recommend you leave the city center early enough to get to Hout Bay to catch one of the morning boats if you want to see the seals on Duiker Island—a 45-minute straight drive without stops.

Plan where you want to go for lunch too—many restaurants on the Peninsula are listed in Chapter 6, The Best Dining (see p 79).

Alternatively, you can join a tour, which costs in the region of R600. Daytrippers (☎ 021-511-4766; www.daytrippers.co.za) and Downhill Adventures (☎ 021-422-0388; www.downhilladventures.com) also include a couple of hours of cycling on mountain bikes in the Cape of Good Hope Nature Reserve.

The more sedate can opt to go with Cape Rainbow, (☎ 021-448-3117; www.tourcapers.co.za), Hylton Ross (☎ 021-511-1784; www.hyltonross.com), or Springbok Atlas (☎ 021-460-4700; www.springbokatlas.com).

Road, well-toned bodies playing volleyball on the sand, and a clutch of white-washed mansions with glittering swimming pools climbing up the hill, Camps Bay has a wonderful Californian feel. ⏱ *10 min to drive through.*

⑤ kids ★★ Hout Bay. The road from Camps Bay to Hout Bay has the magnificent **Twelve Apostles** (a chain of mountains that make up the spine of the peninsula) on the left and the crashing waves and boulder-strewn coastline of the Atlantic on the right. Park at Hout Bay's harbor and admire the colorful fishing boats, and take a 35-minute round boat trip to **Duiker Island**, where thousands of Cape fur seals bask. Be warned, they can be a bit smelly. ⏱ *1 hr. Drumbeat Charters, Hout Bay Harbor.* ☎ *021-791-4441. www.drumbeatcharters.co.za. R50 adults, R25 kids. Boats depart daily 8.30am, 9.15am, 10am, and 10.45am.*

⑥ ★★★ kids Chapman's Peak Drive. With sheer cliffs both above and below the road and with 114 bends, this dramatic 9km (5.6 miles) road passes over the rocky outcrop of Chapman's Peak. In parts the road has, incredibly, been carved into the mountain. Pull over at one of the lookouts as you descend for views of wide and sandy Noordhoek Beach. The road frequently closes in bad weather so check it's open before departing. ⏱ *45 min to drive through.* ☎ *021-790-9163. www.chapmanspeakdrive.co.za. R24 per car.*

Boats in Hout Bay harbor with Chapman's Peak Drive in the background.

Statue of Just Nuisance at Simon's Town.

From Chapman's Peak, follow the M65 via Kommetjie and Scarborough to:

7 ★★★ **kids** **Cape of Good Hope Nature Reserve.** Part of the Table Mountain National Park (see p 10, **1**), this reserve encompasses 7,750 hectares (19,150 acres) of low-lying *fynbos* vegetation, deserted beaches, storm-battered cliffs, and jaw-dropping ocean views. Animals found here include a number of species of antelope, Cape mountain zebra, ostriches, and baboons. At the southern tip is the beach at The Cape of Good Hope. You'll see it to the right of the road, and it was so named by early Portuguese sailors because rounding it was seen as a milestone on a voyage to the Far East. At the very end is **Cape Point**. Walk up the series of paved footpaths or ride the funicular railway to the lighthouse at the top for sweeping views of False Bay. In the car park are some souvenir shops and the Two Oceans Restaurant. The **Cape Point Ostrich Farm** is near the entrance. ⏱ *2 hrs.* ☎ *021-701-8692. www.sanparks.org. R70 adults, R10 kids (under 12). Daily Oct–Mar 6am–6pm, Apr–Sep 7am–5pm. Funicular railway R32 return, R24 single.*

Head 15 minutes along the M4 to Miller's Point:

8 ★★ **Black Marlin.** This is a popular late-lunch stop for seafood on the Cape Peninsula tour. Start with prawns or calamari and then ask about the catch-of-the-day. The lovely outside terrace is a good vantage spot to watch whales in season (June to November). *Main Rd, Miller's Point.* ☎ *021-786-1621. www.blackmarlin.co.za. $$$.*

9 ★★★ **kids** **Boulders Beach.** Look a penguin in the eye and watch these comical little characters surfing in the waves, waddling along the beach, or simply standing alone on a rock contemplating life. A visitor's center tells you all you need to know about African penguins and a boardwalk takes you down to the beach to see the little fellows. Rather staggeringly, the colony has grown from just two breeding pairs in 1982 to more than 3,000 penguins today. ⏱ *1 hr.* ☎ *021-786-2329. www.sanparks.org. R30 adults, R10 kids. Daily Oct–Mar 8am–6.30pm, Apr–Sep 8am–5pm.*

10 ★★ **kids** **Simon's Town.** Established in 1743 as an alternative port to Table Bay during windy Cape winters, this town features an attractive line of Victorian buildings

African penguin colony at Boulders Beach.

Fishing boat in Kalk Bay.

along the main street, and the Quay-side Centre is a modern mall with shops and restaurants. Look out for the statue of Just Nuisance—a Great Dane dog who, in the 1930s and 1940s, would guide inebriated sailors home and would get in the way by lying across gangplanks. He is the only (sea) dog in the world to have been given a military funeral. ⏱ *30 min.*

⓫ **kids** **Fish Hoek.** There's not much to detain you in Fish Hoek, but the beach here has fine white sand and is good for swimming. Sea temperatures here are lower than the Atlantic Seaboard. ⏱ *20 min to drive through.*

⓬ ★★ **kids** **Kalk Bay.** This is one of the most attractive fishing villages on the False Bay coast. Many of the Victorian buildings have been converted into shops selling antiques, gifts, furniture, books, and bric-a-brac and are well worth a browse. There are also a number of cafés and restaurants to be found here. Between Kalk Bay and Muizenberg (see ⓭) look out for the sign on the left to Boyes Drive— this road takes only 10 minutes to Muizenberg and, as an alternative to the often-busy lower coast road, offers great views of False Bay. ⏱ *45 min.*

⓭ **kids** **Muizenberg.** This is the last town on False Bay, but it is a faded, scruffy resort without much appeal. However the beach (see p 71) is magnificent, with powdery white sand sloping down to the rolling waves. Look out too for the famous, postcard-pretty row of brightly painted beach huts. It is a popular surfing spot; so much so that a shark-spotting team is deployed here. From Muizenberg it's a 30-minute drive back to central Cape Town on the M3 Highway. ⏱ *15 min to drive through.*

Muizenberg Beach.

The Best **in Three Days**

1. Rhodes Memorial
2. Rhodes Memorial Restaurant
3. Irma Stern Museum
4. Kirstenbosch National Botanical Garden
5. Fynbos Deli
6. Groot Constantia
7. Klein Constantia
8. Constantia Uitsig

- *i*   Information
- *Beach*
- *Diving*
- *Lighthouse*
- *Peak*
- *Camp / Caravan*

This tour is best taken on a sunny day, when you can really enjoy the scenery at Kirstenbosch National Botanical Garden and the wine estates in Constantia Valley. The vineyards here were originally planted to provide wine for sailors on passing ships—red wine was drunk to fight off scurvy. START: **Take the M3 out of the city.**

① ★★ Rhodes Memorial. Built on the spot where Cecil John Rhodes (1853–1902) used to sit and look over early Cape Town when he was prime minister of the Cape (1890–95), this impressive granite memorial was built by Sir Herbert Baker and Sir Francis Macey in 1912. The 49 steps—one for each year of Rhodes' short life—are flanked by four bronze lions with a statue of Rhodes on horseback at the base. The views here over the northern suburbs and Cape Flats are outstanding and there are a number of footpaths leading up **Devil's Peak**. ⏱ *45 min. Clearly signposted off Rhodes Dr (M3), Rondebosch.* ☎ *021-689-9151. www.rhodesmemorial. co.za. Admission free. Nov–Apr 7am–7pm, May–Oct 8am–6pm.*

②ᴾ Rhodes Memorial Restaurant. This lovely spot behind the Memorial has outside tables set among blue hydrangeas. It serves

View from Rhodes Memorial.

breakfast, light lunches, good coffees, and wine. The blueberry cheesecake is to die for, or ask the waiter when the scones are coming out of the oven. ☎ *021-689-9151. $.*

On the other side of the M3:

③ Irma Stern Museum. Located in the house she lived in for 38 years, this museum displays paintings of acclaimed South African artist Irma Stern (1894–1966), plus her fine antique furniture and tribal artifacts collected from across Africa. Her portraits and landscapes are quite striking but you may find the religious paintings a little disturbing. ⏱ *30 min. Cecil Rd, Rosebank.* ☎ *021-685-5686. www.irmastern.co.za. Admission R10 adults, R5 kids. Tues–Sat 10am–5pm.*

Back on the M3, take the turnoff on to the M63 to:

④ kids ★★★ Kirstenbosch National Botanical Garden. Cecil Rhodes presented the people of South Africa with this land in 1895, and the gardens opened in 1913. This is South Africa's oldest botanical garden, in a delightful setting on the sheltered eastern contours of Table Mountain (see p 78, **⑥**). The manicured lawns, flower and herb beds, orchards, and cycad and aloe gardens join seamlessly with forests full of waterfalls and mountain *fynbos* on the higher slopes. During summer, don't miss the Sunday concerts on the lawns (see p 111). There are two restaurants, and you can book guided tours by golf cart. ⏱ *2–3 hrs. Rhodes Dr, Newlands.* ☎ *021-799-8783. www.sanbi.org. Admission R32 adults,*

Kirstenbosch National Botanical Garden on the eastern slopes of Table Mountain.

R10 children (aged 6–17), free for under-6s. Sep–Mar 8am–7pm (later for concerts), Apr–Aug 8am–6pm.

5 **Fynbos Deli.** Grab a bite to eat at the Fynbos deli in the Kirstenbosch gardens, and fill up before heading off to the wine estates, or pack a picnic to take with you. ☎ 021-762-9585. $.

Take the M63, going southwest, turn left onto M41 and follow signs for:

6 ★★★ **Groot Constantia.** Founded in 1685, this is South Africa's oldest wine estate and one of its most beautiful, with commanding Cape Dutch-style whitewashed buildings, established gardens, and a

sweeping driveway lined with oaks, all flanked by rows of grapes. Check out the visitor's center, the museum in the manor house (which is full of period furniture), taste some of the wines, or go on a cellar tour. ⏱ *1 hr. Groot Constantia Rd, Constantia.* ☎ *021-794-5128. www.groot constantia.co.za. Admission is free to the estate, R10 museum, R25 wine tasting, R30 cellar tours. Sep–Mar 8am–7pm, Apr–Aug 8am–6pm.*

7 ★ **Klein Constantia.** This attractive, hilly estate, which dates back to 1689, is famous for its dessert wine, which reputedly was Napoleon's favorite tipple. Its tasting center has good views of False Bay. ⏱ *30 min. Klein Constantia Rd, Constantia.* ☎ *021-794-5188. www. kleinconstantia.com. Tasting R25. Mon–Fri 9am–5pm, Sat 9am–1pm.*

Follow the M42 for 2.5km until you see the sign on the right for:

8 ★★ **Constantia Uitsig.** This beautiful estate, where the lines of vines stretch up the mountainside, was originally part of Groot Constantia (see **6**). The Cape Dutch-style manor house was built in 1894, and now, as well as wine tasting, it offers luxury accommodation (see p 124) and the award-winning La Colombe restaurant (see p 90). ⏱ *30 min. Spaanschemat Rd, Constantia.* ☎ *021-794-1810. www. constantia-uitsig.com. Tasting free. Mon–Fri 9am–5pm, Sat–Sun 10am–5pm.* ●

View of the eastern side of Table Mountain from Constantia Uitsig.

Cape Town's Apartheid History

Map legend:
- (i) Information
- ⬕ Beach
- ⬳ Diving
- 🗼 Lighthouse
- ▲ Peak

1 District Six Museum
2 District Six Museum Café
3 Townships

Apartheid policies (apartheid means 'being apart' in Afrikaans) governed South Africa from 1948 until 1994, and affected every facet of life, including where people lived, with the Group Areas Act assigning separate and inferior areas to non-whites. Learn this history on a township tour, beginning with a visit to the excellent District Six Museum. START: **City Center.**

1 ★★★ District Six Museum. In the 1950s and 1960s, **District Six** was a vibrant, cosmopolitan neighborhood known for its jazz music, which attracted a lively mix of people, including bohemian whites. Its very success in showing that mixed races could live together unhappily proved to be its downfall. In 1966, some 60,000 black and colored residents were forcibly relocated to the **Cape Flats** by the government

Street signs serve as a reminder of homes razed to the grounds in District Six.

Township Tour Operators

Half-day tours cost in the region of R360 per person. Some of the better ones are Andulela (☎ 021-790-2592; www.andulela.com); Cape Capers (☎ 021-448-3117; www.tourcapers.co.za); and Zibonele Tours (☎ 021-551-4263; www.ziboneletours.com).

and the suburb was razed to the ground. This museum brings District Six evocatively to life using photographs, original street signs, and audio and video accounts of former residents, and shows how the Group Areas Act tore communities apart. Township tours include a brief stop at the museum, although I suggest you visit independently to fully absorb everything. ⏱ 90 min. 25a Buitenkant St. ☎ 021-461-8745. www.districtsix.co.za. Admission R30 adults, R5 kids. Mon 9am–3pm, Tues–Sat 9am–4pm.

2 **District Six Museum Café.** Grab a coffee and a koeksister—a spongy, syrupy traditional Cape Malay donut dusted with cinnamon—from the museum's café and then browse in the excellent bookshop. $.

3 ★★ **Townships.** Tours drive out of the city to the Cape Flats and through the formal townships (proper houses) of **Langa** and **Guguletu** and the informal settlements (shacks) of **Crossroads** and **Khayelitsha**. At the latter there's an opportunity to walk around and meet some locals, and perhaps visit a school, *shebeen* (pub), craft outlet, or even a *sangoma* (a traditional African healer). These tours offer an informative insight into the lives of a substantial part of Cape Town's population, and part of the tour costs go towards community projects. ⏱ 2–3 hrs.

The acclaimed District Six Museum.

Cape Town for Kids

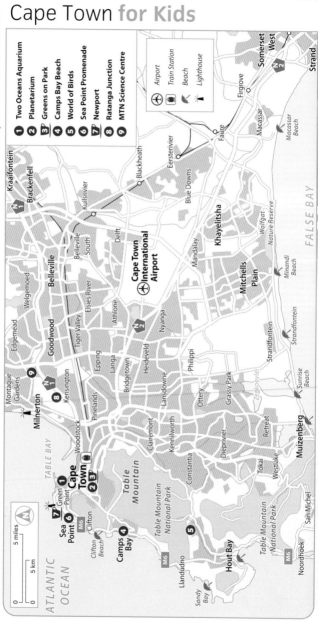

1 Two Oceans Aquarium
2 Planetarium
3 Greens on Park
4 Camps Bay Beach
5 World of Birds
6 Sea Point Promenade
7 Newport
8 Ratanga Junction
9 MTN Science Centre

Airport
Train Station
Beach
Lighthouse

Cape Town is perfect for family holidays and many Cape Town activities not listed here are still exciting for kids—taking the cableway up Table Mountain (p 10) or visiting the penguins (p 18) for example. This tour offers different options at the end, which can be added to some of the other tours listed in this book.
START: **V&A Waterfront.**

1 kids ★★★ Two Oceans Aquarium. The aquarium at the V&A Waterfront was built with children in mind, and they love seeing penguins, seals, and sharks close up. Activity books focus on environmental issues and youngsters can dabble in the touch pool. ⏱ *90 min. See p 12,* **16**.

From the V&A Waterfront, the Planetarium in the city center is a 10-minute drive.

2 kids ★★ Planetarium. Every weekend, Davy the Dragon holds special kids' (for 5- to 10-year-olds) shows at the Planetarium. Davy provides an entertaining early-learning lesson on astronomy so that he can become 'the best flying dragon ever'. The Planetarium's other shows are suitable for teenagers and first-time star-gazing adults. ⏱ *1 hr. Admission R6 kids, R10 adults accompanying kids. Noon, Sat and Sun. See p 49,* **15**.

Sunset on Camps Bay Beach.

3 ★★ Greens on Park. A short stroll from the Planetarium and just off Kloof Street, kids will enjoy the all-day breakfasts, tasty pizzas, and gourmet burgers here and you can sit outside on a sunny day. *5 Park Rd, Gardens.* ☎ *021-422-4415. $–$$.*

From the city center, drive 10 minutes over Kloof Nek Road to:

4 kids ★★★ Camps Bay Beach. This postcard-perfect beach has powdery white sand (perfect for building sand castles), and the ocean is a stunning aquamarine color. The Atlantic is too cold for swimming, but kids can paddle in the tidal pool and families can relax at the picnic spots among the rocks at the south end of the beach. ⏱ *1–2 hrs. Victoria Rd, Camps Bay.*

City Sightseeing Tour Bus

You can visit all the attractions on the Cape Town with Kids tour on the City Sightseeing bus (p 12). From the stop outside the Two Oceans Aquarium (p 12), take the Red Route to the Planetarium and continue to Camps Bay. From there, switch to the Blue Route to Hout Bay and the World of Birds. Then you can take the Blue Route back to the city and get off at one of the stops on the Promenade in Sea Point. Finish by jumping on again to the stop outside the Two Oceans Aquarium; or alternatively you could walk—the 'prom' is stroller/pedestrian welcoming.

Continue south to Hout Bay on the M6.

5 kids ★ **World of Birds.** Here you can walk through several large aviaries with more than 3,000 species of birds. Look out for the elegant crowned crane, South Africa's national bird. There are also a number of species of small mammals such as comical meerkats, bat-eared foxes, and cheeky little squirrel monkeys, which have been known to steal earrings or pens from visitors. The City Sightseeing bus stops

A crowned crane at the World of Birds.

here (p 12). ⏱ *1–2 hrs. Valley Rd, Hout Bay.* ☎ *021-790-2730. www. worldofbirds.org.za. Admission R59 adults, R37 kids (aged 4–17). Daily 9am–5pm.*

Follow the M6 back to the city along the coast via Sea Point or on a rainy day head to MTN Science Centre (**9**). Teenagers might want to head to Ratanga Junction (**8**).

6 kids ★★ **Sea Point Promenade.** Take the kids for a walk from the candy-striped lighthouse at Mouille Point (see p 53, **11**) along the 6km (3.7 miles) promenade to the open-air swimming pool. You can enjoy ocean views from the promenade, or climb down to the beach to explore the rock pools at low tide. Near the lighthouse is a putt-putt (mini-golf) course with 18 holes. The promenade itself is lined with several play areas with swings and climbing frames, and there's a mini Blue Train near the lighthouse. Indulge yourself with an ice cream from one of the promenade vendors. The crystal-clear Olympic-sized Sea Point Swimming Pool, positioned right on the edge of the ocean, has two splash pools for youngsters and a springboard diving pool (and temperatures can be warmer than the sea). ⏱ *2–3 hrs.*

Beach Rd, Sea Point Putt-putt.
📞 *021-434-6805. Admission R10.50.
Daily 9am–9pm. Swimming pool*
📞 *021-434-3341. Admission R9.50
adults, R6 children (under-16s). Daily
Oct–April 7am–7pm, April–Oct
8.30am–5pm.*

7 Newport. Perfect for picking
up picnic items, this light and airy
deli offers freshly baked bread,
cookies and muffins as well as cold
meats and cheese. Kids will enjoy
the adjoining ice cream parlor. *47
Beach Rd, Mouille Point.* 📞 *021-
439-1538. $.*

Little kids will enjoy the mini Blue Train.

8 kids ★★ Ratanga Junction.
This theme park has plenty to keep
both kids and adults occupied,
although it's nothing close to Dis-
neyland. There's a water ride, roller-
coaster, giant swinging pirate ship,
and tamer mini-rides for youngsters.
🕐 *2–3 hrs. N1, Sable Rd turnoff,*
📞 *021-550-8500. www.ratanga.
co.za. Admission R130 over 1.3m
tall, R60 under 1.3m tall. Daily Nov–
Jan and open during other South
African school holidays.*

**9 kids ★★ MTN Science Cen-
tre.** Mums can go shopping at
Canal Walk (p 32) and drop off dads

and kids at this interactive science
center. Most of the 280 exhibits
involve hands-on activities and
bright youngsters can learn how a
hot air balloon or a nuclear reactor
works. There's also a kids' construc-
tion zone and Nintendo Wii games
to keep little minds occupied—
although Dads will probably be
equally enthralled. 🕐 *1–2 hrs.
Upper level, Canal Walk, Century
City.* 📞 *021-529-8100. www.mtn
sciencecentre.org.za. Admission R22
adults, R28 kids (aged 3–17), R86 2
adults 2 kids or 1 adult 3 kids. Sun–
Thurs 9am–6pm, Fri–Sat 9am–9pm.*

Babysitting & Nannies

Some of the larger hotels can provide babysitting services,
otherwise **Sitter 4 U** (📞 083-691-2009; www.sitters4u.co.za) can
provide experienced and trained babysitters at hotels for R100 per
hour before midnight and R120 per hour after midnight. If parents
want to go on more adult orientated activities—wine tasting or to
Robben Island, for example—**The Holiday Nanny** (📞 021-556-
8361; www.theholidaynanny.com) will take kids for their own special day out to many of the attractions listed on these pages. A daily
rate of R1200 per child (aged 4–12) includes transport, lunch and
snacks, entry fees, and a CD of photos.

Cape Town for Shopaholics

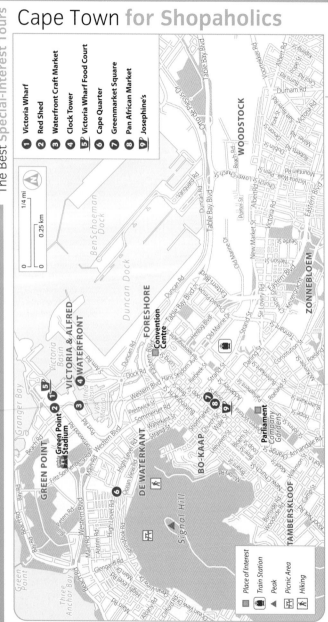

1 Victoria Wharf
2 Red Shed
3 Waterfront Craft Market
4 Clock Tower
5 Victoria Wharf Food Court
6 Cape Quarter
7 Greenmarket Square
8 Pan African Market
9 Josephine's

1/4 mi
0
0.25 km
0

BenSchoeman Dock

Duncan Dock

Victoria Basin

Granger Bay

Green Point

Three Anchor Bay

GREEN POINT
Green Point Stadium

VICTORIA & ALFRED WATERFRONT

Alfred Basin

FORESHORE
Convention Centre

Duncan Dock

DE WATERKANT

BO-KAAP

Signal Hill

TAMBERSKLOOF

Parliament
Company Gardens

WOODSTOCK

ZONNEBLOEM

Place of Interest
Train Station
Peak
Picnic Area
Hiking

Prices in South Africa are favorable if you're visiting from Europe or North America, and international visitors can claim back any VAT (value added tax) paid (p 66). Good buys include diamonds and quality African curios. Any proper shopping tour should start at the Waterfront. Individual shops are listed in the Best Shopping p 55. START: **V&A Waterfront.**

1 ★★★ Victoria Wharf. Cape Town's premier luxury shopping mall has two levels of international and local specialist shops, two cinema complexes, and some of the city's best (and most expensive) restaurants (81). You'll find plenty of souvenir shops and the fashion mall features high-end stores such as Jimmy Choo and Burberry. ⏱ *2–3 hrs. Breakwater Boulevard, V&A Waterfront. ☎ 021-408-7600. www.waterfront.co.za. Daily 9am–9pm.*

2 Red Shed. Adjoining Victoria Wharf, this is a collection of upmarket stalls selling touristy (and sometimes tacky) items such as African carvings set in picture frames, jewelry, leather goods, African textiles, safari clothes, and the like. If you're looking for a tea towel with an elephant on it, this is where you'll find it. ⏱ *30 min. Breakwater Boulevard, V&A Waterfront. ☎ 021-408-7600. www.waterfront.co.za. Daily 9am–9pm.*

3 ★ Waterfront Craft Market. A large indoor market located in a bright blue shed near the Aquarium, the Craft Market sells items designed for tourists, as well as clothes and home furnishings. At the **Wellness Market** you can buy natural remedies or a pack of tarot cards, and weary shoppers can stop for a quick foot or neck and shoulder massage. ⏱ *45 min. Dock Rd,*

Red Shed craft market.

V&A Waterfront. ☎ 021-408-7600. www. waterfront. co.za. Daily 9am–9pm.

From Alfred Basin cross the swing bridge to East Quay.

4 ★★ Clock Tower. The high-end stores found here include two of the city's best diamond dealers—*Diamonds of Africa* and *Shimansky* (see p 65). There's a VAT refund desk here and a branch of Cape Town Tourism, and you'll also find some fine, but very expensive, art galleries. ⏱ *45 min. Clock Tower, V&A Waterfront. ☎ 021-408-7600. www. waterfront.co.za. Daily 9am–9pm.*

Traditional African mask.

5 Victoria Wharf Food Court.
Pop back to the Food Court adjoining the Red Shed, where busy shoppers can refuel from a range of quick choices—grab a slice of pizza, Turkish kebab, yoghurt smoothie, or box of Asian noodles and sit at the sunny tables outside. *Victoria Wharf, V&A Waterfront.* $.

From the V&A Waterfront, take a taxi to the stylish De Waterkant area in Green Point.

6 ★★★ Cape Quarter. This stylish development has excellent décor and gift shops, art galleries, and delis set around a delightful paved courtyard ringed by *al fresco* restaurant tables. It incorporates some of the original Cape Malay architecture found in this area, and is currently being extended to Main Road Green Point, where the original Victorian façades will be included in the design. ⏱ *1 hr. 72 Waterkant St.* ☎ *021-529-9699. www.capequarter.co.za. Shops, daily 10am–5pm, restaurants variable.*

From Cape Quarter take a stroll through the Bo-Kaap along Rose Street and turn left on Shortmarket Street to:

7 ★★★ Greenmarket Square.
This daily (except Sundays) flea market sits on the cobbles of a square originally built in the 17th century (see p 41). The warren of stalls sells typical African curios. Do try to come here on a sunny day when street performers add to the lively atmosphere. ⏱ *45 min. Off Long St, between Shortmarket and Longmarket Sts.* ☎ *021-423-3266.*

T-shirt for sale at the Pan African Market.

Shopping Malls

Cape Town has a number of large, glitzy shopping malls, which also have cinemas and restaurants. Opened in 2000, Canal Walk (Century City, Century Boulevard; ☎ 021-529-9699; www.canal walk.co.za; daily 9am–9pm) is the biggest, with more than 400 stores. There's a huge choice of restaurants, the central atrium features events such as local talent shows, and on Saturday afternoon live rugby is shown on giant TV screens to keep bored husbands occupied. Shuttle buses will pick you up from numerous hotels in Cape Town—timetables are available from Cape Town Tourism (p 42) and the website.

    Cavendish Square (Dreyer St, Claremont; ☎ 021-657-5620; www.cavendish.co.za; Mon–Sat 9am–7pm, Sun 9am–5pm) is a stylish mall with more than 200 stores that caters to the affluent Southern Suburbs. The boutiques here have a great choice of clothes and Cavendish Connect, linked to the main mall by walkways, sells some international labels.

Weekend Markets

On Saturdays, don't miss the Neighbourgoods Market at the Old Biscuit Mill (p 35, ❷) in Woodstock, or Porter Estate Produce **Market** (9 Chrysalis Academy Grounds, Tokai Rd; ☎ 021-781-0144; www.pepmarket.co.za) in Constantia, an indoor food market, with a range of stalls selling breakfasts, coffees, cheese, meat, fish, and vegetables open until 1pm. There's also a play area for youngsters.

On Sundays, **Green Point Market,** presently operating from 9am to 4pm on Green Point Common, will soon move to a new site near Green Point Stadium. Here, you'll find a large selection of African crafts and curios, and bear in mind that prices are negotiable. One 'lane' is dedicated to food stalls, should you need a pick-me-up snack. **Hout Bay Market** (Village Green, Chapmans Peak Dr, Hout Bay; Sun 10am–4pm) is a popular craft market run by the local Lions Club selling curios, clothes, secondhand books, plants, and toys, and there's a bouncy castle and pony rides for kids.

www.greenmarketsquare.net. Mon–Sat 9am–5pm.

One block east on Long Street is:

❽ ★★★ Pan African Market. This all-under-one-roof market has arts and crafts from across the continent. Listen out for the infectious chatter of Senegalese or Swahili among many other African languages. From here you can wander up and down Long Street to visit its many other interesting shops. ⏱ *45 min. 76 Long St.*

☎ *021-426-4478. www.panafrican. co.za. Mon–Sat 10am–6pm.*

From Long Street follow Short-market Street for four blocks to:

❾ ★★ Josephine's. A little piece of Paris in the heart of Cape Town offering baguettes, croissants, macaroons, and pretty cakes, and also selling homemade jams, exotic teas, and fresh flowers. *The Piazza, Parliament St.* ☎ *021-469-9750. $–$$.*

Bangles for sale at Greenmarket Square craft market.

Gourmet **Cape Town**

1 Giovanni's Deliworld
2 The Old Biscuit Mill
3 Melissa's
4 Vaughn Johnson Wine & Cigar Shop
5 Caroline's Fine Wine
6 Atlas Trading Store
7 Mount Nelson Hotel

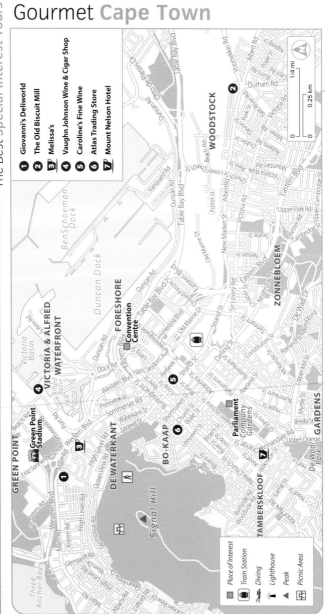

Place of Interest
Train Station
Diving
Lighthouse
Peak
Picnic Area

Foodies will be in heaven in Cape Town. As well as fine chef-driven restaurants and cafés, you will discover a number of delis and specialist grocery stores—perfect places to stock up on delicious picnic items or simply mingle with the regulars at lunchtime. The wine stores can offer advice about the best of South African wines. START: **Green Point.**

1 ★★★ Giovanni's Deliworld. Start the day with coffee at Giovanni's. The genuine Italian baristas serve the best espressos and cappuccinos in Cape Town at the buzzy outdoor coffee bar, and the long deli counter has mounds of salamis, hams, cheeses, tapas, and delicious readymade meals to eat in or take out. The shelves are stacked from floor to ceiling with every imaginable import from Italy, including the finest olive oils, Rioja wines, olives, truffles, and foie gras. ⏱ *45 min.* *103 Main Rd, Green Point.* ☎ *021-434-6893. Daily 7.30am–9pm.*

From Green Point drive through the city center and then follow the R1102 for approximately 4km (2.5 miles) to Woodstock.

2 kids ★★★ The Old Biscuit Mill. Set in a converted biscuit factory, this little 'village' has a number of original and stylish lifestyle and décor shops, which are also open during the week. On Saturday mornings, the Neighbourgoods Market (p 33) held here is the place to be seen. Along with clothing and jewelry stalls, there are a variety of food options on

Melissa's offers fine home-made food.

offer. These range from a half-dozen oysters with a glass of fizz to a Greek lamb kebabs, seared tuna sandwiches, Mexican wraps, or Cape Malay curries—and the Bloody Marys are to die for. Sociable seating is on hay bales at trestle tables. Stock up on fine cheese, homemade bread, organic fruit and vegetables, and fresh flowers. Note: be prepared to compete for a parking space in the surrounding streets. ⏱ *2 hrs.* *375 Albert Rd, Woodstock.* ☎ *021-462-6361. www.theoldbiscuitmill.* *co.za. Sat 9am–2pm.*

The Old Biscuit Mill is popular on Saturday morning.

From Woodstock drive to the V&A Waterfront.

3 ★★ **Melissa's.** Stop here for a daily lunch buffet of quiches, casseroles, and salads. This deli also sells gourmet ready-made meals, interesting blends of herbs and spices, and homemade pickles and relishes. Their cookies, meringues, and nougat are ideal for picnics or as gifts. *Shop 6195, Victoria Wharf, V&A Waterfront.* ☎ *021-418-0255. $.*

4 ★ **Vaughn Johnson Wine & Cigar Shop.** A veritable institution, and experts on wine from top-of-the-range limited vintages to every day drinking palate-pleasers. Shipping can be arranged to destinations around the world. ⏱ *45 min. Dock Rd, V&A Waterfront.* ☎ *021-419-2121. www.vaughnjohnson.com. Daily 10am–5pm.*

5 ★★★ **Caroline's Fine Wine.** This is arguably Cape Town's best wine shop. Caroline has an exceptional nose for fine wines and not just those from South Africa—there's a top-class selection of Bordeaux, Burgundy, and Champagne and Spanish, Italian, and South American wines here too. *Shop 8, Victoria Wharf, V&A Waterfront.* ☎ *021-425-5701. Mon–Fri 9am–8pm, Sat–Sun 9am–5pm.* ⏱ *1 hr. A second branch is at*

High tea at the Mount Nelson Hotel is a real treat.

62 Strand St. ☎ *021-419-8984. www. carolineswine.com. Mon–Fri 9am–5.30pm, Sat 9am–1pm.*

From the V&A Waterfront, drive to Bo-Kaap and park on Wale Street.

6 ★ **Atlas Trading Store.** Sniff out some Cape Malay ingredients in this 60-year-old spice shop, which is stuffed to the gills with sacks of rice, jars of pickles, and tins of coconut milk. At the back, look at and taste the colorful spices used in Cape Malay cooking (see p 52) stored in rows of wooden boxes. ⏱ *30 min. 94 Wale St.* ☎ *021-423-4361. Mon–Fri 8.30am–5pm, Sat 8.30am–12.45am.*

From Wale Street, drive towards the mountain up Buitengracht, and then turn left at Buitensingel to the Mount Nelson Hotel on Orange Street.

7 ★★★ **Mount Nelson Hotel.** Afternoon tea at Cape Town's top luxury hotel is a special experience. Choose from a selection of dainty sandwiches and savories, still warm scones, and delectable cakes, while a piano tinkles away in the background. *76 Orange St, Gardens.* ☎ *021-483-1948. Daily 2.30–5pm. $$.* ●

Relishes and spices at Atlas Trading, Bo-Kaap.

3 The Best
Neighborhood Walks

City **Center**

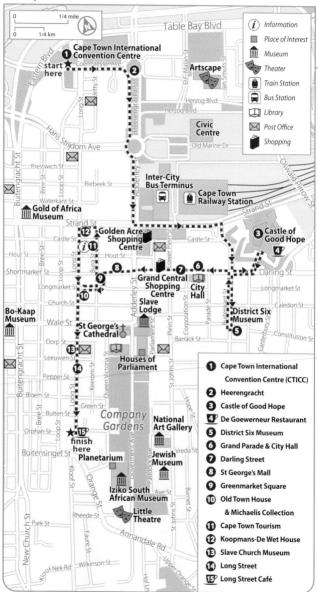

(i)	Information
■	Place of Interest
🏛	Museum
🎭	Theater
🚉	Train Station
🚌	Bus Station
📖	Library
✉	Post Office
📕	Shopping

1 Cape Town International Convention Centre (CTICC)
2 Heerengracht
3 Castle of Good Hope
4 De Goewerneur Restaurant
5 District Six Museum
6 Grand Parade & City Hall
7 Darling Street
8 St George's Mall
9 Greenmarket Square
10 Old Town House & Michaelis Collection
11 Cape Town Tourism
12 Koopmans-De Wet House
13 Slave Church Museum
14 Long Street
15 Long Street Café

The commercial center of the city is a grid of high-rise offices interspersed with Victorian and Art Deco buildings. All within an easy walk, you'll find prominent architecture, shopping districts, and South Africa's oldest colonial structure, the Castle of Good Hope, which once flanked the coast before much of this area was reclaimed. START: **Lower Long Street.**

❶ ★★ Cape Town International Convention Centre (CTICC). Grab a coffee, look at the modern art in the foyer, and check out what's on at the CTICC. Opened in 2003, this vast center holds public events throughout the year including the Book Fair, Women's Show, Fashion Week, Good Food and Wine Show, Design Indaba, and even the popular SEXPO. ⏱ *20 min. 1 Lower Long St.* ☎ *021-410-5000. www.cticc.co.za. Opening times vary.*

❷ ★ Heerengracht. Although the 1970s' tower blocks are an eyesore, this grand, palm-lined boulevard has two large grassy ornate roundabouts which are worth looking at. The first features a **statue of Bartolomeu Dias** (c.1451–1500), who was the first Portuguese mariner to round the Cape of Good Hope in 1488, and on the second is a **statue of Jan van Riebeeck** (1619–1677) and his wife, the first Europeans to settle in the Cape in 1652. **Cape Town Station** is the

The impressive Cape Town International Convention Centre.

main train station and also the city's transport hub for long-distance buses and city minibus taxis. The station is linked by a skywalk and

Statue of Jan van Riebeeck, founder of Cape Town.

subterranean shopping tunnels to the **Golden Acre Shopping Complex** on the other side of Strand Street. Outside is an informal **flea market** (daily, except Sunday) that seems to sell mainly cheap goods made in China.

③ ★★★ kids Castle of Good Hope. Built by the Dutch East India Company between 1666 and 1679, this star-shaped garrison (not actually a castle) is well worth an hour or two of exploration. For some 150 years, up to the early 19th century, it was the seat of the Cape's administration, as well as the center for the city's social and economic life. The impressive entrance gate, still adorned with the original coat of arms of the United Netherlands, leads to a grassy enclave, which is sliced in half by a 12m (40ft) wall known as the *kat*. Cannons used to be fired from the top, and ordinances were announced from the balcony. Guided tours take you to the torture chambers, dungeons, battlements, and ornamental lakes, or maps are provided for self-guided tours. At noon, watch the changing of the guard, and listen out for the Noon Day Gun—a cannon fired off Signal Hill. The **Military Museum** houses regimental displays of medals and uniforms, while the **William Fehr Collection** has an impressive display of period furniture and paintings. ⏱ *1–2 hrs. Buitenkant St.* ☎ *021-787-1249. www.castleof goodhope.co.za. Admission R20 adults, R10 children. Daily 9am–4pm. Guided tours Mon–Sat 11am, 12am, and 2pm.*

④ ★★ De Goewerneur Restaurant. I love the castle's restaurant. Tables are set outside, or inside in grand old rooms decorated with friezes and paintings. Dishes include South African fare such as bredie and

babotie (see box p 52) or opt for tea and freshly baked scones. *Castle of Good Hope.* ☎ *021-787-1249. $$.*

⑤ ★★★ District Six Museum. Located three blocks south of the castle on Buitenkant Street. *See p 24, ①.*

⑥ Grand Parade & City Hall. Once a parade ground for troops in the 19th century, the **Grand Parade** is a big space and has been upgraded to host a fan park for the 2010 FIFA World Cup South Africa tournament. Meanwhile, it serves as a car park with a tatty flea market along the eastern edge, Plein Street. Overlooking it is the elegant façade of the Italian Renaissance-style **City Hall**, built in 1905 from honey-colored limestone imported from Bath in England. Best known as the balcony where Nelson Mandela addressed the nation for the first time after his release from prison, today City Hall is the principal venue of the Cape Town Philharmonic Orchestra. ⏱ *20 min.*

⑦ Darling Street. On the corner of Parliament Street, the **Old Post Office** is now a shopping mall. Opposite, at 14 Darling Street, is the impressive Art Deco **Mutual Heights,** which at 91.4m (300ft) was the tallest building in Africa, after Egypt's pyramids, when it was built in 1940. Once the headquarters for an insurance firm, it's been converted to loft-style apartments. On the corner of Adderley Street is the **Standard Bank,** built in 1880 after the diamond wealth generated in Kimberley filtered down to Cape Town. A statue of Britannia sits on the dome and the vast banking hall retains many of its Victorian features. Alongside the bank, look out for the **flower market** at Trafalgar Place where traders are surrounded

The elegant façade of Cape Town City Hall.

by buckets of blooms. On the corner of Adderley and Shortmarket Streets is the fine sandstone **First National Bank,** the last building to be built in South Africa by acclaimed architect Herbert Baker in 1933. ⏱ *10–20 min.*

8 ★ St George's Mall. Running parallel to Adderley Street, St George's Mall is a pleasant, tree-lined pedestrian zone with the usual

St George's Mall.

chain stores, cafés, fast food outlets, and street stalls, where the occasional busker performs. The stores are better in the malls, but it's a pleasant place to wander. ⏱ *15 min. St George's St. Shops open Mon–Fri 9am–5.30pm, Sat 9am–1pm.*

9 ★★★ kids Greenmarket Square. Early farmers once sold their produce on the cobbles here and the square was the site of the declaration of the abolition of slavery in 1834. Today there's a popular African souvenir market (*see p 32,* **7**), where you're likely to hear a myriad of African languages spoken by traders from around the continent. The western side is flanked by the Art Deco former **Shell Building** (now a hotel) with its giant clock, while on the southeast corner is the **Old Town House** (see **10**). There are a number of cafés around the perimeter and drummers, mime artists, and jugglers entertain the crowds. ⏱ *45 min. Between Shortmarket and Longmarket Sts.*

10 ★★ Old Town House & Michaelis Collection. Built in 1755, one of Cape Town's first

Victorian, Art Deco and modern buildings ring Greenmarket Square.

double-storey buildings is a fine example of Cape Dutch architecture. Over the centuries, it has served as a police station, magistrate's court, and the City Hall. Today it houses the **Michaelis Collection** of 17th-century art bequeathed to the city in 1914 by Max Michaelis, a German diamond-mining magnate. Rembrandt is one of the Masters on show among other Dutch and Flemish artists. Look out for the lavish sweeping staircase. There's an outdoor café in the courtyard during summer. 🕐 *30 min. Greenmarket Square.* ☎ *021-481-3933, www.iziko.org.za/* michaelis. Admission free. Mon–Fri 10am–5pm, Sat 10am–4pm.

⓫ ★★★ Cape Town Tourism. Pop into Cape Town Tourism if you haven't already done so. *See box Cape Town Tourism, below.*

⓬ ★ Koopmans-De Wet House. Built around 1700 and named after a popular 19th-century socialite who was the last to live here, Marie Koopmans-De Wet, this historical home has a collection of antiques, silverware, and some priceless Japanese porcelain. At the back you can see the stables with the old slave accommodation

Cape Town Tourism

The principal office of Cape Town Tourism (☎ 021-487-6800; www.tourismcapetown.co.za; Mon–Fri 8am–7pm, Sat 8.30am–2pm, Sun 9am–1pm) is on the corner of Burg and Castle Streets. It's an excellent resource, and they will book tours, activities, and accommodation for you. You can pick up information on restaurants and nightlife, check your email, have a coffee in the café, or browse in the small gift shop for locally made crafts. There's also an accommodation booking desk for South Africa National Parks (SAN-Parks) and you will find the Namibia Tourist Office downstairs. Cape Town Tourism has a second office (☎ 021-405-4500; daily 9am–9pm) at the Clock Tower at the V&A Waterfront (p 31).

Long Street Nightlife

At the top end of Long Street, where it meets Kloof Street, there's a profusion of bars and nightclubs. This area can get very busy, with revelers milling around until dawn on weekends. Venues come and go and offer anything from R&B and deep house to local *kwaito* rap and student grunge rock. A good place to start is the café **Mr Pickwicks,** (158 Long St; ☎ 021-423-37100; Mon–Sat 8.30am–late), where you can quiz the waiting staff about what clubs are 'in' and pick up some flyers. Note: exercise caution after dark and always take a taxi.

above. ⏱ 40 min. 35 Strand St. ☎ 021-481-3935. www.iziko.org.za/koopmans. Admission R10 adults, free for under-16s. Tues–Thurs 10am–5pm.

⑬ ★ Slave Church Museum. The city's first slave church was built in 1804 by the South African Missionary Society, and slaves were taught literacy and Christianity here. Today you can find out more about the missionaries on the Cape through the small exhibition. Also note the impressive pulpit fashioned as an angel in flight. ⏱ 10 min. 40 Long St. ☎ 021-423-6755. Admission free. Daily 9am–4pm.

⑭ ★★★ Long Street. End this walk with a stroll up and down Long Street—there's plenty to distract you. Lined with multi-colored Victorian buildings with wrap-around balconies in various states of repair, Long Street stretches 3.8km (1.7 miles) from the Foreshore to Gardens. In the 1960s, it was a sleazy alley of brothels and drinking holes and, although in parts the seediness remains, today, fashionable boutiques, trendy cafés, and boutique hotels mix with adult shops, pawnbrokers, and bottle stores. You'll also find a clutch of backpackers' hostels, budget travel agencies,

music stores, and some excellent secondhand bookshops, and overall it has a youthful, bohemian vibe. It's also a popular street for film shoots—it's not unlike a Manhattan street—and you may see models or actors strutting their stuff. p 60, 63, 64, 66.

⑮ ★★ Long Street Café. Trendy spot with large Art Deco windows, polished wooden floors, tall stools, and glamorous waiting staff. Open all day from breakfast until well into the night for cocktails including their famous Long Street Iced Tea. 259 Long St. ☎ 021-424-2464. $$.

Long Street by night.

Government **Avenue**

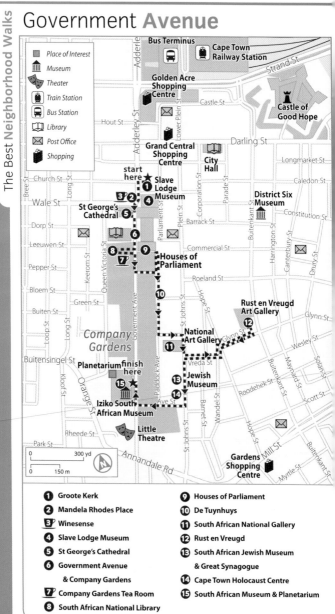

1. Groote Kerk
2. Mandela Rhodes Place
3. Winesense
4. Slave Lodge Museum
5. St George's Cathedral
6. Government Avenue
   & Company Gardens
7. Company Gardens Tea Room
8. South African National Library
9. Houses of Parliament
10. De Tuynhuys
11. South African National Gallery
12. Rust en Vreugd
13. South African Jewish Museum
    & Great Synagogue
14. Cape Town Holocaust Centre
15. South African Museum & Planetarium

From Long Street, this walk retraces your steps back to the corner of Wale and Adderley Streets, and then up Government Avenue, which as the name suggests is the location of government buildings, as well as some museums. It will take you through Company Gardens, with its ponds and fountains, and looking up, you'll see the top cableway of Table Mountain. START: **Adderley Street.**

① ★★ Groote Kerk. The Large Church, as it is called in English, is South Africa's oldest church and was completed in 1703 and rebuilt around 1840. Only the original steeple with its clock remains. The soaring pulpit is supported by a pair of teak lions with their mouths agape, and the giant organ and fine vaulted ceiling are worth a look. Look out for the pews with their own locked doors—built for wealthy families who didn't want to pray with mere commoners. ⌚ *20 min. 39 Adderley St.* ☎ *021-422-0569. Admission free. Mon–Fri 10am–2pm. Sun services.*

② ★★ Mandela Rhodes Place. Constructed within the original façades of seven prominent buildings, this development is named after two of the very different personalities who helped shape South Africa: Nelson Mandela and Cecil Rhodes. It features a luxury hotel, rooftop spa, 180 serviced apartments, and a gym. Pop into the

Groote Kerk.

foyer where there are a number of shops and restaurants, and stop by the **Signal Hill Winery,** which

Desmond Tutu

Desmond Tutu was the Secretary General of the South African Council of Churches from 1978, and became Anglican Archbishop of Cape Town in 1986.

A tireless anti-apartheid activist, he called for non-violent change and economic sanctions against South Africa, for which he won the Nobel Peace Prize in 1984. In 1996, he chaired the Truth and Reconciliation Commission, which helped investigate crimes against humanity committed during the Apartheid regime.

Today, as a member of The Elders (a group of older public figures), he is involved in conflict resolution and human rights issues.

stocks wine from small independent wine producers with vines on Signal Hill. ⏱ *5 min to peek inside. Corner of Adderley and Wale Sts. www. mandelarhodesplace.co.za.*

3 ★★ **Winesense.** This trendy wine bar is popular at lunchtime. Try a selection of tapas, such as olives, dips, sticky chicken wings, and beef satay; or the generous club sandwich or Caesar salad. A wide selection of wine is available by the glass. *Closed weekends. Mandela Rhodes Place, corner of Adderley and Wale Sts.* ☎ *021-422-0695. $$.*

4 ★★★ **Slave Lodge Museum.** This fascinating museum has recently been given a 21st-century revamp and now the film footage, sound, and creative lighting really do bring the impressive exhibitions to life. I recommend paying the small extra fee for the audio guide. Housed in the Slave Lodge built in 1679 by the Dutch East Africa Company, this museum tells the story of how slaves from the Far East were kept in inhumane conditions, and how they went on to contribute to the building of Cape Town and helped shape the Cape's community. ⏱ *45 min–1 hr.*

Corner Adderley and Wale Sts. ☎ *021-460-8242. www.iziko.org.za/ slavelodge. Admission R15 adults, free for children under-16s. Mon–Sat 10am–5pm.*

5 ★ **St George's Cathedral.** This Anglican cathedral was designed by Herbert Baker in the Gothic style and built in 1901. Stalwart anti-apartheid activist Desmond Tutu (see box, p 45) hammered on the doors in 1986 demanding to be the country's first black Archbishop. Three years after he was made bishop, he led a demonstration of 30,000 people from the cathedral to the Grand Parade (see p 40, **6**) where his speech included the words, 'We are the rainbow people…', which spawned the famous description of South Africa as the 'Rainbow Nation'. A highlight of the cathedral is the fine stained glass windows depicting early pioneers of the Anglican Church. ⏱ *30 min. 5 Wale St.* ☎ *021-424-7360. www.stgeorges cathedral.com. Admission free. Mon–Fri 8.30am–4.30pm.*

6 ★★★ **kids** **Government Avenue & Company Gardens.** From the top end of Adderley Street, Government Avenue runs

Slave Lodge and statue of Jan Smuts.

Company Gardens.

through the delightful Company Gardens. At the entrance, there's a **statue of Jan Smuts** (1870–1950) the former Boer War general and South African Prime Minister (1919–1924 and 1939–1948). The name refers to the Dutch East India Company, who first planted a vegetable garden in 1652 to supply passing ships. Today you can enjoy the lawns, rose garden, labeled trees, koi ponds, aviary, and statues of past Cape governors, including Cecil Rhodes, or simply sit on a bench and watch the world go by. It's popular with office workers at lunchtime, as well as picnicking families and courting couples at the weekend. ⏲ *To take in all the attractions allow at least half day. Daily 7am–7pm.*

7 ★ **Company Gardens Tea Room.** Take a break at this pleasant little café and opt for an outside table under shady well-established trees. If you are lucky you might spot a cute little gray squirrel. *$.*

8 ★ **South African National Library.** Behind St George's Cathedral, this is one of the oldest libraries in Africa, built in 1822 and funded by a tax on wine. It's home to an extensive collection of antique and modern reference books, but is only mildly interesting to visitors. ⏲ *5 min to walk past. 5 Queen Victoria St.* ☎ *021-424-6320. Admission free. Mon–Fri 9am–6pm, Sat 9am–1pm.*

9 ★★ **Houses of Parliament.** Although Tshwane (formerly Pretoria) is South Africa's seat of government, Parliament still sits in Cape Town. Among the offices and debating chambers, the most impressive is the 1885 Parliament building (best viewed from Plein Street) with its lovely central dome, gleaming white pillars, and Corinthian porticos. Phone ahead to see whether Parliament is in session if you want to attend the public gallery. ⏲ *20 min to walk past. 90 Plein St.* ☎ *021-403-2201.*

De Tuynhuys.

⑩ ★ De Tuynhuys. Beyond Parliament, on Government Avenue, peer through locked iron gates at the startlingly white offices of the President. First built as a guesthouse in 1716 for visiting dignitaries of the Dutch East India Company, *De Tuynhuys* was modified and expanded in the 18th and 19th centuries. Surrounded by well-tended flowerbeds, the name means 'Garden House'. ⏱ *5 min. Government Ave.*

⑪ ★★★ South African National Gallery. The gallery was established in 1871 in a striking building with an impressive set of steps. Today you'll find permanent galleries of French, Dutch, Flemish, and South African Masters, and temporary exhibition spaces for modern art and contemporary photography. In recent years, it has focused on developing its collection of indigenous art, particularly beadwork and sculpture, and there are ongoing efforts to repatriate African works of art from other countries. Don't miss the gallery of powerful Ernest Cole photographs taken in the townships during apartheid. I recommend you pop into the shop—there are some good art books and quality crafts for sale. ⏱ *1 hr. Government Ave.* ☎ *021-467-4660. www.iziko.org.za/ sang. Admission R15 adults, free for under-16s. Tues–Sun 10am–5pm.*

⑫ ★★ Rust en Vreugd. A couple of blocks east from the South African National Gallery, this pretty Cape Dutch style 18th-century house displays paintings, etchings, and engravings, giving an insight into life in Cape Town's early colonial heyday, during both Dutch and British occupation. Some of the early pictures feature ships in Table Bay and dolphins frolicking in the ocean. The name is Dutch for 'rest and peace', which is best appreciated in the lovely garden with its crunchy gravel paths, bay and lemon trees, rosemary and lavender bushes, a lawn with a gazebo, and the odd duck wandering around. ⏱ *45 min. 78 Buitenkant St.* ☎ *021-464-3280. www.iziko.org.za/rustvreugd. Admission free. Tues–Thurs 10am–5pm.*

⑬ ★★★ South African Jewish Museum & Great Synagogue.

Although on Government Avenue, the Great Synagogue is accessed through the museum entrance on Hatfield Street. It was built in 1905 next to an older synagogue dating to the mid-19th century that is now part of the museum. Features include stained glass windows, gold-leaf friezes, and polished mahogany pews. Although its central theme is Cape Town's Jewish community, the excellent museum sheds light on the Cape's history as a whole including the role of Jews in building South Africa's gold wealth and the part they played in the struggle against apartheid. The café serves kosher food. ⏱ *45 min. 84 Hatfield St.* ☎ *021-465-1546. www.sajewish museum.co.za. Admission R35 adults, R15 children under 16, free under 6. Sun–Thurs 10am–5pm, Fri 10am–2pm.*

⑭ ★★★ Cape Town Holocaust Centre.

Be prepared for a stirring of the emotions, especially when looking at the rows of photographs of families that met their untimely death in the gas chambers. The museum documents the rise of anti-Semitism in Europe, the creation of ghettos and death camps, the horrors of the Final Solution, and the liberation at the end of World War II. It also covers racism in general and the similarities of apartheid with Nazi Germany. Interestingly, the South African Air Force took the first aerial photographs of Auschwitz. The use of hi-tech multimedia equipment really drives the message home. ⏱ *30 min. 88 Hatfield St.* ☎ *021-462-5553. www.ct holocaust.co.za. Admission free. Sun–Thurs 10am–5pm, Fri 10am–1pm.*

⑮ ★★ kids South Africa Museum & Planetarium.

Predominantly covering South Africa's natural history, the museum entertains children with stuffed animals, dissected creatures in jars, and giant dinosaur and whale skeletons. Excellent displays about various ethnic groups include replicas of San rock art (the San were the first people to inhabit what is now South Africa). Equipped with a star map from the entrance desk, you can look for constellations and planets in the adjoining planetarium, which also holds occasional events for kids (see p 27). ⏱ *45 min or 1 hr for a show. 25 Queen Victoria St.* ☎ *021-481-3800. www.iziko.org.za/sam. Admission R15 adults, free for under-16s. Daily 10am–5pm. The Sky Tonight, Sat–Sun 1pm. Admission R20 adults, R6 children under 16.*

The Great Synagogue

Bo-Kaap **to Green Point**

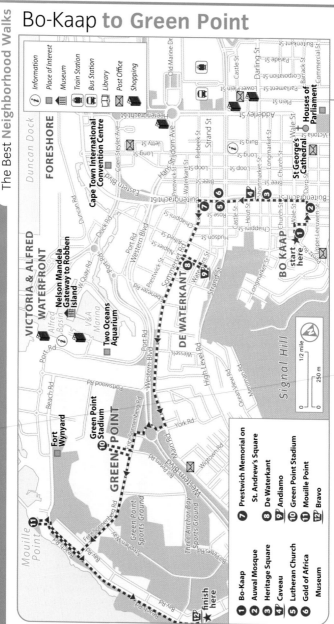

Legend
- (i) Information
- ■ Place of Interest
- 🏛 Museum
- 🚉 Train Station
- 🚌 Bus Station
- 🏤 Library
- ✉ Post Office
- 🛍 Shopping

FORESHORE

Duncan Dock

Cape Town International Convention Centre

VICTORIA & ALFRED WATERFRONT

Nelson Mandela Gateway to Robben Island

Two Oceans Aquarium

Alfred Basin

V&A Marina

DE WATERKANT

BO KAAP start here

Houses of Parliament

St George's Cathedral

Signal Hill

GREEN POINT

Green Point Stadium

Green Point Sports Ground

Three Anchor Bay Sports Ground

Fort Wynyard

Mouille Point

finish here

0   1/2 mile
0   250 m

1. Bo-Kaap
2. Auwal Mosque
3. Heritage Square
4. Caveau
5. Lutheran Church
6. Gold of Africa Museum
7. Prestwich Memorial on St. Andrew's Square
8. De Waterkant
9. Andiamo
10. Green Point Stadium
11. Mouille Point
12. Bravo

Walk through the residential districts that wind their way west of the city towards the Atlantic Seaboard. The Bo-Kaap retains a historical charm, while De Waterkant is home to city slickers and good nightlife. Gleaming white apartment blocks in Green Point and Sea Point hug the slopes of Signal Hill, and the long promenade has great mountain and ocean views. START: **Wale Street.**

❶ ★★ **Bo-Kaap.** Painted in a colorful array, these boxy, single-story Georgian and Cape Dutch houses are traditionally home to the Muslim Cape Malay community—descendants of slaves from Indonesia and Malaysia in the 1600s. After their emancipation in 1834, many settled on the lower slopes of Signal Hill, and Bo-Kaap (meaning 'Upper Cape') developed as a working-class district. The tiny **Bo-Kaap Museum** is furnished as a wealthy Muslim merchant's house from the 19th century, and a room at the back has some interesting photographs of today's residents. Pop into **Atlas Trading** (see p 36) a spice shop across the road full of marvelous aromas—Cape Malay cooking uses a lot of spices and herbs (see box p 52, Cape Malay cuisine)—and

One of the many mosques in Bo-Kaap.

from here climb the hill for one block. On your left is a row of pastel-colored houses, while on the right is a cobbled street of photogenic homes in orange, lime, and sky-blue. The residents are happy for you to snap away. The most atmospheric time to visit Bo-Kaap is during prayer time (5 times a day), when old robed men in skullcaps climb the hills to the district's 10 mosques and the air rings with *muezzin* calls. ⏱ *30 min. Bo-Kaap Museum, 71 Wale St.* ☎ *021-481-3939. www. iziko.org.za/bokaap. Admission R10 adults, free for children under 16, free on Sat. Mon–Sat 9am–5pm.*

❷ **Auwal Mosque.** South Africa's oldest mosque was founded in 1794, but it's a plain and unassuming building and non-Muslims are not permitted inside. ⏱ *5 min. 43 Dorp St.*

❸ ★★ **Heritage Square.** This is not a square as such, but a renovated block of historical Dutch and Georgian townhouses surrounding a courtyard built in the 17th to 18th centuries. Originally housing a snuff maker, wheelwright, and undertakers and later a boarding house, it's now home to a collection of restaurants, such as the Africa Café (see p 85), as well as the Cape Heritage Hotel (see p 123). The atmospheric cobbled courtyard has the oldest vine in South Africa, planted in 1781. Look through the glass on the right down into the only operating blacksmiths in Cape Town. ⏱ *20 min. Corner Bree & Shortmarket Sts.*

Cape Malay Cuisine

Many of the original Malay slaves were craftspeople, and their skills were passed down through the generations. The men were tailors, carpenters, and coopers (cask-makers), and the women were renowned for their cooking. In the kitchen, it was the slave who ruled the master, and a Malay influence in South African cooking continues to this day. Curries are served with an array of *sambals* (condiments made from chilies) and *atjars* (oily vegetable relishes), and fruit is often cooked with meat. My favorite dishes include tomato *bredie* (stew), normally made from mutton, with cinnamon, cardamom, ginger, and cloves, and *babotie*, a Malay improvement on shepherd's pie with chutney, almonds and sultanas, and savory custard instead of mashed potato on top.

4 Caveau. If you haven't had breakfast, stop here for croissants and coffee with the locals (see p 88). *92 Bree St, Heritage Square.* 📞 *021-422-1367. www.caveau. co.za. $.*

5 ★ Lutheran Church. The Dutch Reformed Church relinquished their monopoly on religion

The Heritage Square vine.

and permitted free worship in the Cape in 1771. Subsequently, this church on the Eastern edge of Bo-Kaap was converted from a barn in 1785 into a church for a mostly German congregation. Note the striking pale gray bell tower and, inside, the impressive pulpit with its carved cherubs. 🕐 *15 min. Corner of Buitengracht and Strand Sts.*

6 ★★★ kids Gold of Africa Museum. The glittering booty on display here is so impressive that you'll wonder why it's not in a bank vault. Located in the striking yellow Martin Melck House, built in 1793, which I think is one of the finest examples of early Cape domestic architecture in the city, the museum showcases the history of gold mining and gold craftsmanship in Africa as far back as ancient Egypt. There's a particularly good collection of 19th- to 20th-century West African pieces, including jewelry, statues, and masks. Make time for the restaurant offering Cape Malay dishes (see box above, Cape Malay Cuisine). If you have time, enquire about the unique evening tours, when you can explore the museum by torch-light. 1–2 hrs. 96 Strand St. 021-405-1540. www.goldofafrica.com. R25 adults, children under 16 free. Mon–Sat 9.30am–5pm.

Golden Lion at the Gold of Africa Museum.

7 ★ Prestwich Memorial on St. Andrew's Square.
Excavations in 2003 revealed some 2,000 graves in and around Green Point's Prestwich Street. Many believe they belong to slaves who died during a smallpox epidemic that hit Cape Town in the 18th century. The remains found here have now been interred in this new memorial, set in a peaceful garden. 5 min. Somerset Rd.

8 ★★★ De Waterkant.
The brightly colored houses of the trendy De Waterkant are similar in architecture to Bo-Kaap but have been luxuriously renovated. It's a fashionable residential area, and the cobbled streets are worth a wander. This is also the epicenter for Cape Town's gay nightlife (see p 102). The **Cape Quarter** (see p 32, 6) is a stylish shopping mall that has a number of restaurants and home décor shops around a leafy courtyard. 30 min. Somerset Rd.

9 ★ Andiamo.
In the Cape Quarter's central courtyard, with tables on the cobbles under giant umbrellas, this is a good spot for a healthy lunch of skinny latte and generously stuffed ciabattas or focaccias, and pizzas. Cape Quarter, 74 Waterkant St. 021-421-3687. $$.

10 ★★★ kids Green Point Stadium.
A 10-minute walk from De Waterkant brings you to Green Point's looming and unmissable new soccer stadium. In their trademark red-striped overalls and yellow hard hats, Team Green Point have been building the white concrete and steel complex since 2007 in readiness for the 2010 soccer World Cup. The Visitor Centre displays photographs of South African soccer stars and information on the event. On Sundays the popular Green Point Flea Market is held nearby on Green Point Common (see p 16, 1). 021-430-0410. www.greenpointstadiumvc.co.za. Admission R40 adults, R20 kids (under-16s). Tours Mon–Fri 10am and 2pm, Sat 10am and 12am.

11 ★★ kids Mouille Point.
Beyond the stadium, a promenade curves its way around Mouille Point

Andiamo's tables, Cape Quarter, The Waterkant.

Joggers on the promenade at Mouille Point.

and to a red-and-white candy-striped lighthouse. If you have an hour or two to spare you can walk its length (see p 28, ❻)—along with dog walkers, joggers, and rollerbladers—while enjoying views of Robben Island, licking on an ice cream and playing on the swings. Green Point was originally Cape Town's founder Jan van Riebeeck's (see box below) farm. **Mouille Point Lighthouse** was built in 1824, electrified in 1929, and is South Africa's oldest active lighthouse. *Beach Rd, Green Point.*

12P ★ **Bravo.** A lovely informal café/bar to end this walk, preferably in time to enjoy a sunset over the ocean—ask for one of their bright red blankets if you want to sit out in winter. It's best known for its thin-crust pizzas served on wooden boards. *121 Beach Rd, Mouille Point.* ☎ *021-439-5260. $$.* ●

Jan van Riebeeck

Born in the Netherlands, Jan van Riebeeck (1619–67) was sent by the Dutch East India Company to establish a settlement to service its ships as they rounded the Cape of Good Hope en route to the Far East. He arrived in 1651 and was Commander of the Cape from 1652 to 1662, when he was charged with building a fort, improving the natural anchorage at Table Bay, planting fruit and vegetables, and obtaining livestock from the indigenous Khoi people. The Castle of Good Hope (see p 40, ❸), South Africa's oldest building, which was built between 1666 and 1679, several years after Van Riebeeck's departure, replaced the original fort.

Shopping Best Bets

Best **Books on Africa**
★★★ Exclusive Books, *Shop 6160, Victoria Wharf, V&A Waterfront* (p 61)

Best **Trinkets & Collectibles**
★ Long Street Antiques Arcade, *127 Long St (p 60)*

Best **African Arts & Crafts**
★★★ Greenmarket Square, *off Long St, between Shortmarket and Longmarket Sts (p 32)*

Best **Outdoor Clothing & Equipment**
★★ Cape Union Mart, *Quay 4, V&A Waterfront (p 62)*

Best **Pampering Goodies**
★★★ Wellness Warehouse, *Lifestyle Centre, Kloof St, Gardens (p 64)*

Best **Exquisite Diamonds**
Diamonds of Africa, *Shop 119, Clock Tower, V&A Waterfront (p 65)*

Best **Trendy Kids' Clothes**
★★ Naartjie, *Shop 117, Victoria Wharf, V&A Waterfront (p 66)*

Best **Young South African Designers**
★ Young Designers Emporium, *Shop F50, Cavendish Square, Dreyer St, Claremont (p 63)*

Best **Music from Across Africa**
★★★ The African Music Store, *134 Long St (p 66)*

Best for **a Red Carpet Dress**
★★ Marion & Lindie, *Shop G102, Cavendish Sq, Dreyer St, Claremont (p 63)*

Best for **Yummy Mummies**
★★★ Kids Emporium, *18 Somerset Sq, Highfields Rd, Green Point (p 66)*

Best **Glamorous Jewelry**
★★★ Shimansky Collection, *Top Floor, Clock Tower, V&A Waterfront*

Greenmarket Square for African Arts & Crafts.

V&A Waterfront & Southern Suburbs Shopping

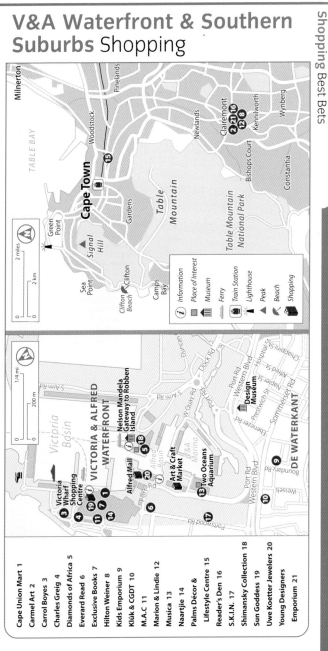

Cape Union Mart 1
Carmel Art 2
Carrol Boyes 3
Charles Greig 4
Diamonds of Africa 5
Everard Read 6
Exclusive Books 7
Hilton Weiner 8
Kids Emporium 9
Klûk & CGDT 10
M.A.C 11
Marion & Lindie 12
Musica 13
Naartjie 14
Palms Décor &
Lifestyle Centre 15
Reader's Den 16
S.K.I.N. 17
Shimansky Collection 18
Sun Goddess 19
Uwe Koetter Jewelers 20
Young Designers
Emporium 21

City Center Shopping

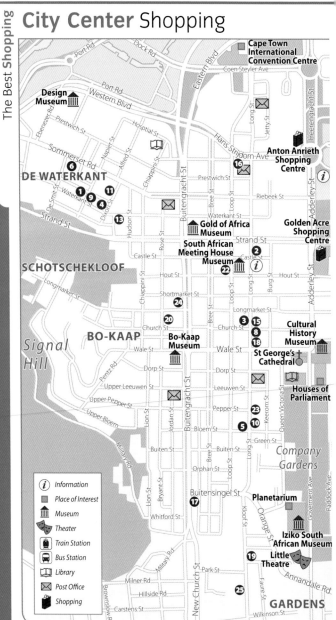

Cape Town International Convention Centre

Coen Steyler Ave

Port Rd

Dock Rd

Eastern Blvd

Port Rd

Western Blvd

Hans Strijdom Ave

Jetty St

Long St

Heerengracht St

Design Museum

Prestwich St

Ebenezer Rd

Sommerset Rd

Hosptial St

Napier St

Alfred St

Chiappini St

Anton Anrieth Shopping Centre

(i)

16

Prestwich St

Riebeek St

Adderley St

DE WATERKANT

Waterkant St

De Smit St

Dixon St

Buitengracht St

Bree St

Loop St

1 9 11

13

Hudson St

Rose St

Waterkant St

Gold of Africa Museum

South African Meeting House Museum

Strand St

Golden Acre Shopping Centre

Strand St

SCHOTSCHEKLOOF

Castle St

Longmarket St

Castle St

22

(i)

Hout St

Burg St

Adderley St

Chiappini St

Shortmarket St

Hout St

Long St

24

Longmarket St

Bree St

20

Church St

BO-KAAP

Church St

3 15

8

Cultural History Museum

Wale St

Bo-Kaap Museum

Wale St

18

St George's Cathedral

Signal Hill

Pentz Rd

Dorp St

Dorp St

Upper Leeuwen St

Leeuwen St

Buitengracht St

Jordan St

Houses of Parliament

Upper Pepper St

Pepper St

Keerom St

Queen Victoria St

23

Upper Bloem

Lion St

Bloem St

5 10

Buiten St

Bree St

Buiten St

Green St

Long St

Company Gardens

Military Rd

Orphan St

Loop St

Goverment Ave

Raddock Ave

(i)	Information
■	Place of Interest
🏛	Museum
🎭	Theater
🚆	Train Station
🚌	Bus Station
📖	Library
✉	Post Office
🛍	Shopping

Lion St

Bryant St

Whitford St

Buitensingel St

17

Planetarium

Kloof St

Orange St

Iziko South African Museum

Military Rd

Brownslow Rd

Park St

19

Little Theatre

Faure St

Annandale Rd

Milner Rd

Hillside Rd

New Church St

25

Wilkinson St

GARDENS

Carstens St

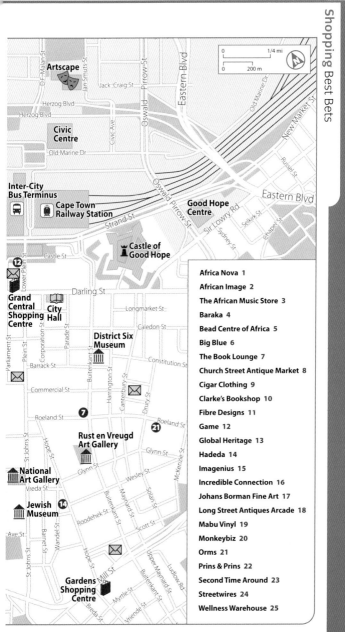

Africa Nova 1
African Image 2
The African Music Store 3
Baraka 4
Bead Centre of Africa 5
Big Blue 6
The Book Lounge 7
Church Street Antique Market 8
Cigar Clothing 9
Clarke's Bookshop 10
Fibre Designs 11
Game 12
Global Heritage 13
Hadeda 14
Imagenius 15
Incredible Connection 16
Johans Borman Fine Art 17
Long Street Antiques Arcade 18
Mabu Vinyl 19
Monkeybiz 20
Orms 21
Prins & Prins 22
Second Time Around 23
Streetwires 24
Wellness Warehouse 25

Cape Town **Shopping A to Z**

Antiques

★ **Church Street Antique Market** CITY CENTER Trestle tables are piled high with jewelry, ceramics, glassware, and unusual items such as nautical instruments and microscopes. Open daily except Sundays. *Church Street Mall.* ☎ *021-438-8566. No credit cards. Map p 58.*

★ **Global Heritage** ATLANTIC SEABOARD This is the only place in South Africa to buy rare items from the Ming Dynasty (1368–1644) and each piece is certified. Can arrange international shipping. *Cape Quarter, Dixon St, Green Point.* ☎ *021-418-3133. www.globalheritage.co.za. AE, DC, MC, V. Map p 58.*

★ **Long Street Antiques Arcade** CITY CENTER This small and narrow arcade has a cluster of stores selling antiques and collectables. You can pick up anything from ornate ostrich eggs and vintage shoes to war medals and Victorian costume jewelry. *127 Long St.* ☎ *021-422-0226. AE, DC, MC, V. Map p 58.*

Art Galleries

★ **Carmel Art** SOUTHERN SUBURBS Paintings by leading South African contemporary artists are for sale here, and include Pieter van der

Church Street Antique Market.

Westhuizen, one of the country's most popular artists, who works with a variety of mediums, including etchings and oils. *66 Vineyard Rd, Claremont.* ☎ *021-671-6601. www.carmelart.co.za. AE, DC, MC, V. Map p 57.*

★★ **Everard Read** V&A WATERFRONT This upmarket gallery sells contemporary art from around southern Africa, and exhibits a number of Cape Town artists. Do

Shopping Malls & Markets

Many of the stores listed here are in the large shopping malls. For details of these, as well as details about markets, see **Cape Town for Shopaholics**, p 30. Stores in the larger shopping malls such as Victoria Wharf, Cavendish Square, and Canal Walk are open daily until as late as 9pm. All other stores are generally open from 9am to 5.30pm Monday to Friday, and 9am to 1pm on Saturday.

Woolworths

There are more than 50 branches of 'Woolies' in and around Cape Town. For UK visitors, this store is more similar to the Marks & Spencer, rather than the former Woolworths, and sells quality food, clothing, and homeware, while offering excellent customer service. The larger stores have restaurants and the branch at the V&A Waterfront has a wine bar. Visit the website for a store locator: www.woolworths.co.za.

have a look at the lovely sculpture garden at the back. *3 Portswood Rd.* ☎ *021-418-4527. www.everard-read-capetown.co.za. AE, DC, MC, V. Map p 57.*

★ **Johans Borman Fine Art** CITY CENTER Owned by one of the country's leading art dealers, this gallery sells Old Masters and contemporary paintings and sculptures by South African artists. *In-Fin-Art Building, Upper Buitengracht St.* ☎ *021-432-6075. www.johansborman. co.za. AE, DC, MC, V. Map p 58.*

Books

★★ **Clarke's Bookshop** CITY CENTER Established in 1956, this store specializes in new, secondhand, and out-of-print books on southern

Africa, covering every conceivable subject from history and genealogy to ornithology and art. *211 Long St.* ☎ *021-423-5791. www.clarkesbooks. co.za. MC, V. Map p 58.*

★★★ **Exclusive Books** V&A WATERFRONT South Africa's best bookstore chain has branches at the V&A and all other shopping malls, and a full range of international books and magazines. Head here for souvenir coffee-table books on Cape Town. *Shop 6160, Victoria Wharf.* ☎ *021-419-0905. www. exclusivebooks.co.za. AE, DC, MC, V. Map p 57.*

★ **Reader's Den** SOUTHERN SUB-URBS Avid collectors of *Marvel* and other cult magazines, plus graphic Japanese novels and action

A larger Woolworths store.

figures head to this specialist comic store. Enthusiasts may find some rare items here, and they do mail order. *Shop G10, Stadium on Main, Main Rd, Claremont.* ☎ *021-671-9551. www.readersden.co.za. DC, MC, V. Map p 57.*

★ **The Book Lounge** CITY CENTER This independent bookseller, with knowledgeable staff and an elegant wood-paneled interior, specializes in local authors. You won't leave empty-handed. *71 Roeland St.* ☎ *021-462-2425. MC, V. Map p 58.*

Chain Stores

Game CITY CENTER You'll find branches of this very large hypermarket chain in the larger shopping malls and a store housed in Cape Town's old post office in the city center. Sells anything from sweets to sofas, but no perishable food. *Corner of Plein and Darling Sts.* ☎ *021-467-1800. www.game.co.za. AE, DC, MC, V. Map p 58.*

Incredible Connection CITY CENTER Great for cameras, computer software, games, and cell phones with branches in all the shopping malls. This is a great place to shop for accessories for your laptop, phone, or camera that you may have left at home. *SHG Building, Lower Loop St.* ☎ *021-441-2420. www.incredible.co.za. AE, DC, MC, V. Map p 58.*

Fashion & Accessories
★★ **Big Blue** ATLANTIC SEABOARD Girls and boys wear from home grown designers; includes retro shirts, African print skirts, funky bags, and structured shoes. Come here for a one-off designer T-shirt. *47 Somerset Rd, Green Point.* ☎ *021-425-1179. www.bigblue. co.za. AE, DC, MC, V. Map p 58.*

★★ **Cape Union Mart** V&A WATERFRONT This store sells a full

range of outdoors items such as backpacks, camping equipment, and accessories. Do look out for their stylish, good quality Old Khaki clothes brand. *Quay 4.* ☎ *021-425-4559. www.capeunionmart.co.za. AE DC, MC, V. Map p 57.*

★★ **Cigar Clothing** ATLANTIC SEABOARD Women with style and money to burn head to this sexy little store in the heart of the trendy Cape Quarter. Mostly imported from Paris, the clothes are stylishly feminine and well cut. *Cape Quarter, 72 Waterkant St.* ☎ *021-418-4846. www.cigarwomen. co.za. AE, DC, MC, V. Map p 58.*

★★ **Hilton Weiner** SOUTHERN SUBURBS Informal men's and women's fashions here use good quality fabrics such as linen and metallic prints in muted and natural colors, with good classic cuts and tailoring. *Shop G3, Cavendish Square, Dreyer St, Claremont.* ☎ *021-683-3069. www.hiltonweiner.co.za. AE, MC, V. Map p 57. A second location is at Shop 550B, Canal Walk.* ☎ *021-552-0083.*

★★★ **Klûk & CGDT** ATLANTIC SEABOARD A favorite at Cape Town

Outdoor gear at Cape Union Mart.

Cape Town Fashion Week

Established in 2003, and held at the Cape Town International Convention Centre (CTICC) in August, Cape Town Fashion Week (www.capetownfashionweek.com) has become Africa's biggest fashion event, and celebrates designers from across southern Africa. It attracts a number of local and international buyers. The local celeb-studded after-parties are legendary. Tickets can be bought from Computicket (p 114).

Fashion Week, these designers create beautifully feminine creations in delicate fabrics. *Portside Centre, Main Rd, Green Point.* ☎ *021-418-4846. www. kluk.co.za. AE, MC, V. Map p 57.*

★★ **Marion & Lindie** SOUTHERN SUBURBS Interesting fabrics and hand finished details from award-winning designers who represent South Africa at its most fashion-conscious. This is the place to come for a goddess-inspired gown. *Shop G102, Cavendish Square, Dreyer St, Claremont.* ☎ *021-674-1436. www. marionandlindie.co.za. AE, DC, MC, V. Map p 57. A second location is at Shop 231, Victoria Wharf, V&A Waterfront.* ☎ *021-419-4251.*

★★★ **Second Time Around** CITY CENTER A little Aladdin's Cave of a store that sells vintage men's and women's clothing and jewelry from the 1920s to the 1980s. They rent out dressing up party outfits too. *196 Long St.* ☎ *021-423-1674. V. Map p 58.*

★★ **Sun Goddess** V&A WATERFRONT This husband and wife duo put a modern twist on both men and women's traditional African clothing. *Shop 243, Victoria Wharf.* ☎ *021-421-7620. www.sungoddess. co.za. AE, DC, MC, V. Map p 57.*

★ **Young Designers Emporium** SOUTHERN SUBURBS The playful,

brightly colored fashions in YDE are, as the name suggests, designed by young designers who rent out individual rails in this super trendy store. *Shop F50, Cavendish Square, Dreyer St, Claremont.* ☎ *021-683-6177. www.yde.co.za. AE, DC, MC, V. Map p 57. Another branch at Shop 432, Canal Walk* ☎ *021-555-2090.*

Gift & Souvenir Stores
★ **Africa Nova** ATLANTIC SEABOARD Here you will find recycled crafts inspired by township culture, contemporary African ceramics, West African cloth, and tribal art. *Cape Quarter. 72 Waterkant St, Green Point.* ☎ *021-425-5123. www.africa nova.co.za. AE, DC, MC, V. Map p 58.*

★ **African Image** CITY CENTER This treasure trove of a store is crammed with African tribal art from all over Africa. Less touristy than most, it specializes in antiques and one-off pieces. *Corner of Castle and Burg Sts.* ☎ *021-423-8385. www.african-image.co.za. AE, DC, MC, V. Map p 58.*

★★ **Carrol Boyes** V&A WATERFRONT One of South Africa's best known exports, this chain store sells beautiful pewter and chrome giftware, flatware, and tableware in modern designs. The platters, bowls, and cutlery make great wedding gifts and the jewelry is inventive. *Shop 6180, Victoria Wharf.* ☎ *021-418-0595. www.carrolboyes. co.za. AE, DC, MC, V. Map p 57.*

★★★ **Imagenius** CITY CENTER This wonderfully eclectic store is on three floors in a 19th-century house, and sells well-chosen homeware, gifts, art, ceramics, and jewelry. Look out for the multi-colored lampshades and antique wind-up toys. *117 Long St.* ☎ *021-423-7870. www.imagenius.co.za. AE, DC, MC, V. Map p 58.*

★★ **Monkeybiz** CITY CENTER This store supports some 450 disadvantaged women by selling their home-made beaded crafts. I like the elongated African dolls. *65 Rose St.* ☎ *021-426-0636. www. monkeybiz.co.za. MC, V. Map p 58.*

★★ **Streetwires** CITY CENTER A studio that supports over 100 bead and wire artists, some of whom you can chat with while they work. They make anything from animals—I love the sheep—to lighting, jewelry, flowers, and tables. No credit cards but they have an ATM. *77 Shortmarket St.* ☎ *021-426-2475. www. streetwires.co.za. Map p 58.*

Knitted toys at Monkeybiz.

Health & Beauty

★★ **M.A.C** V&A WATERFRONT This international brand has a small store at the V&A, with helpful and beautifully made-up staff, and plenty of make-up to play around with. *Shop 6140, Victoria Wharf.* ☎ *021-421-4886. AE, DC, MC, V. Map p 57.*

★★ **S.K.I.N.** V&A WATERFRONT A bright white relaxing spa offering numerous treatments for both men and women. It also sells international products such as Dermalogica and Danne. *Dock Rd.* ☎ *021-425-3551. AE, DC, MC, V. Map p 57.*

★★★ **Wellness Warehouse** CITY BOWL For all your health and beauty needs, this one-stop store has a pharmacy and alternative health zone, a spa, and gym and exercise equipment as well as organic fresh food for sale. Try a delicious and healthy smoothie in the café. *Lifestyles on Kloof, 50 Kloof St, Gardens.* ☎ *021-487-5422. A second location is at Shop F8, Cavendish Connect, Dreyer St, Claremont. www.wellnesswarehouse. com. AE, DC, MC, V. Map p 58.*

Home Décor

★★ **Baraka** ATLANTIC SEABOARD This store is crammed with interesting décor and gift items such as intricate toy airplanes, distressed wooden picture frames, and bowls made from Masai beads. Look out for the gorgeous leather-bound photo albums. *Cape Quarter. 72 Waterkant St, Green Point.* ☎ *021-425-8883. AE, DC, MC, V. Map p 58.*

★ **Fibre Designs** ATLANTIC SEABOARD Luxury hand-woven carpets, with contemporary, fresh modern patterns and motifs: like a fashion label, this store produces various collections each year. *16 Dixon St, De Waterkant, Green Point.* ☎ *021-418-1054. www.fibredesigns. co.za. AE, DC, MC, V. Map p 58.*

Eastern inspired trinkets at Baraka.

★★★ **Hadeda** GARDENS With its ochre walls, pink floral cushions, pewter platters, and brass-studded mirrors, this store celebrates all thing Mexican and Peruvian. It's a favorite with Cape Town's top interior decorators. *Dunkley Sq, 3 Wandel St, Gardens.* 📷 *021-465-8620. www.hadeda.net. AE, DC, MC, V. Map p 58.*

Palms Décor & Lifestyle Centre CITY CENTER There are a number of designer décor stores here clustered around a central courtyard. Stop for a cappuccino in the downstairs café, and flick through glossy magazines for inspiration. *145 Sir Lowry Rd.* 📷 *021-462-0394. Credit cards vary per store. www. palms.co.za. Map p 57.*

Jewelry

★ **Bead Centre of Africa** CITY CENTER This distinctively colorful store is filled to the brim with beads and jewelry-making accessories. The gallery of African jewelry from the Masai, Yoruba, and Tuareg people will inspire you to create your own unique piece. *223 Long St.*

📷 *021-423-4687. www.bead merchantsofafrica.com. AE, DC, MC, V. Map p 58.*

★★ **Charles Greig** V&A WATERFRONT A family company with a good reputation for design and quality and specializing in diamonds from South Africa and tanzanite from Tanzania. Look out for the unique yellow diamond collection and the bronze African wildlife sculptures by Donald Greig. *Shop 6224, Victoria Wharf.* 📷 *021-418-4515. www.charlesgreig.co.za. AE, DC, MC, V. Map p 57.*

Diamonds of Africa V&A WATERFRONT This is a quality jewelers/gemologists specializing in diamonds, gold, and platinum and they are frequent De Beers Shining Light Award winners for their designs. They also sell loose diamonds. *Shop 119, Clock Tower.* 📷 *021-421-1852. www.diamonds-of-africa.co.za. AE, DC, MC, V. Map p 57.*

★★ **Prins & Prins** CITY CENTER Located in a historic house built in 1792, this jewelers sells a range of diamond, ruby, tanzanite, emerald, and pearl jewelry. They also custom-design engagement and wedding rings. *66 Loop St.* 📷 *021-422-1090. www.prinsandprins.com. AE, DC, MC, V. Map p 58.*

★★★ **Shimansky Collection** V&A WATERFRONT South African-born Hollywood actress Charlize Theron owns a Shimansky diamond. Watch diamonds being cut and polished or discover the history of South African diamonds in this glamorous showroom. *Top Floor, Clock Tower.* 📷 *021-421-2778. www.shimansky.co.za. AE, DC, MC, V. Map p 57.*

★ **Uwe Koetter Jewelers** V&A WATERFRONT Another quality jewelers at the V&A, which again has a good range of diamonds and tanzanite pieces and a varied gents range: can also arrange workshop tours. *Shop 14, V&A Arcade.* ☎ *021-421-1039. www.uwekoetter.co.za. AE, DC, MC, V. Map p 57.*

Kids

★ **Kids Emporium** ATLANTIC SEA-BOARD You will find plenty of yummy mummies here shopping for designer baby wear, eco-friendly nappies, and stylish nursery furnishings. Good gift wrapping too. *18 Somerset Sq, Highfield Rd, Green Point.* ☎ *021-418-7636. www.kidsemporium.co.za. AE, DC, MC, V. Map p 57.*

★★ **Naartjie** V&A WATER-FRONT Incredibly cute children's and babies clothes and accessories in colorful prints. Your child will certainly stand out in a crowd. *Shop 117, Victoria Wharf.* ☎ *021-421-5819. AE, DC, MC, V. Map p 57.*

Music

★ **Mabu Vinyl** GARDENS Vinyl lovers will be in heaven in this retro store, with its stacks of vintage LPs and 12 inch singles, plus independent CD releases from up and coming South African artists. You'll find cassettes, comics, and T-shirts too. *2 Rheede St.* ☎ *021-423-7635.*

www.mabuvinyl.co.za. No credit cards. Map p 58.

★ **Musica** V&A WATER-FRONT Housed in an impressive restored red brick warehouse, the Musica megastore has some contemporary South African options, and a nice selection of traditional African music. There's also a pleasant café. *Dock Rd Complex, Nobel Square.* ☎ *021-425-6300. AE, DC, MC, V. Map p 57.*

★★★ **The African Music Store** CITY CENTER World music fans will enjoy the vast choice of CDs and DVDs from across the continent and the staff are well-informed and helpful. Do take a listen to kwaito—a South African take on hip hop and rap. *134 Long St.* ☎ *021-426-0857. www.africanmusicstore.co.za. MC, V. Map p 58.*

Photography

★★ **Orms** CITY CENTER This is Cape Town's best photography store and lab. They stock the latest gear and professional photographers head here for the state-of-the-art printing. *Shop 5, Roeland Square.* ☎ *021-465-3573. www.orms.co.za. AE, DC, MC, V. Map p 58.* ●

VAT Refunds

Visitors (i.e. non South African residents) can claim refunds for the 14% VAT (value added tax) paid on all purchases if they are taken out of the country. This is done at the airport, where you need to get receipts stamped by customs officers before you check in. Once airside, present receipts to the VAT refund desk where you'll be issued a check in rands, which you can pay into your home bank account, cash at a bureau de change at the airport, or have the amount debited to your Visa or MasterCard. There is a preprocessing VAT refund desk in the Clock Tower (p 31) at the V&A Waterfront, to get your receipts stamped, but you still have to claim the refund at the airport, and you must show your passport and air ticket. For more information, visit www.taxrefunds.co.za.

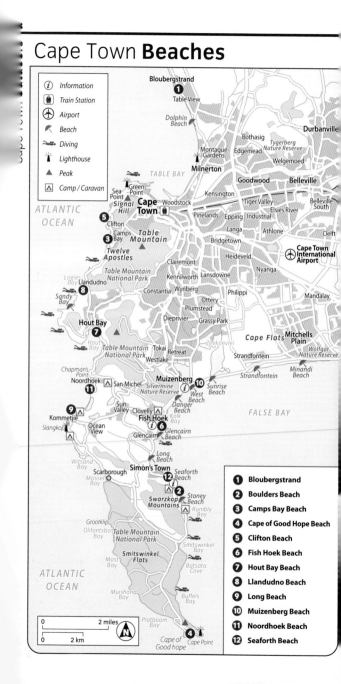

Cape Town **Beaches**

Legend:
- (i) Information
- Train Station
- Airport
- Beach
- Diving
- Lighthouse
- ▲ Peak
- Camp / Caravan

1. **Bloubergstrand**
2. **Boulders Beach**
3. **Camps Bay Beach**
4. **Cape of Good Hope Beach**
5. **Clifton Beach**
6. **Fish Hoek Beach**
7. **Hout Bay Beach**
8. **Llandudno Beach**
9. **Long Beach**
10. **Muizenberg Beach**
11. **Noordhoek Beach**
12. **Seaforth Beach**

A common misconception is that **Cape Point is the place where the Indian and Atlantic oceans meet,** but that is actually at Cape Agulhas, a few hours southeast of Cape Town. As such, the whole Cape Peninsula is surrounded by the Atlantic, which can make it too cold for swimming, although it is slightly warmer and calmer on the False Bay side. Cape Town's beaches are ideal for a few hours of relaxation.

1 `kids` ★★ **Bloubergstrand.** About 25km (16 miles) north of the city center, this beach offers the quintessential view of Table Mountain in all its glory. There are miles and miles of sand for beach walks, but it can sometimes be a little too windy for sunbathing. It's popular for flying kites and kite-surfing. *See p 143,* **1**.

2 `kids` ★★★ **Boulders Beach.** Access to the beach is restricted to protect the colony of African penguins residing here, but you can view them from the boardwalk that slopes down the sand dunes. *See p 18,* **9**.

3 ★★★ `kids` **Camps Bay Beach.** You may recognize the beautiful arc of Camps Bay Beach's white sand because it's frequently the backdrop for film shoots. Lined with palms, the beach is overlooked by the magnificent Twelve Apostles, the spine of mountains along the peninsula, and across the road are fashionable restaurants. Umbrellas and deck chairs can be hired. Look to the left of the mountains and you'll see the back view of the Table Mountain Aerial Cableway as it reaches the Upper Cableway Station. Across the boulders at the northern end is Glen Beach, which is also lovely but better known as a surfer's domain.

4 `kids` ★★ **Cape of Good Hope Beach.** A lovely half-moon of

Penguins at Boulders Beach.

Top Tips on the Beach

The South African sun is strong, and so wear sun block at all times. Avoid taking valuables to the beach and don't leave items such as cell phones unattended. The Atlantic current is strong and so swim in designated places only, where life guards are on duty. Great White sharks are present in the waters around the Cape Peninsula, but shark attacks on swimmers and surfers are extremely rare. Shark-spotters are deployed at key beaches popular for surfing to warn surfers of any impending danger.

brilliant white sand, found at the tip of the Cape Peninsula, and a great place for a picnic while admiring Cape Point towering above. *See p 18,* **7**.

5 ★★★ **kids** **Clifton Beach.** Come here to pose with the beautiful people at the four beautiful sandy coves below Clifton's luxury houses and apartments. The sand is powder soft and the waves gentle, and if the southeasterly wind is blowing Clifton is more sheltered than some of the other beaches. Clifton Fourth Beach has the best facilities for families, with changing rooms, toilets, and kiosks.

Beach at Cape Point.

6 **kids** ★★★ **Fish Hoek Beach.** Set in a wide sheltered bay, this flat and sandy beach is good for swimming because the waves are relatively gentle and the water is a few degrees warmer than at other beaches on the Cape Peninsula.

7 **kids** ★★ **Hout Bay Beach.** Popular with dog walkers and joggers, and a good spot for families to build sandcastles. The north end of this beach is good for swimming, because the waves are gentle. Kids will enjoy exploring the dunes, and if you look up there are great views of Chapman's Peak Drive (p 17). Look out for Fish on the Rocks *(Harbour Rd, Hout Bay.* ☎ *021-790-0001)*. This charming yellow shed has rickety wooden outside tables that overlook the fishing boats. Enjoy simple, traditional fish or calamari and chips (fries) served with a wedge of lemon.

8 ★★ **Llandudno Beach.** This is one of the most picturesque beaches on the Cape Peninsula, although it's difficult to find parking. This is a beautiful spot to watch the sunset and the sand is flanked by rocky coves on either end that invite further exploration. Sandy Bay is about 20 minutes walk to the south, surrounded by dunes, and sheltered and quiet. It's Cape Town's nudist beach, although you don't have to take your clothes off.

9 kids ★ **Long Beach.** This beach, found at Kommetjie, is an isolated stretch of sand perfect for a beach walk. The waves here are popular with surfers and in a couple of places reach up to 5m (16ft) in height.

10 kids ★ **Muizenberg Beach.** Running along the northern shore of False Bay, this magnificent swathe of sand is pounded by waves; hence its popularity for surfing. The promenade is looking a little seedy, however, and so it's not as popular as some of the other beaches. Look out for the row of brightly painted Victorian changing huts; they make a perfect photo.

11 ★★ **Noordhoek Beach.** Large rollers break on this vast expanse of white sand and it's perfect for a long walk or horse ride (p 76). It stretches 6km (3.75 miles) from the foot of Chapmans Peak and features The Hoek, one of the best surfing right hand breaks in South Africa. As

Relaxing on Long Beach, Kommetjie.

you walk through the wetlands to get to the beach, look out for birds, including the rare oystercatcher.

12 kids ★★★ **Seaforth Beach.** Next to Boulders Beach, this small sandy beach is clustered with giant rocks, which form shallow, calm bays that are perfect for paddling and swimming. You may bump into a stray penguin in the water.

Surf's Up

Cape Town is one of the world's top spots for surfing and there are a number of famous swells around the Cape Peninsula. The water is cold, and so full wetsuits are required. There are almost 50 surf spots around Cape Town, which are listed at www.wavescape.co.za. Beginners should head for Muizenberg Beach or Long Beach, while experienced surfers could try Dungeons near Hout Bay where waves break at 8m (26ft) and occasional international big wave competitions are held. **Downhill Adventures** (p 17) offer courses and equipment, and **Homeland Tours** (305 Long St; ☎ 021-426-0294; www.homeland.co.za) rents out boards and wetsuits.

Cape Town **Adventures**

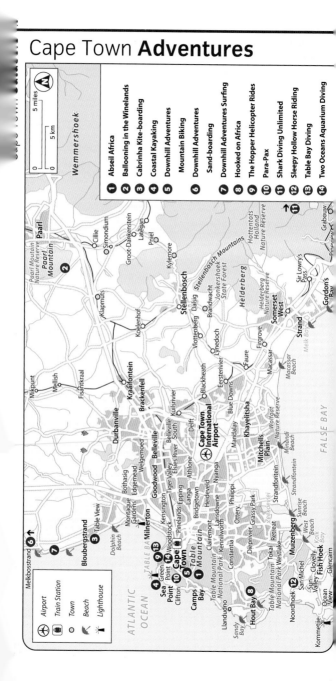

1. Abseil Africa
2. Ballooning in the Winelands
3. Cabrinha Kite-boarding
4. Coastal Kayaking
5. Downhill Adventures
   Mountain Biking
6. Downhill Adventures
   Sand-boarding
7. Downhill Adventures Surfing
8. Hooked on Africa
9. The Hopper Helicopter Rides
10. Para-Pax
11. Shark Diving Unlimited
12. Sleepy Hollow Horse Riding
13. Table Bay Diving
14. Two Oceans Aquarium Diving

- ✈ Airport
- 🚉 Train Station
- ○ Town
- 🏖 Beach
- 🔆 Lighthouse

Cape Town has a wealth of activities for the thrill-seeker—such as abseiling off the face of Table Mountain, diving with Great White sharks, cantering on horseback along an empty beach, or drifting over Lions Head on a tandem paraglide. Day trips are easily organized and so there's no reason not to explore the adventurous character of the Mother City.

1 ★★★ Abseil Africa. At 112m (367ft) this is the longest commercial abseil in the world. You jump off the west face of Table Mountain—certainly an unbeatable location—where you'll get an incredible rush of adrenalin when you take the first step and rappel into vertical space. This can be combined with a guided walk up the mountain via the Platteklip Gorge. The company also organizes 1-day *kloofing* at Kamikaze Kanyon outside Cape Town—this involves hiking, scrambling over rocks, jumping into rock pools, and abseiling over waterfalls. ⏲ *1–4 hrs. Upper Cableway Station, Table Mountain.* ☎ *021-424-4760. www.abseilafrica.co.za. Abseil R495, walk and abseil R650 (excluding Cableway), Kamikaze Kanyon day trip R695.*

Abseiling from Table Mountain.

2 ★★ Ballooning in the Winelands. A wonderful way to enjoy an early-morning sunrise over the beautiful Paarl winelands, the flight takes an hour and is followed by a champagne breakfast. ⏲ *4 hrs. Paarl.* ☎ *021-863-3192. www.kapinfo.com. Cost R2640. Nov–April only.*

A perfect opportunity to learn to surf.

③ ★★ Cabrinha Kite-boarding. The wide beach at Table View is a perfect place to learn the sport and after three 2-hour lessons you should be able to take to the ocean. Experienced kite-boarders can rent equipment. ⏱ *2 hrs. Shop 4, Marine Promenade, Porterfield Rd, Table View.* ☎ *021-556-7910. www.cabrinha.co.za. Lessons R495.*

④ ★★ Coastal Kayaking. Take a guided 2-person kayak trip along the 3km (nearly 2 miles) stretch of coastline from Three Anchor Bay to Clifton, and there's an excellent chance you'll spot seals, penguins, and a number of sea birds. If you're lucky, dolphins may accompany you on your paddle. ⏱ *2 hrs. 179 Beach Rd, Three Anchor Bay.* ☎ *021-439-1134. www.kayak.co.za. Cost R250.*

⑤ ★ Downhill Adventures Mountain Biking. Starting at the Lower Cableway Station, Downhill Adventures organizes guided mountain bike trips on off-road trails around Devil's Peak. They also include biking on their day tours of the Cape Peninsula (p 17). ⏱ *3 hrs. Lower Cableway Station.* ☎ *021-422-0388. www.downhilladventures.com. Cost R495.*

⑥ ★ Downhill Adventures Sand-boarding. Downhill Adventures will take you up the north coast, to a bank of brilliant white sand dunes, for a day of sand-boarding. It's like snow-boarding, but not as fast, and equipment, instruction, lunch, and drinks are included. Just bring thick socks. ⏱ *1 day. Atlantis, 1 hr drive north of Cape Town.* ☎ *021-422-0388. www.downhilladventures.com. Cost R655.*

⑦ ★ Downhill Adventures Surfing. It's those guys at Downhill again who promise to get surf virgins up and balancing on a wave in one day. Most trips go to Big Bay, north of the city, and include

Paragliding over Camps Bay.

instruction by an experienced surf rat, plus lunch. ⏱ *1 day. Big Bay, Table View.* ☎ *021-422-0388. www.downhilladventures.com. Cost R655.*

⑧ ★★ Hooked on Africa. Wrestle with one of the world's toughest fighting fish, yellowfin tuna (which can reach up to weights of 80kg (/176lb)), on this deep-sea fishing day trip, which departs from Hout Bay. The season runs from September to June. At other times of the year you can fish for crayfish, dorado, marlin, mako shark, or *snoek*—a local fish similar to cod. ⏱ *1 day. Hout Bay Harbor.* ☎ *021-790-5332. www.hookedonafrica.co.za. From R8,000 per boat, 1–4 people.*

⑨ ★★★ The Hopper Helicopter Rides. This is a fantastic way to see the geography of Table Mountain, and the views of the city, beaches, Robben Island, and the Twelve Apostles are simply tremendous. Even grandmothers will enjoy this and it makes an ideal surprise gift too. ⏱ *15 min. Quay 5, V&A Waterfront.* ☎ *021-419-8851. www.thehopper.co.za. Cost R500.*

10 ★★★ Para-Pax. Soar from Lion's Head over the beautiful beaches of Clifton and Camps Bay on a tandem paraglide. The views are astounding and the excursion includes refreshments. ⏱ *90 min. Pick-ups arranged to Lion's Head.* ☎ *082-881-4724. www.para-pax. co.za. Cost R950.*

11 ★★★ Shark Diving Unlimited. About a 2-hour drive from Cape Town, Shark Alley lies off the coast at Gansbaai and is world-renowned for the Great White sharks that feed on seals on nearby Geyser Island. Boats go out daily to view the sharks, and adrenaline junkies can get terrifyingly close by diving in a cage from the boat. The excursion includes transport from Cape Town. ⏱ *1 day. Gansbaai.* ☎ *082-441-4555. www.sharkdiving unlimited.com. Cost R1500.*

12 ★★ Sleepy Hollow Horse Riding. Noordhoek Beach on the Cape Peninsula is an 8km (5 miles) expanse of pristine beach best explored on horseback. Ride through wetlands and over sand dunes and then trot through the waves. The well-schooled horses are suitable for novices 14 years and older, and lessons and pony rides are offered for youngsters. ⏱ *2 hrs. Sleepy Hollow Lane, Noordhoek.* ☎ *021-789-2341. www.sleepy hollowhorseriding.co.za. Cost from R300.*

13 ★ Table Bay Diving. There are a number of dive sites around the Cape Peninsula, including some interesting wreck and kelp forest dives, but bear in mind that the water is very cold. This PADI center arranges off-shore or boat dives. ⏱ *From 1 hr. Quay 5, V&A Waterfront.* ☎ *021-419-8822. www.table baydiving.com. Cost per dive from R300.*

14 ★★★ Two Oceans Aquarium Diving. Experienced scuba divers can dive among Ragged Tooth sharks in the Predator Tank, or swim among thousands of fish in the kelp tank. This unique opportunity must be pre-booked and the cost includes wetsuit and equipment. You'll be putting on a show for other visitors to the aquarium too. ⏱ *30 min. Dock Rd, V&A Waterfront.* ☎ *021-418-3823. www. aquarium.co.za. Cost R485. Daily 9am, 11am, and 1pm.*

Horse riding on the beautiful swathe of beach at Noordhoek.

Cape Town **Parks & Reserves**

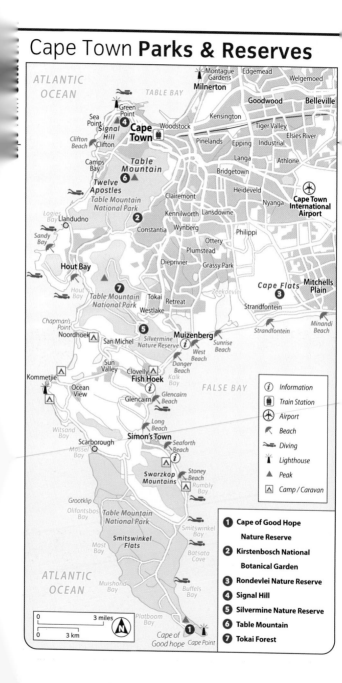

ⓘ	Information
🚉	Train Station
✈	Airport
🏖	Beach
🤿	Diving
🗼	Lighthouse
▲	Peak
🏕	Camp / Caravan

1 Cape of Good Hope
Nature Reserve

2 Kirstenbosch National
Botanical Garden

3 Rondevlei Nature Reserve

4 Signal Hill

5 Silvermine Nature Reserve

6 Table Mountain

7 Tokai Forest

From anywhere in Cape Town, look up to see an incredible vista of mountain scenery. Table Mountain National Park, from Signal Hill in the north to Cape Point in the south, encompasses the coastline of the Cape Peninsula. There are a number of different areas as well as smaller independent reserves, which make ideal outdoor excursions from the city. Activities include hiking, picnicking, and in places, mountain-biking.

❶ kids Cape of Good Hope Nature Reserve. Usually visited as part of a day tour around the Cape Peninsula, you can hike on laid out paths between the Cape of Good Hope and Cape Point. If you're in your own car you can also explore the minor roads and deserted beaches well away from the tourist buses. *1–2 hrs. See p 18, ❼.*

❷ kids ★★★ Kirstenbosch National Botanical Garden. Visit the Medicinal Plants Garden and the Fragrance Garden, or follow the lovely path through ferns and past a tumbling stream in The Dell. In the conservatory, see plants from South Africa's different habitats. *2–3 hrs. See p 21, ❹.*

❸ kids Rondevlei Nature Reserve. This area of wetlands and sand dunes is one of the best places in Cape Town for bird-watching; some 230 species of birds have been recorded. From bird hides and lookout towers equipped with telescopes, you can spot flamingoes, pelicans, African spoonbills, and Caspian terns. The best time to visit is

Kirstenbosch National Botanical Garden.

from January to March when many European migrants are present. You may also see the occasional hippo in the lake. *1–2 hrs. Fisherman's*

Two Oceans Marathon

Some 10,000 runners participate in the **Old Mutual Two Oceans Marathon** held annually on Easter Saturday (☎ 021-685-2030; www.twooceansmarathon.org), which runs on a scenic course around the Cape Peninsula. Rightly dubbed 'the world's most beautiful marathon', the full race is 56km (36 miles) or you can opt for the 21km (13 miles) half-marathon.

Cape Argus Pick 'n' Pay Cycle Tour

The biggest timed cycling event in the world, attracting more than 40,000 participants each year, is the **Cape Argus Pick 'n' Pay Cycle Tour** (☎ 021-685-6551; www.cycletour.co.za), This event, held every March, follows 109 km (68 miles) of the Cape Peninsula and is an enjoyable day for participants and the spectators that line the route cheering the cyclists on.

Walk, Zeekoevlei. ☎ *021-706-2404. www.rondevlei.co.za. Admission R5 adults, R2 kids (aged 3–13). Daily 7.30am–5pm.*

4 **kids** ★★★ **Signal Hill.** Follow the road as it winds its way around Signal Hill—be sure to stop at the view points—to the car park at the 350m (1,150ft) summit. Like the top of Table Mountain, the views are incredible and at sunset watch a fiery sun sink into the Atlantic. On the lower slopes of the hill, the Noon Day Gun has been operational since 1806 and is fired every day except Sunday. ⏱ *45 min. Signal Hill Rd. ww.sanparks.org.*

5 ★ **Silvermine Nature Reserve.** Hikers head here to enjoy the *fynbos* vegetation and wild flowers, plus great views across False Bay. There are several marked trails, picnic sites, and a boardwalk next to the reservoir. ⏱ *2–3 hrs. Off Ou Kaapseweg Rd (M64).* ☎ *021-701-8692. www.san parks.org. Daily May–Aug 8am–5pm, Sep–April 7am–6pm.*

6 ★★★ **Table Mountain.** A Cape Town must-do is to go to the top, either by the Aerial Cableway (p 10) or on foot. It takes about three hours to walk up and you need to be reasonably fit. The most popular route is up the north face via **Platteklip Gorge,** which starts 1.5km (1 mile) beyond the Lower Cableway Station, and there are two

other fairly strenuous routes— **Nursery Ravine** and **Skeleton Gorge**—from Kirstenbosch National Botanical Garden (p 21, **4**). At the top, there are a number of paths to explore and you always have the option of taking the Cableway back down. Note: the weather can change without warning, so never hike alone and take wet weather gear, sun-block, plenty of water, and punch this emergency number into your phone: ☎ 021-480-7700. ⏱ *3–5 hrs. See p 10,* **1**.

7 **kids** ★ **Tokai Forest.** This pine forest was first planted in 1883 and offers a pleasant ramble on well-established paths. Mountain biking is also allowed, and permits are available at the gate. ⏱ *1–2 hrs. Tokai Rd, Tokai.* ☎ *021-712-7471. www.san parks.org. Daily dawn to dusk.* ●

Exploring the top of Table Mountain.

Southern Suburbs & Cape Peninsula Dining

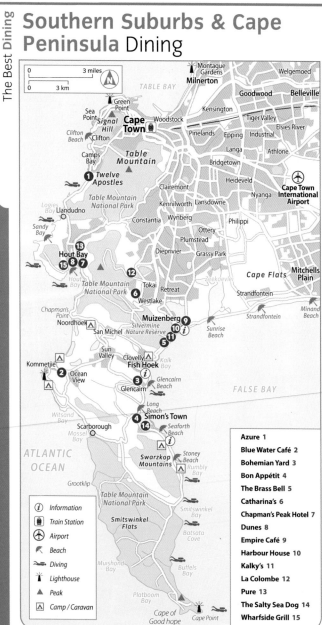

Azure 1

Blue Water Café 2

Bohemian Yard 3

Bon Appétit 4

The Brass Bell 5

Catharina's 6

Chapman's Peak Hotel 7

Dunes 8

Empire Café 9

Harbour House 10

Kalky's 11

La Colombe 12

Pure 13

The Salty Sea Dog 14

Wharfside Grill 15

V&A Waterfront & Atlantic Seaboard Dining

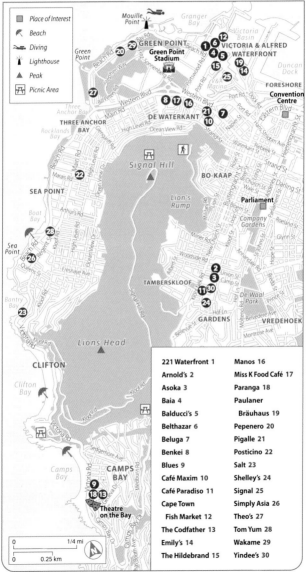

221 Waterfront 1	Manos 16
Arnold's 2	Miss K Food Café 17
Asoka 3	Paranga 18
Baia 4	Paulaner
Balducci's 5	Bräuhaus 19
Belthazar 6	Pepenero 20
Beluga 7	Pigalle 21
Benkei 8	Posticino 22
Blues 9	Salt 23
Café Maxim 10	Shelley's 24
Café Paradiso 11	Signal 25
Cape Town	Simply Asia 26
Fish Market 12	Theo's 27
The Codfather 13	Tom Yum 28
Emily's 14	Wakame 29
The Hildebrand 15	Yindee's 30

City Center Dining

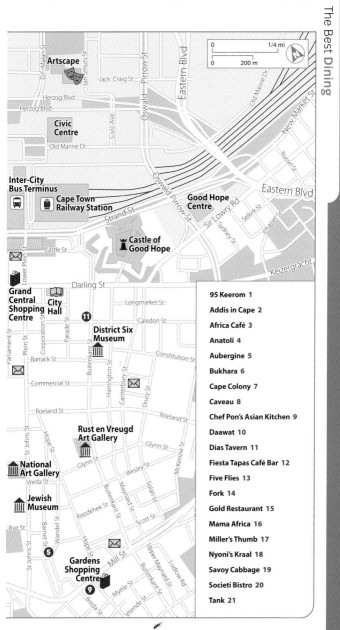

95 Keerom 1

Addis in Cape 2

Africa Café 3

Anatoli 4

Aubergine 5

Bukhara 6

Cape Colony 7

Caveau 8

Chef Pon's Asian Kitchen 9

Daawat 10

Dias Tavern 11

Fiesta Tapas Café Bar 12

Five Flies 13

Fork 14

Gold Restaurant 15

Mama Africa 16

Miller's Thumb 17

Nyoni's Kraal 18

Savoy Cabbage 19

Societi Bistro 20

Tank 21

Dining Best Bets

Best **Impressing Your Date**
★★★ Pigalle $$$ *57 Somerset Rd, Green Point (p 92)*

Best **Wine by the Glass**
★ Belthazar $$$ *153 Victoria Wharf, V&A Waterfront (p 86)*

Best **Cheap Asian Food**
★ Chef Pon's Asian Kitchen $$ *12 Mill St, Gardens (p 89)*

Best **Gourmet Dining**
★★★ Catharina's $$$$ *Steenberg Hotel, Tokai Rd, Constantia (p 88)*

Best **Winery Dining**
★★★ La Colombe $$$$$ *Constantia Uitsig, Spaanschemat River Rd, Constantia (p 90)*

Best **Build Your Own Seafood Platter**
★★★ The Codfather $$$$ *37 The Drive, Camps Bay (p 89)*

Best **Designer Tapas**
★ Fork $$$ *84 Long St (p 90)*

Best **Indian in South Africa**
★★★ Bukhara $$$$ *33 Church St (p 87)*

Best **V&A Waterfront Restaurant**
★★★ Baia $$$$$ *6262 Victoria Wharf, V&A Waterfront (p 86)*

Best **Traditional African Food**
★★ Africa Café $$$ *110 Shortmarket St (p 85)*

Best **Family Breakfast**
Dunes $$ *1 Hout Bay Beach, Hout Bay (p 89)*

Best **Sushi Fix**
★★★ Tank $$$$ *Cape Quarter, 72 De Waterkant St, Green Point (p 94)*

Best **People Watching**
★★ Blues $$$ *The Promenade, Victoria Rd, Camps Bay (p 87)*

Fine dining at Savoy Cabbage.

Best **Gorgeous Décor**
★★★ Pure $$$$ *Hout Bay Manor, Baviaanskloof, Hout Bay (p 92)*

Best **Fine Dining**
★★★ Savoy Cabbage $$$ *101 Hout St (p 93)*

Best **Hotel Restaurant**
★★★ Cape Colony $$$$$ *Mount Nelson Hotel, 76 Orange St, Gardens (p 88)*

Best **Scenic Views**
★★★ Azure $$$$ *12 Apostles Hotel & Spa, Victoria Rd, Camps Bay (p 86)*

Best **Family Steakhouse**
★ Theo's $$$ *163 Beach Rd, Mouille Point (p 94)*

Best **Cooking-school Eatery**
★★ Emily's $$$$ *202 The Clock Tower, V&A Waterfront (p 89)*

Best **Asian Fusion**
★★ Wakame $$$ *Beach Rd, Mouille Point (p 94)*

Cape Town Dining **A to Z**

★★ 221 Waterfront V&A WATER-FRONT *INTERNATIONAL* Serves a fusion of foods from across the globe and presentation is inventive. Huge glass panels slide back to reveal excellent harbor views, and décor is modern and bright. *221 Victoria Wharf.* ☎ *021-418-3633. www.221waterfront.co.za. Entrees R80–125. AE, DC, MC, V. Lunch and dinner daily. Map p 81.*

★★ 95 Keerom CITY BOWL *ITAL-IAN* Authentic Italian from a Milanese chef in a converted 17th-century stables with bare-brick walls. I recommend the white and dark chocolate soufflés. *95 Keerom St, Gardens.* ☎ *021-422-0765. www.95keerom. com. Entrees R80–100. AE, DC, MC, V. Lunch and dinner, Mon–Fri, dinner only Sat. Map p 82.*

★ Addis in Cape CITY CENTER *ETHIOPIAN* Try Ethiopia's national dish here, chicken *doro wot* (spicy stew) served with *injera* (flat bread) and finish off with a traditional coffee ceremony. Vegetarians are well catered for and vegans can order in advance. *41 Church St.* ☎ *021-424-5722. www.addisincape.co.za. Entrees* R70–90. AE, DC, MC, V. Lunch and dinner Mon–Sat. Map p 82.

★★ kids Africa Café CITY CENTER *AFRICAN* This themed restaurant has a buffet featuring dishes from all over Africa, from Moroccan salads to Ethiopian black bean stew. It can be a bit touristy but is loads of fun. *108 Shortmarket St, Heritage Square.* ☎ *021-422-0221. www.africacafe. co.za. Set menus R180. AE, DC, MC, V. Dinner daily. Map p 82.*

★★ Anatoli ATLANTIC SEABOARD *TURKISH* Begin with a selection of *mezes* (appetizers) and fresh-baked flat bread, then follow with traditional kebabs or baked fish. Sample the Turkish *Efes* lager. *Napier St, Green Point.* ☎ *021-419-2501. www. anatoli.co.za. Entrees R70–R100. AE, MC, V. Dinner Mon–Sat. Map p 82.*

kids Arnold's CITY BOWL *INTERNA-TIONAL* Arnold's is very popular with locals—you may have to queue for a table. Offers great value all-day breakfasts, plus pastas, burgers, salads, and grills, and service is attentive. *60 Kloof St, Gardens.* ☎ *021-424-4344. www.arnolds.co.za.*

Outside tables at 221 Waterfront.

Light interior of Aubergine.

Entrees R20–130. MC, V. Breakfast, lunch and dinner daily. Map p 81.

★★ Asoka CITY BOWL *INTERNATIONAL* This tapas and cocktail bar is set in a beautifully restored Victorian house. Indian, Japanese, Thai, Moroccan, and other international dishes come in mini sizes. It gets very busy on weekend nights. Ask about winter specials. *68 Kloof St, Gardens.* ☎ *021-422-0909. www. asokabar.co.za. Tapas R30–50 each. AE, DC, MC, V. Dinner daily. Map p 81.*

★★★ Aubergine CITY BOWL *GOURMET* Expect the likes of quail with potato puree and asparagus, or medallion of venison with an apple and date confit, at fairly high prices. The dishes are beautifully presented. *39 Barnet St, Gardens.* ☎ *021-464-4090. www.aubergine. co.za. Entrees R100–165. AE, DC, MC, V. Lunch Weds–Fri, dinner Mon–Sat. Map p 82.*

★★★ Azure CAPE PENINSULA *GOURMET* Dine in luxury while looking out onto stunning ocean views. Dishes fuse different cuisines with great success; try the 'four of the best' desserts on one plate. *12*

Apostles Hotel & Spa, Victoria Rd, Camps Bay. ☎ *021-437-9000. www. 12apostleshotel.com. Entrees R100– 220. AE, DC, MC, V. Breakfast, lunch and dinner daily. Map p 80.*

★★★ Baia V&A WATERFRONT *SEAFOOD* Specializes in seafood such as West Coast mussels, Mozambiquan prawns and crayfish, Knysna oysters, and a good range of local fish. The lobster *thermidor* is always a winner. *6262 Victoria Wharf.* ☎ *021-491-0935. Entrees R95–260. AE, DC, MC, V. Lunch and dinner daily. Map p 81.*

★★ Balducci's V&A WATERFRONT *INTERNATIONAL* Choose to sit in a plush velvet booth or at an outside table. Service is sleek and the menu has seafood and sushi, plus sandwiches, gourmet pizzas, and luxury burgers. *6162 Victoria Wharf.* ☎ *021-421-6002. www.balduccis. com. Entrees R75–165. AE, DC, MC, V. Breakfast, lunch and dinner daily. Map p 81.*

★ Belthazar V&A WATERFRONT *INTERNATIONAL* Light meals include salads or grilled sole, while the hungry can opt for a game meat skewer or giant sirloin kebab. More than 100 wines are served by the glass. *153 Victoria Wharf.* ☎ *021-421-3753. www.belthazar.co.za. Entrees R80–160. AE, DC, MC, V. Lunch and dinner daily. Map p 81.*

★★★ **Beluga** ATLANTIC SEA-BOARD *GOURMET* A super-sexy and stylish spot that's seen the likes of Bill Clinton and Tiger Woods; you'll need to dress to impress. The menu features caviar, seafood, grills, and decadent desserts. *The Foundry, Prestwich St, Green Point.* ☎ *021-418-2948. www.beluga. co.za. Entrees R90–300. AE, DC, MC, V. Lunch and dinner daily. Map p 81.*

Benkei ATLANTIC SEABOARD *JAP-ANESE* Benkei offers the most affordable sushi in town, plus soups, noodles, tempura, and teppanyaki dishes. *105 Main Rd, Green Point.* ☎ *021-439-4918. Entrees R35–130. AE, MC, V. Lunch and dinner daily. Map p 81.*

★★ **Blues** CAPE PENINSULA *INTER-NATIONAL* This is a trendy spot on the Camps Bay strip with beach views. The menu features seafood, salads, pastas, and grills. Try a delicious cocktail. *The Promenade, Victoria Rd, Camps Bay.* ☎ *021-438-2040. www.blues.co.za. Entrees R85–180. AE, DC, MC, V. Lunch and dinner daily. Map p 81.*

kids Blue Water Café CAPE PEN-INSULA *INTERNATIONAL* Set in a charming old Cape Dutch home-stead, this café opens early for eggs Benedict or fluffy omelets, and at lunchtime has specials such as Cape Malay chicken curry. *Imhoff Farm, Kommetjie Rd, Kommetjie.* ☎ *021-783-2007. Entrees R45–95. MC, V. Breakfast and lunch daily. Map p 80.*

★ **Bohemian Yard** CAPE PENIN-SULA *MEDITERRANEAN* With its lovely antiques, overstuffed sofas, and chandeliers, I think this is an

atmospheric venue. The modern Mediterranean menu changes sea-sonally. *16 Kommetjie Rd, Fish Hoek.* ☎ *021-782-7773. Entrees R55–120. AE, MC, V. Breakfast and lunch Tues–Sun, dinner Tues–Sat. Map p 80.*

★★ **Bon Appétit** CAPE PENIN-SULA *FRENCH* Run by a chef from Brittany, and so you can expect the likes of pork fillet with prune *confit* or beef fillet stuffed with oyster mushrooms. Leave room for the irresistible desserts. *90 George's Rd, Simon's Town.* ☎ *021-786-2412. Entrees R85–130. AE, DC, MC, V. Din-ner Tues–Sat. Map p 80.*

kids The Brass Bell CAPE PENIN-SULA *INTERNATIONAL* You will find the formal seafood restaurant upstairs and cheaper pizzas and pub grub downstairs and on the ter-race. It backs on to some tidal pools where youngsters can paddle. *Main Rd, Kalk Bay.* ☎ *021-788-5455. www. brassbell.co.za. Entrees R35–185. AE, MC, V. Lunch and dinner daily. Map p 80.*

★★★ **Bukhara** CITY CENTER *INDIAN* This is the best Indian in the city and is consistently packed to the gills so do book in advance. Watch the chefs in the glass-fronted kitchen, and try one of the Asian beers. *33 Church St.* ☎ *021-434-0000. www.bukhara.com. Entrees R110–170. AE, DC, MC, V. Lunch daily, din-ner Mon–Sat. Map p 82.*

★★ **Café Maxim** ATLANTIC SEA-BOARD *FRENCH* Pop into this *boulangerie* for croissants, filled baguettes, and salads, or try a slice of delicate nougat imported from Paris. *126 Waterkant St, Green Point.* ☎ *021-425-5102. www.cafemaxim.co.za. Entrees R30–60. AE, DC, MC, V. Break-fast and lunch Tues–Sun. Map p 81.*

★★ **Café Paradiso** CITY BOWL *FRENCH* This is good for rich and tasty duck, lamb, beef, and rabbit dishes but also try the *flammekue-chen*, a French-style flat pizza spread with yoghurt, cream cheese, and a variety of toppings. *110 Kloof St, Gardens.* ☎ *021-423-8653. Entrees R50–110. AE, DC, MC, V. Breakfast Sat–Sun, lunch and dinner daily. Map p 81.*

★★★ **Cape Colony** CITY BOWL *GOURMET* Frequently rated by travel magazines as one of the world's top restaurants, dine out here on hearty fare such as beef Wellington or roast lamb in a setting with a wonderfully old-fashioned feel—chandeliers, sweeping drapes, and cutlery from old cruise ships. *Mount Nelson Hotel, 76 Orange St, Gardens.* ☎ *021-483-1948. www. themountnelson.co.za. Entrees R150. AE, DC, MC, V. Dinner daily. Map p 82.*

★★ **Cape Town Fish Market** V&A WATERFRONT *SEAFOOD* You can pick out your own seafood from the chilled cabinets, then sit at the large circular rotating sushi bar and watch the chefs at work. This is the best of many branches around the city. *159 King's Warehouse.* ☎ *021-418-5977. www.ctfm.co.za. Entrees*

R50–190. AE, DC, MC, V. Lunch and dinner daily. Map p 81. Also at 21 The Promenade, Victoria Rd, Camps Bay. ☎ *021-438-1866.*

★★★ **Catharina's** CAPE PENINSULA *GOURMET* A top-notch spot where the chef enhances the dishes with *jus*, sauces, and foams. Try the sought-after Steenberg Sauvignon Blanc Reserve; only 2,000 cases are produced each year. *Steenberg Hotel, Tokai Rd, Constantia.* ☎ *021-713-2222. www.steenberghotel.com. Entrees R110–140. AE, DC, MC, V. Lunch and dinner daily. Map p 80.*

Caveau CITY CENTER *INTERNATIONAL* Very popular with locals and so arrive early to sit outside as bookings are not taken for parties of less than six people. The courtyard has a distinctly European air, and the food is bistro style and written up on chalk boards. *92 Bree St, Heritage Square* ☎ *021-422-1367. www. caveau.co.za. Entrees R50–105. AE, MC, V. Breakfast, lunch and dinner Mon–Sat. Map p 82.*

★ **Chapman's Peak Hotel** CAPE PENINSULA *INTERNATIONAL* This restaurant is famous for its calamari served in frying pans; the seafood

Roast line-fish at Catharina's.

platters are good value too. Sit in the wood-paneled dining room or casual outside terrace. *Chapmans Peak Rd, Hout Bay.* ☎ *021-790-1036. www.chapmanspeakhotel.co.za. R70–110. AE, MC, V. Lunch and dinner daily. Map p 80.*

★ **Chef Pon's Asian Kitchen** CITY BOWL *ASIAN* A Cape Town institution due to its affordable and excellent Thai, Chinese, Japanese, and Indonesian food. The Thai curries and crispy duck are unbeatable. *12 Mill St, Gardens.* ☎ *021-465-5846. www.chefponsasiankitchen.co.za. Entrees R50–80. MC, V. Dinner daily. Map p 82.*

★★ **The Codfather** CAPE PENINSULA *SEAFOOD/INTERNATIONAL* Expensive but superb seafood and fish, which you pick out and have cooked to your liking. It's almost impossible to resist a snack at the sushi bar while you wait. *37 The Drive, Camps Bay.* ☎ *021-438-0782. Entrees R100–300. AE, DC, MC, V. www.thecodfather.co.za. Lunch and dinner daily. Map p 81.*

★★ **Daawat** CITY CENTER *PAKISTANI* The only Pakistani restaurant in Cape Town has a good range of curries, kebabs, and tandoori dishes. The lamb chop masala and the butter chicken are popular. *Dockside Building, 37 Buteingracht St.* ☎ *021-421-9017. www.daawat.co.za. Entrees R65–110. AE, DC, MC, V. Lunch and dinner daily. Map p 82.*

Dias Tavern CITY CENTER *INTERNATIONAL* Rub shoulders with the regulars at this old-fashioned pub, which is decorated like a Portuguese taverna. There's a good choice of pub grub and the sole, kingklip and sardines are especially good. *15 Caledon St.* ☎ *021-465-7547. Entrees R45–90. MC, V. Lunch and dinner Mon–Sat. Map p 82.*

kids Dunes CAPE PENINSULA *INTERNATIONAL* This restaurant is perched in the sand dunes, and has pub style fare such as fish 'n' chips (fries), calamari, and rump steak. Take the kids—there's a jungle gym and kiddies' menu. *1 Hout Bay Beach, Hout Bay.* ☎ *021-790-1876. www.dunesrestaurant.co.za. Entrees R55–140. MC, V. Lunch and dinner Mon–Fri, breakfast, lunch and dinner Sat–Sun. Map p 80.*

★★ **Emily's** V&A WATERFRONT *INTERNATIONAL* Emily's is a sophisticated, award-winning establishment run by a restaurant school, and specializes in game and seafood. Ask for a table in the window for good views over the V&A Waterfront. *202 The Clock Tower.* ☎ *021-421-1133. www.emily-s.com. Entrees R95–125. AE, DC, MC, V. Lunch and dinner Mon–Sat. Map p 81.*

kids Empire Café CAPE PENINSULA *INTERNATIONAL* Popular with surfers for breakfast, this spacious café serves light meals until 4pm. Daily specials are written up on blackboards. *11 York Rd, Muizenberg.* ☎ *021-788-1250. www.empirecafe.co.za. Entrees R20–100. MC, V. Breakfast and lunch daily. Map p 80.*

★ **Fiesta Tapas Café Bar** ATLANTIC SEABOARD *MEDITERRANEAN* The tapas here include grilled prawns, corn cakes and *chorizo* sausage. A lively spot, with tables spilling out into the Cape Quarter courtyard, and open until 2am. *Cape Quarter, 72 Waterkant St, Green Point.* ☎ *021-418-5121. www.fiesta-tapas.co.za. Entrees R50–105; tapas from R30 each. AE, DC, MC, V. Lunch and dinner daily. Map p 82.*

★★ **Five Flies** CITY CENTER *GOURMET* The menu features the likes of warm goat's cheese, gorgonzola salad, roast lamb, or duck breast, although the desserts lack flair. There is a formal wood-paneled

Delicate dessert at Fork.

dining room or cobbled square out back. *14 Keerom St.* ☎ *021-424-4442. www.fiveflies.co.za. Set meals R150–260. AE, DC, MC, V. Lunch Mon–Fri, dinner daily. Map p 82.*

★ **Fork** CITY CENTER *MEDITERRA-NEAN* A great place to share a meal, as the menu features an array of Mediterranean tapas. Portions are generous, and the décor is bare brick walls and booth seating. There's a good selection of wine by the glass. *84 Long St.* ☎ *021-424-6334. www.fork-restaurants.co.za. Tapas R25–55 each. MC, V. Lunch and dinner Mon–Sat. Map p 82.*

★★ **Gold Restaurant** CITY CEN-TER *AFRICAN* Located in the rear courtyard of the Gold of Africa Museum (see p 52), under trees full of twinkly lights, this restaurant serves fantastic African food. Try out some drumming, and ask about the occasional Mali puppetry performances. *Gold of Africa Museum, 96 Strand St.* ☎ *021-421-4653. www. goldrestaurant.co.za. Entrees R75–220. AE, DC, MC, V. Lunch and din-ner daily. Map p 82.*

★ **Harbour House** CAPE PENIN-SULA *SEAFOOD* You'd be hard pressed to find restaurant tables so close to the sea anywhere else in Cape Town. The menu has a strong emphasis on seafood straight from the harbor and caught by the res-taurant's own fishermen. *Kalk Bay Harbour, Kalk Bay.* ☎ *021-788-4133. www.harbourhouse.co.za. Entrees R80–300. AE. MC, V. Lunch and din-ner daily. Map p 80.*

★★ **The Hildebrand** V&A WATER-FRONT *ITALIAN/SEAFOOD* Try a plate of antipasti, a crusty loaf, and a chilled bottle of wine for lunch or opt for the legendary chateaubriand flamed at your table for dinner. The Hildebrand has a great location right on the water's edge. *Pier Head.* ☎ *021-425-3385. www.hildebrand. co.za. Entrees R70–120. AE, DC, MC, V. Lunch and dinner daily. Map p 81.*

kids Kalky's CAPE PENINSULA *SEAFOOD* Simple but tasty tradi-tional fish 'n' chips is served here with plastic cutlery in a colorful wooden shack. Tables spill out onto the quayside. Look out for seals in the harbor. *Kalk Bay Harbour, Kalk Bay.* ☎ *021-788-1726. Entrees R30–70. No credit cards. Lunch and din-ner daily. Map p 80.*

★★★ **La Colombe** CAPE PENIN-SULA *FRENCH* One of Cape Town's finest restaurants. The superb menu incorporates bursts of flavor such as lavender, berries, and lemon in spring or the earthy flavors of truffle and mushroom in the autumn. *Con-stantia Uitsig, Spaanschemat River Rd, Constantia.* ☎ *021-794-6500. www.constantia-uitsig.com. Entrees R110–160. AE, DC, MC, V. Lunch and dinner daily. Map p 80.*

★ **Mama Africa** CITY CENTER *AFRICAN* Try traditional South Afri-can food such as *samp* (maize with the husk and germ removed) and beans, Cape Malay curries and game meat, and leave room for the delicious *malva* pudding (sponge with apricot jam). A lively marimba bands plays in the evening. *178 Long St.* ☎ *021-426-1017. www. mamaafricarest.net. Entrees R60– 130. AE, DC, MC, V. Dinner Mon–Sat. Map p 82.*

Manos ATLANTIC SEABOARD *MEDITERRANEAN* Try the beef carpaccio or a salad, followed by fillet with béarnaise sauce or line fish. The menu is short, but dishes are imaginative and affordable. *39 Main Rd, Green Point.* ☎ *021-434-1090. Entrees R50–120. AE, MC, V. Lunch and dinner Mon–Sat. Map p 81.*

★ **Miller's Thumb** CITY BOWL *INTERNATIONAL* Husband and wife team, Solly and Jane, create a cozy atmosphere at this firm favorite of Cape Town locals. Seafood is cooked Cajun style, and the Mississippi mud pie is to die for. *10b Kloofnek Rd, Gardens.* ☎ *021-424-3838. Entrees R50–130. AE, MC, V. Lunch Tues–Fri, dinner Mon–Sat; closed July. Map p 82.*

Miss K Food Café ATLANTIC SEABOARD *INTERNATIONAL* A weekend breakfast hotspot with freshly squeezed juices, decadent orange polenta cakes, and lemon tarts. Look out for the giant tea-cup in the doorway. *65 Main Rd, Green Point.* ☎ *021-439-9559. Entrees R20–50. MC, V. Breakfast and lunch Tues–Sun. Map p 81.*

★ **Nyoni's Kraal** CITY CENTER *AFRICAN* Come here for African cuisine such as *mealie pap* (maize porridge), pickled fish, *smiley's* (sheep's head) or mopani worms. The less brave can opt for curries or calamari, though there's not much choice for vegetarians. *98 Long St.* ☎ *021-422-0529. www.nyoniskraal. co.za. Entrees R65–110. AE, DC, MC, V. Breakfast and lunch Mon–Sat, dinner daily. Map p 82.*

★★ **Paranga** CAPE PENINSULA *INTERNATIONAL* This is a super place to watch the sunset on a balmy summer's evening. There's a long menu of salads, pastas, seafood, sushi, and grills. A trendy spot, and even the waiting staff are

The glamorous Pigalle.

Opulent décor at Pure.

super-glamorous. *The Promenade, Victoria Rd, Camps Bay.* ☎ *021-438-0404. www.paranga.co.za. Entrees R70–140. AE, DC, MC, V. Breakfast, lunch and dinner daily. Map p 81.*

★ **Paulaner Bräuhaus** V&A WATERFRONT *GERMAN*   The drill is simple here—sausages, sauerkraut, and frosty beer. Bang your beer flagons together at the long wooden tables and giggle at the over-the-top Bavarian costumes worn by the staff. *18 Clock Tower.* ☎ *021-418-9999. www.paulaner.co.za. Entrees R45–100. AE, DC, MC, V. Lunch and dinner daily. Map p 81.*

★ **Pepenero** ATLANTIC SEABOARD *SEAFOOD/ITALIAN*   Enjoy seafood with great views of Table Bay. The crayfish and seared tuna are sublime; finish with a luxurious dessert made from Lindt chocolate. *Two Oceans House, Beach Rd, Mouille Point.* ☎ *021-439-9027. www.pepenero.co.za. Entrees R60–180. AE, DC, MC, V. Lunch and dinner daily. Map p 81.*

★★★ **Pigalle** ATLANTIC SEA-BOARD *MEDITERRANEAN*   This glamorous dinner/dance venue has chandeliers, velvet banquettes, a live jazz band, and a spacious dance floor. The menu features a good range of seafood and Portuguese dishes. *57 Somerset Rd, Green Point.* ☎ *021-421-4848. www.pigalle restaurants.co.za. Entrees R90–150. AE, DC, MC, V. Lunch and dinner Mon–Sat. Map p 81.*

Posticino ATLANTIC SEABOARD *ITALIAN*   One of my favorite good-value Italian bistros. You can make up your own pasta sauce—some may work, some may not. Sit next to the crackling fire in winter and in summer, order a jug of icy sangria. *323 Main Rd, Sea Point.* ☎ *021-439-4014. www.posticino.co.za. Entrees R30–80. AE, MC, V. Lunch and dinner daily. Map p 81.*

★★★ **Pure** CAPE PENINSULA *INTERNATIONAL*   You will find fine dining here with a carefully thought-out menu and beautifully dressed plates. The breathtakingly opulent all-silver décor is impressive, and is even found in the bathrooms. *Hout Bay Manor, Baviaanskloof, Hout Bay.* ☎ *021-790-0116. www.hout baymanor.co.za. Entrees R120–160. AE, DC, MC, V. Lunch Sun, dinner Tues–Sat. Map p 80.*

★★★ **Salt** CAPE PENINSULA *INTER-NATIONAL*   A sample menu could have smoked salmon with arti-chokes, followed by slow roasted pork with apple mash and chilled lime soufflé. Watch the sun set over Table Bay from your table. *34 Victoria Rd, Bantry Bay.* ☎ *021-439-7258. www.saltrestaurant.co.za. Entrees R90–130. AE, DC, MC, V. Lunch and dinner daily. Map p 81.*

kids The Salty Sea Dog CAPE PENINSULA *SEAFOOD* Simple and delicious fish or calamari and fries are served here, accompanied by bread and butter, mushy peas, and pickled onions. *6 Wharf St, Simon's Town.* ☎ *021-786-1918. Entrees R35–60. No credit cards. Lunch daily. Map p 80.*

★★★ Savoy Cabbage CITY CENTER *INTERNATIONAL* The Savoy Cabbage offers excellent main courses and delicate, beautifully presented desserts in a bare-brick, industrial steel décor, with cabbage-shaped chandeliers and open-plan kitchen. *101 Hout St.* ☎ *021-424-2626. www.savoycabbage.co.za. Entrees R95–160. AE, DC, MC, V. Lunch Mon–Fri, dinner Mon–Sat. Map p 82.*

Shelley's CITY BOWL *INTERNATIONAL* A sunny café offering good breakfasts, particularly the buttermilk pancakes with syrup and berries, plus sandwiches, light meals, cakes, and freshly squeezed

juices and smoothies. *90 Kloof St, Gardens.* ☎ *021-424-2470. Entrees R25–50. MC, V. Breakfast and lunch daily. Map p 81.*

★★★ Signal V&A WATERFRONT *INTERNATIONAL* Smart hotel restaurant with chandeliers, crisp white linen, and gourmet food. Also does a good afternoon tea with a glass of bubbly. *Cape Grace Hotel, West Quay Rd.* ☎ *021-410-7040. www. capegrace.com. Entrees R90–250. AE, DC, MC, V. Breakfast, lunch and dinner daily. Map p 81.*

★ Simply Asia ATLANTIC SEABOARD *ASIAN* Rapid service and cheap, tasty, and filling food is the order of the day here. Thai noodles are cooked in front of you and served in square boxes; choose chicken, beef, or prawns and nibble on sushi while you wait. *84 Regent Rd, Sea Point.* ☎ *021-439-0160. www.simplyasia.co.za. Entrees R30–65. MC, V. Lunch and dinner daily. Map p 81. There are other branches in the shopping malls.*

★ Societi Bistro CITY BOWL *FRENCH/ITALIAN* Choose the eggs Benedict or Florentine for breakfast and classic meals such as steak au poivre or pasta carbonara later in the day. You'll get a blanket outside if it's

Restaurant Reviews

Capetonians love to eat out, and it's easy to find information on dining in print and on the web. The annual **Eat Out** (www.eatout. co.za) magazine reviews the top restaurants in South Africa, while its sister magazine **Eat In** (www.eat-in.co.za) reviews delis, markets, and specialist food stores. They are available in all bookshops. **Dining Out** (www.dining-out.co.za) reviews hundreds of restaurants across the country and features photos and menus. The annual **TimeOut for Visitors** magazine has a great overview of restaurants in Cape Town.

chilly. *50 Orange St, Gardens.* ☎ *021-424-2100. www.societi.co.za. Entrees R70–130. Breakfast Tues–Sat, lunch and dinner Mon–Sat. Map p 82.*

★★★ **Tank** ATLANTIC SEABOARD *JAPANESE* The Japanese chef here has a cult following and the *sashimi* literally melts in your mouth. The décor is white and minimalist, but the clientele are rather pretentious. *Cape Quarter, 72 De Waterkant St, Green Point.* ☎ *021-419-0007. www.the-tank.co.za. Entrees R65–190. AE, DC, MC, V. Lunch and dinner daily. Map p 82.*

★ kids **Theo's** ATLANTIC SEABOARD *STEAKHOUSE/SEAFOOD* Casual and unpretentious, Theo's serves seafood and grills and is best known for melt-in-the-mouth steaks with creamy sauces and an array of toppings. *163 Beach Rd, Mouille Point.* ☎ *021-439-3494. Entrees R60–150. AE, DC, MC, V. Lunch Mon–Fri, dinner daily. Map p 81.*

Tom Yum ATLANTIC SEABOARD *THAI* Affordable Thai food and has bright orange décor. The fiery red and green curries, *tom yum* (hot and sour) soup and crispy duck pancakes are especially good. *72 Regent Rd, Sea Point.* ☎ *021-434-8139. Entrees R40–80. MC, V. Lunch and dinner daily. Map p 81.*

★★ **Wakame** ATLANTIC SEABOARD *ASIAN* You get great sea views from the rooftop deck and a pleasant place to spend a sunny afternoon. Food is Asian fusion; the signature dish is tea-smoked salmon and there's a long sushi menu. *Beach Rd, Mouille Point.* ☎ *021-433-2377. www.wakame.co.za. Entrees R70–160. AE, DC, MC, V. Lunch and dinner daily. Map p 81.*

★★ kids **Wharfside Grill** CAPE PENINSULA *SEAFOOD* Family restaurant with cozy booths or outside tables overlooking the fishing boats in the harbor. Staff wear jaunty blue-and-white sailor outfits. The chowders are great. *Mariner's Wharf, Hout Bay.* ☎ *021-790-1100. www.marinerswharf.com. Entrees R45–115. DC, MC, V. Lunch and dinner daily. Map p 80.*

★★ **Yindee's** CITY BOWL *THAI* This is Cape Town's best Thai restaurant. The very long menu has all the usual favorites and garlic and chili can be adjusted. The chef's recommendations are worth investigating. *39 Camp St, Gardens.* ☎ *021-422-1012. Entrees R70–100. AE, DC, MC, V. Lunch Mon–Sat, dinner daily. Map p 81.* ●

The Best Nightlife

City Center, City Bowl & V&A

Alba Lounge 1

Asoka Son of Dharma 2

Bascule Bar 3

Beulah Bar 4

Bronx Action Bar 5

Buena Vista Social Café 6

Café Manhattan 7

Chrome 8

Ferryman's Tavern 9

Fireman's Arms 10

Hemisphere 11

Jo'burg 12

The Loft Lounge 13

Marimba 14

Mercury Live & Lounge 15

Mitchell's Brewery 16

Neighbourhood Bar
 & Lounge 17

The Nose Restaurant
 & Wine Bar 18

Planet Champagne Bar 19

Rafiki's 20

Relish 21

Tobago's 22

Vertigo 23

Zula Sound Bar 24

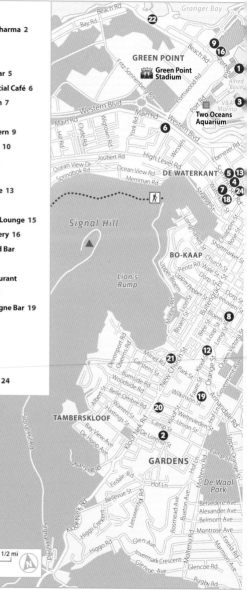

Waterfront Nightlife

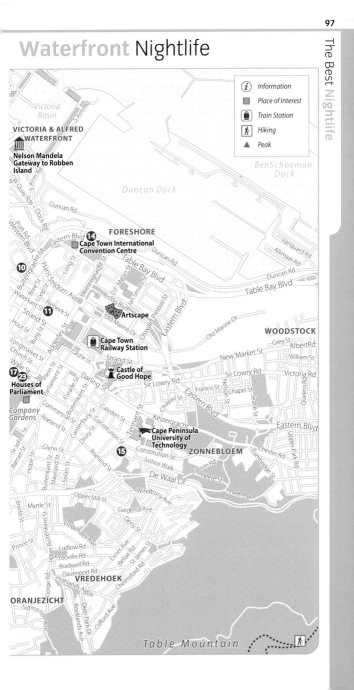

Nightlife Best Bets

Best **English Pub for Watching the Big Match**
★★ Fireman's Arms, *25 Mechau St (p 100)*

Best **Jaw-dropping City Views**
★★★ Hemisphere, *31st Floor, Absa Building, 2 Riebeeck St (p 102)*

Best **Sundowners**
★★★ Tobago's, *Radisson SAS Hotel, Beach Rd, Granger Bay (p 103)*

Best **Mixing with the Beautiful People**
★★★ Café Caprice, *37 Victoria Rd, Camps Bay (p 99)*

Best **Wine Bar**
★★ The Nose, *Cape Quarter, 72 De Waterkant St, Green Point (p 100)*

Best **Live Indie Music**
★ Mercury Live & Lounge, *43 De Villiers St (p 104)*

Best **Champagne Bar**
★★★ Planet Champagne Bar, *Mount Nelson Hotel, 76 Orange St, Gardens (p 103)*

Best **Variety of Whiskies**
★★★ Bascule Bar, *Cape Grace, West Quay, V&A Waterfront (p 103)*

Mitchell's brews its own beer.

Best **Student Grunge**
Jo'burg, *218 Long St (p 103)*

Best **Home-brewed Beer**
★ Mitchell's Brewery, *East Pier Rd, V&A Waterfront (p 100)*

Best **Mainstream Nightclub**
Chrome, *6 Pepper St (p 101)*

Best **Cigars & Latino Music**
★★ Buena Vista Social Café, *81 Main Rd, Green Point (p 99)*

Best for **a Pint While the Wife Goes Shopping**
Ferryman's Tavern, *East Pier Rd, V&A Waterfront (p 100)*

Best for **a Game of Blackjack**
GrandWest Casino, *1 Vanguard Dr, Goodwood (p 101)*

Best **Gay & Lesbian Sophisticated Lounge**
★★ The Loft Lounge, *24 Napier St, Green Point (p 103)*

Best **Shaken not Stirred Martinis**
★★★ Leopard Lounge *Twelve Apostles Hotel, Victoria Rd, Camps Bay (p 103)*

Southern Suburbs & Cape Peninsula Nightlife

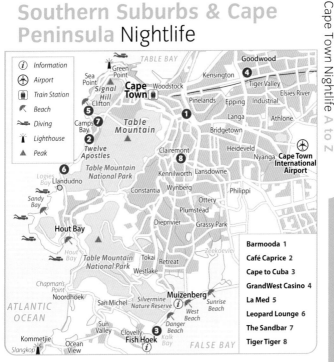

ⓘ	Information
✈	Airport
🚉	Train Station
⌂	Beach
⚑	Diving
🗼	Lighthouse
▲	Peak

Barmooda 1
Café Caprice 2
Cape to Cuba 3
GrandWest Casino 4
La Med 5
Leopard Lounge 6
The Sandbar 7
Tiger Tiger 8

Cape Town Nightlife A to Z

Bars & Pubs

★★★ **Alba Lounge** V&A WATER-FRONT Chilled cocktail lounge with stylish sofas, warm and cold finger food, and good Waterfront views. It's popular with a professional post-work, pre-party crowd. *Pierhead.* ☎ *021-425-3385. www.albalounge. co.za. Map p 96.*

★ **Asoka Son of Dharma** CITY BOWL Very elegant Eastern décor designed with Feng Shui principles, and there's a real tree in the center covered in twinkly lights. The cocktails are legendary and there's a long menu of Asian tapas snacks. *68 Kloof St.* ☎ *021-422-0909. www. asokabar.co.za. Map p 96.*

★★ **Buena Vista Social Café** ATLANTIC SEABOARD Lively Cuban-themed bar and restaurant with balcony, bare-brick walls and a cigar menu. Tables are pushed back later for dancing to Latin music. *81 Main Road, Green Point.* ☎ *021-434-6196. www.buenavista.co.za. Map p 96.*

★★★ **Café Caprice** CAPE PENIN-SULA *The* place to be seen in Camps Bay—you'll rub shoulders

The Best Nightlife

with models and Ferrari owners—with bright blue-and-white décor, cube-shaped seats, trendy cocktails, good food, and slick service. *37 Victoria Rd, Camps Bay. ☎ 021-438-8315. www.cafecaprice.co.za. Map p 99.*

Cape to Cuba CAPE PENINSULA Colorful restaurant and bar decorated in a Cuban/Havana mansion style with mismatched outside tables set among palms, and great ocean views. Cuban music, good cocktails, and cigars are available. *Main Rd, Kalk Bay. ☎ 021-788-1566. www.capetocuba.co.za. Map p 99.*

Ferryman's Tavern V&A WATERFRONT With a host of beers on tap, and several TVs tuned to sports, this has a real British pub feel and attracts expats who come to watch the soccer. Better for drinking as the food is mediocre. *East Pier Rd. ☎ 021-419-7748. www.ferrymans.co.za. Map p 96.*

★★ Fireman's Arms CITY CENTER Set in what was Cape Town's first fire station 140 years ago, this homely pub has great food and TVs for watching sport. Look out for the

The Fireman's Arms.

original fireman's pole, which you can climb if you're drunk enough. *25 Mechau St. ☎ 021-419-1513. www.firemansarms.co.za. Map p 96.*

La Med CAPE PENINSULA Youthful and known for its raucous parties in summer, La Med is sundowner territory and in winter a drunken rugby-watching venue. There are great ocean views and simple food such as calamari and fries or giant burgers. *Glen Country Club, Victoria Rd, Clifton. ☎ 021-438-5600. www.lamed.co.za. Map p 99.*

★ Mitchell's Brewery V&A WATERFRONT English wood-paneled pub with home-brewed beer on tap, including bitter and stout; both of which are rare in South Africa. The Forester's lager is also tasty and there's pub fare such as lasagne and fish 'n' chips. *East Pier Rd. ☎ 021-419-5074. Map p 96.*

★ Neighbourhood Bar & Lounge CITY CENTER The balcony here overlooks lively Long Street, and inside is table football and a pool table. Happy hour is 4–7pm with two cocktails for the price of one. *163 Long St. ☎ 021-424-7620. Map p 96.*

★★ The Nose Restaurant & Wine Bar ATLANTIC SEABOARD Great setting in Cape Quarter's atmospheric piazza, and with more than 40 wines by the glass, cocktails, and good food. Try the gourmet burger. *Cape Quarter, 72 De Waterkant, Green Point. ☎ 021-425-2200. www.thenose.co.za. Map p 96.*

Rafiki's CITY BOWL There's always a buzzy vibe on the wraparound balcony here, and food includes good pizzas, burgers, or buckets of Mozambique prawns. An open fire burns in winter. *13b Kloof Nek Rd, Tamboerskloof. ☎ 021-426-4731. www.rafikis.co.za. Map p 96.*

The Nose Restaurant & Winebar at Cape Quarter.

★ **Relish** CITY BOWL A retro spot set on 3 floors with industrial-style steel décor. Take a strawberry daiquiri or jug of Pimm's to the top floor lounge and deck for great views of Table Mountain. *70 New Church St, Tamboerskloof.* ☎ *021-422-3584. www.relish.co.za. Map p 96.*

★★ **The Sandbar** CAPE PENINSULA Another good option in Camps Bay and a little less pretentious than some of its neighbors, with good food and tables on the pavement. Order a mojito cocktail, made with fresh strawberries. *31 Victoria Rd, Camps Bay.* ☎ *021-438-8336. www.thesandbar.co.za. Map p 99.*

Casino
GrandWest Casino NORTHERN SUBURBS Huge, brash and hardly classy, but the only casino in Cape Town. It also has restaurants, an ice-rink, and a play center to keep kids occupied while parents feed the slot machines. *1 Vanguard Dr, Goodwood.* ☎ *021-505-7777. www.sun international.com. No cover. Map p 99.*

Dance Clubs
Barmooda SOUTHERN SUBURBS Club with a youthful edge and popular with students from the nearby University of Cape Town, playing high-energy house and hip hop. *86 Station Rd, Observatory.* ☎ *021-447-6752. www.barmooda.co.za. R30 cover. Map p 99.*

★★★ **Chrome** CITY CENTER A large, lavish club with state-of-the-art sound and lighting, VIP rooms with chandeliers, plasma screens, and a mix of R&B and cool lounge music. The crowd is fairly well-heeled.

The Sandbar in Camps Bay.

Gay Events

Cape Town is indisputably the pink capital of Africa, and De Waterkant (see p 53, **8**) in Green Point is dubbed The Gayborhood. **Gay Pride** (www.capetownpride.co.za) takes place towards the end of February and a week of parties and beauty pageants are followed by a procession through Green Point of drag queens, floats, bands, decorated convertibles, and people dressed in outrageous costumes. Then, there's a street fair in De Waterkant that turns into a party at night. The highlight of the year, and held in December, is the fabulous **Mother City Queer Project** (www.mcqp.co.za), a huge party with several dance floors and DJs. It changes venue and dress theme each year and attracts tens of thousands of people. Cape Town Tourism (p 42) produces a Pink Map of Cape Town, which lists gay-friendly hotels, bars, and clubs.

6 Pepper St. ☎ 021-422-3368. www.chromect.com. R50–60 cover, Thurs no cover. Map p 96.

★★★ **Hemisphere** CITY CENTER If the marble floors, lavish fabrics, tasty cocktails, and beautiful oval bar don't tempt you, the simply stunning 180° views from 31 floors above the city certainly will. Strict dress code. No under-25s. *Absa Building, 2 Riebeeck St.* ☎ 021-422-3368. www.hemisphere.org.za. R50 girls, R70 guys cover. Map p 96.

★ **Tiger Tiger** SOUTHERN SUBURBS An upmarket club in Claremont with six bars and a spacious sunken dance floor. This is where Prince Harry used to take Chelsy. Music is a bit run-of-the-mill pop though. *The Atrium, Main Rd, Claremont.* ☎ 021-683-2220. www.tigertiger.co.za. R20–40 cover. Map p 99.

Vertigo CITY CENTER A fairly busy club with good lighting, comfortable lounge areas, and an outside balcony. Music is mainstream R&B, hip hop, and house, and there are regular themed nights. *96 Long St.* ☎ 072-323-7621. www.clubtonic.com. R40–50 cover. Map p 96.

Gay & Lesbian

★★ **Beulah Bar** ATLANTIC SEABOARD Stylish upmarket gay and lesbian bar, with DJs at the weekend. It's popular for after-work drinks and things liven up later on. *30 Somerset Rd, Green Point.* ☎ 021-421-6798. www.beulahbar.co.za. No cover. Map p 96.

★★ **Bronx Action Bar** ATLANTIC SEABOARD The oldest gay club in town, which can be a lot of fun whether you're gay or straight. The music is house and R&B, and there's a sweaty dance floor—expect a lot of shirts to be removed. The well-oiled go-go boys have to be seen to be believed. *22 Somerset Rd, Green Point.* ☎ 021-419-9216. www.bronx.com. No cover. Map p 96.

★ **Café Manhattan** ATLANTIC SEABOARD Well-loved by Cape Town's gay community and a focal meeting point, this relaxed restaurant serves steaks and burgers and there's a long wooden bar for socializing. *71 Waterkant St, Green Point.* ☎ 021-421-6666. www.manhattan.co.za. No cover. Map p 96.

★★ The Loft Lounge ATLANTIC SEABOARD Set in the 'Pink Block' along with the Bronx and Beulah, this is a chilled gay and lesbian bar on two floors. It has retro décor in lime green and red, and great mountain views. *24 Napier St, Green Point.* ☎ *021-425-2647. www.loft lounge.co.za. No cover. Map p 96.*

Hotel Bars

★★★ Bascule Bar V&A WATERFRONT This is an opulent bar in the Cape Grace Hotel, with fat leather sofas, chandeliers, and more than 400 whiskies. Rub shoulders with yacht owners here. Regular hotel guests get a lock-up cupboard in the wine cellar to store their wine until they next visit. *Cape Grace, West Quay.* ☎ *021-410-7100. www. capegrace.com. Map p 96.*

★★★ Leopard Lounge CAPE PENINSULA Gorgeous views, so come here for sunset; they also do 'Tea by the Sea' in the afternoon. You'll find a huge choice of drinks, including 76 martinis and 46 ports. *Twelve Apostles Hotel, Victoria Rd,* *Camps Bay.* ☎ *021-437-9000. www. 12apostleshotel.com. Map p 99.*

★★★ Planet Champagne Bar CITY BOWL Dress to impress at this luxurious and glamorous bar, which has stylish modern décor, an attractive terrace, and attentive waiting staff. Perfect for champagne and canapés. *Mount Nelson Hotel, 76 Orange St, Gardens.* ☎ *021-483-1000. www.mountnelson.co.za. Map p 96.*

★★★ Tobago's ATLANTIC SEABOARD Super-stylish hotel bar set around a stunning infinity swimming pool and the perfect spot for sundowners overlooking the ocean. A mixed crowd of holidaymakers and after-work drinkers come here. *Radisson SAS Hotel, Beach Rd, Granger Bay.* ☎ *021-441-3000. www.radissonsas.com. Map p 96.*

Live Music

Jo'burg CITY CENTER Jo'burg in Cape Town is impossible to miss because it's covered in neon. There are live bands in the early evening,

Café Manhattan is a popular gay venue.

followed by DJs, and the restaurant is open until 3.30am. *218 Long St. ☎ 021-422-0142. www.joburgbar. com. Fri and Sat. R20 cover. Map p 96.*

★★★ **Marimba** CITY CENTER Found in the Convention Centre (see p 39) this sexy and stylish cocktail bar and restaurant is a haunt for celeb events. There's live music most nights or DJs reign over the impressive sound system. *Cape Town International Convention Centre, Convention Sq, Lower Long St, ☎ 021-418-3366. www.marimbsa. com. No cover. Map p 96.*

Mercury Live & Lounge CITY CENTER   Although it's a little grungy, this venue showcases some great indie-pop and rock bands from all over South Africa. *43 De Villiers St. ☎ 021-465-2106. www.mercuryl. co.za. R20–50 cover. Map p 96.*

★★ **Zula Sound Bar** CITY CENTER   This is a fashionable bar with several small rooms, a great balcony overlooking Long Street, pool tables, dance floor, and funky lighting. There's live music on some

Champagne cocktails at Mount Nelson Hotel's Planet Champagne Bar.

nights and comedy on Mondays. *196 Long St. ☎ 021-424-2242. www. zulabar.co.za. R30–40 cover for entertainment. Map p 96.* ●

Cover Charges

Most clubs are open Wednesday to Saturday and charge from R30 to R70 entry, but there are sometimes special offers such as you get your first drink free or ladies are free. Bars only really charge entry if an especially well-known band is performing. Gig guides are available on the relevant bar and club websites.

Arts & Entertainment Best Bets

Best **Foot-tapping Jazz**
★★★ Green Dolphin, *Pierhead, V&A Waterfront (p 110)*

Best **Seasonal Event**
★★ Cape Town International Comedy Festival, *Various venues (p 113)*

Best **Jazz**
★★★ Cape Town International Jazz Festival, *Various venues (p 113)*

Best **Large Arts Venue**
★★★ Artscape, *D F Malan St (p 111)*

Best **Atmospheric Theater**
★★★ Theatre On the Bay, *1 Link St, Camps Bay (p 113)*

Best **Summer Music Festival**
★★★ Kirstenbosch National Botanical Garden Summer Concerts, *Rhodes Dr, Newlands (p 111)*

Best **Venue for the Bard**
★★ Maynardville Open Air Theatre, *20 Piers Ave, Wynberg (p 111)*

Best **Cabaret & Comedy**
★★ On Broadway, *88 Shortmarket St (p 114)*

Best **Posh Day Out at the Races**
★★★ J&B Met, Kenilworth Race Course, *Rosemead Ave, Kenilworth (p 114)*

Best **Independent Cinema with a Bar**
★★★ The Labia, *88 Orange St, Gardens (p 110)*

Best for **Moody Foreign Films**
★★ Cinema Nouveau, *Cavendish Sq, 1 Dreyer St, Cavendish (p 110)*

Best **Religious Choral Music**
St George's Cathedral *Wale St (p 110)*

Best **Variety of Entertainment**
★★★ Baxter Theatre, *Main Rd, Rondebosch (p 112)*

Best **Film Festival**
Encounters South African International Documentary Festival, *Various venues (p 111)*

Best for **Pointy Toes & Tights**
★★ Cape Town City Ballet, *Various venues (p 112)*

Summer concert at Kirstenbosch National Botanical Garden.

Southern Suburbs & Cape Peninsula Arts & Entertainment

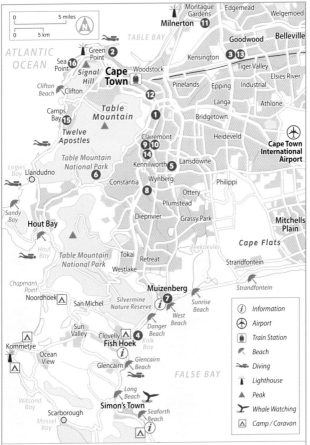

Baxter Theatre 1

Cinema Nouveau 2

GrandArena 3

Kalk Bay Theatre 4

Kenilworth Race Course 5

Kirstenbosch Botanical Gardens
  Summer Concerts 6

Masque Theatre 7

Maynardville Open Air Theatre 8

Newlands Cricket Ground 9

Newlands Rugby Stadium 10

Nu-Metro 11

Obz Café 12

Roxy Revue Bar 13

Ster-Kinekor 14

Theatre On the Bay 15

Winchester Mansions Hotel 16

City Center, City Bowl & V&A

The Best Arts & Entertainment

Amphitheatre at the V&A Waterfront 1

Artscape 2

Cape Town International
 Convention Centre 3

Green Dolphin 4

The Labia 5

The Labia on Kloof 6

Little Theatre 7

Manenberg's Jazz Café 8

On Broadway 9

St George's Cathedral 10

Theatre @ The Pavilion 11

Waterfront A&E

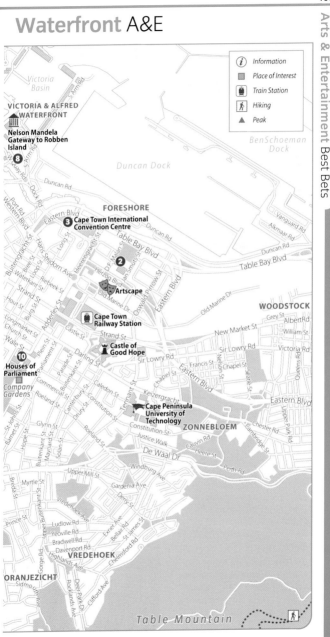

Legend:
- *(i)* Information
- ▢ Place of Interest
- 🚉 Train Station
- 🚶 Hiking
- ▲ Peak

Victoria Basin

VICTORIA & ALFRED WATERFRONT

Nelson Mandela Gateway to Robben Island

8

BenSchoeman Dock

Duncan Dock

FORESHORE

3 Cape Town International Convention Centre

2

Artscape

Cape Town Railway Station

WOODSTOCK

Castle of Good Hope

10 Houses of Parliament

Company Gardens

Cape Peninsula University of Technology

ZONNEBLOEM

De Waal Dr

VREDEHOEK

ORANJEZICHT

Table Mountain

Arts & Entertainment **A to Z**

Film

★★ Cinema Nouveau SOUTH-ERN SUBURBS With branches at the V&A Waterfront and Cavendish Square, this cinema chain shows serious movies and foreign films. *Cavendish Square, 1 Dreyer St, Cavendish.* ☎ *021-671-8042. www. sterkinekor.com. Tickets R35. Map p 107. Lower Level, Victoria Wharf.* ☎ *021-419-9700. Tickets R35. Map p 8.*

Nu-Metro V&A WATERFRONT You'll pretty much find only mainstream Hollywood releases at these multi-screen cinemas. Pre-book tickets through the website or Computicket (see box p 114, Tickets & Bookings).*Upper Level, Victoria Wharf.* ☎ *021-419-9700. www. numetro.co.za. Tickets R35. Map p 107. Upper Level, Canal Walk, Century Boulevard, Century City.* ☎ *021-555-2510. Tickets R35.*

Ster-Kinekor SOUTHERN SUB-URBS This is South Africa's other mainstream cinema chain. *1 Cavendish Square, Dreyer St, Cavendish.* ☎ *021-671-8042. www.sterkinekor. com. Tickets R35. Map p 107.*

★★★ The Labia CITY CENTER Despite the strange name (it was named after an Italian princess), this is a delightful old movie house with a sociable bar, and you can take your drinks into the theater: Cape Town's best independent cinema. *68 Orange St, Gardens.* ☎ *021-424-5927. www.labia.co.za. Tickets R25. Map p 108.*

★★ The Labia on Kloof CITY CENTER More mainstream than the Labia above, there are two screens here and a comfortable bar for pre-movie drinks.

Lifestyle Centre, Kloof St, Gardens. ☎ *021-424-5927. www.labia.co.za. Tickets R35. Map p 108.*

Music: Classical

★★ St George's Cathedral CITY CENTER The rousing and stirring, if not solemn, choir sing Schubert, Hayden, Mozart, and Beethoven. Check the website for programs and notice the superb acoustics in the cathedral. *Wale St.* ☎ *021-424-7360. www.stgeorgescathedral.com. Free. Map p 108.*

Music: Jazz

★★★ Green Dolphin V&A WATERFRONT Foot-tapping live jazz is performed here during dinner and there are three sets every night. Top local and international musicians feature, and the menu is strong on seafood. *Pierhead.* ☎ *021-421-7471. www.greendolphin.co.za. Cover R30–35. Map p 108.*

The Labia is Cape Town's most popular independent movie theater.

Cape Town Film Festivals

The excellent Encounters South African International **Documentary Festival** (www.encounters.co.za) in July screens dozens of documentaries from all over the world at a number of cinemas, including the Nu-Metro at the V&A Waterfront. The **Three Continents Film Festival** (www.3continentsfestival.co.za) in August at Cinema Nouveau at the V&A Waterfront showcases films both about and by developing nations in Africa, Asia, and Latin America. **Out in Africa** (www.oia.co.za) is South Africa's annual gay and lesbian film festival and is held over 10 days in September, again at Cinema Nouveau. International and locally-produced films are sometimes accompanied by panel discussions.

★ **Manenberg's Jazz Café** V&A WATERFRONT This long-standing jazz club has a bright orange stage and spacious dance floor, and there's traditional South African food on offer. Look for the jazz stars' autographs on the walls. *102 Clock Tower.* ☎ *021-421-5639. www. manenbergsjazzcafe.com. Cover R40–80. Map p 108.*

★★ **Winchester Mansions Hotel** ATLANTIC SEABOARD Come here on a sunny Sunday for a lazy brunch and the weekly jazz at the terrace bar. Booking is essential and brunch includes a newspaper and a glass of bubbly. *22 Beach Rd, Sea Point.* ☎ *021-434-2351. www. winchester.co.za. R195. Map p 107.*

Open-air Venues
★★★ kids **Kirstenbosch National Botanical Gardens Summer Concerts** SOUTHERN SUBURBS Nothing beats listening to music with a picnic on a summer's evening. These concerts, held on Sundays in summer, are a favorite with Cape Town residents, and attract a variety of acts from Bryan Adams to the Soweto String Quartet. *Rhodes Dr, Newlands.* ☎ *021-799-8783. www. sanbi.org. Tickets R50–70. Map p 20.*

★★ **Maynardville Open Air Theatre** SOUTHERN SUBURBS The drill is simple; picnic in the park over summer before a performance of ballet or theater. There couldn't be a better venue for Shakespeare on the pretty outdoor stage. *20 Piers Av, Wynberg. Information from Artscape* ☎ *021-410-9800. www. maynardville.co.za. Tickets R60–70. Map p 107.*

Performance Venues
kids **Amphitheatre at the V&A Waterfront** V&A WATERFRONT Right in the heart of the V&A, this amphitheater hosts a number of free events, including concerts at 5pm in summer and fun entertainment for the kids. Plonk yourself down and see what's on. *Quay 4.* ☎ *021-408-7600. www.waterfront. co.za. Free. Map p 108.*

★★★ **Artscape** CITY CENTER This is the city's principal theater venue, and home to the Cape Town City Ballet, Cape Town Opera, and Cape Town Philharmonic Orchestra. Also regularly hosts popular musicals. *D F Malan St, Foreshore.* ☎ *021-410-9800. www.artscape. co.za. Tickets R100–350. Map p 108.*

Free entertainment at the V&A Waterfront Amphitheatre.

★★★ kids Baxter Theatre

SOUTHERN SUBURBS   This theater offers classical music, jazz, plays, comedy, and children's events. The bar, with its giant posters of previous productions, is a good place for a post-show drink. *Main Rd, Rondebosch.* ☎ *021-685-7880. www.baxter.co.za. Tickets R50–200. Map p 107.*

★ Cape Town International Convention Centre

CITY CENTER   Stages occasional concerts and musicals, and events throughout the year such as the Cape Town Book Fair and home, décor, and car shows. *Convention Sq, 1 Lower Long St.* ☎ *021-410-5000. www.cticc. co.za. Tickets R40–150. Map p 108.*

★ GrandArena

NORTHEN SUBURBS   A large venue, has good acoustics, seating, and a standing area, as well as a special wheelchair area. Has hosted the likes of Eddie Grant and home-grown favorites Freshlyground; located at Cape Town's GrandWest casino. *Grand-West Casino, 1 Vanguard Dr, Goodwood.* ☎ *021-505-7777. www. suninternational.com. Tickets R220–320. Map p 107.*

Kalk Bay Theatre

CAPE PENINSULA   This little venue is a converted Dutch Reformed church, and the seats used to be pews. Local acts, from crooners to impersonators, perform. *52 Main Rd, Kalk Bay.* ☎ *073-220-5430. www.kbt. co.za. Tickets R75–150. Map p 107.*

Little Theatre

CITY CENTER   This is the theater for the University of Cape Town's drama department. Performances vary from the traditional to avant-garde. *37 Orange St, Gardens.* ☎ *021-480-7129. www.uct.ac.za. com. Tickets R25–50. Map p 108.*

Cape Town Ballet & Opera

Cape Town City Ballet (www.capetowncityballet.org.za) is South Africa's premier ballet company and usually performs at Artscape, but there are sometimes delightfully romantic performances at the Maynardville Open Air Theatre (see p 111). Classics include *The Nutcracker* and *Sleeping Beauty* or there are modern twists; ballet to the music of hit South African band Freshlyground for example. In 2008, the company made it into the Guinness World Records as the largest ballet class when 989 people danced at Canal Walk shopping center. **Cape Town Opera** (www.cape townopera.co.za) also usually performs at Artscape, and you can expect stirring renditions of *Rigoletto* or *Aida*.

Cape Town Festivals

The New Year starts with the colorful Cape Town Minstrel **Carnival** through the city on 2nd January, when locals dress up and troupes sing and dance. The 4-day free **Jazzathon** (www.jazzathon. co.za) is held at the amphitheater at the V&A Waterfront in January and features session musicians. The **Cape Town International Jazz Festival** (www.capetownjazzfest.com) from late March to early April is a two-day festival held on several stages at the Cape Town International Convention Centre, and there's a free concert on the Grand Parade in the city center. Now in its 10th year, and easily the best jazz festival in Africa, it attracts more than 40 stars from all over the world and more than 30,000 jazz fans. The rip-roaring **Cape Town International Comedy Festival** (www.comedy festival.co.za) is held over three weeks in September at the Baxter Theatre, Grand Arena, and the outdoor amphitheater at the V&A Waterfront.

Masque Theatre CAPE PENINSULA   The theater performances here are by local amateur dramatic groups, so can be a bit hit or miss. Sometimes there are music nights such as flamenco or swing. *37 Main Rd, Muizenberg.* ☎ *021-788-6999. www.muizenberg.info. Tickets R45–55. Map p 107.*

★ **Roxy Revue Bar** NORTHERN SUBURBS   Also located at the GrandWest casino, this venue features cabaret and musical tribute acts, which can be fun if you're in the mood. Although I'm not too sure about the Billy Joel impersonators. *GrandWest Casino, 1 Vanguard Dr, Goodwood.* ☎ *021-505-7777. www. suninternational.com. Tickets R60–70. Map p 107.*

★ **Theatre @ The Pavilion** V&A WATERFRONT   This former IMAX theater now hosts musicals, local bands, and 1980s tribute bands. Eat at a good V&A Waterfront restaurant (see Chapter 6) before or after. *BMW Pavilion.* ☎ *021-505-7777. www.thepavilion.co.za. Tickets R60–70. Map p 108.*

★★★ **Theatre On the Bay** CAPE PENINSULA   This lovely, intimate theater has a sociable bar and restaurant and a good repertoire of comedy and locally written, modern plays. It's always of a high quality, so attracts a regular crowd. *1 Link St, Camps Bay.* ☎ *021-438-3301. www.theatreonthebay.co.za. Tickets R100–250. Map p 107.*

Theatre On the Bay.

Tickets & Bookings

Computicket (www.computicket.co.za) is South Africa's national booking service for all shows, concerts, sporting events, cinema tickets, and festivals. You can book online and they take all major credit cards, or alternatively there are kiosks in all the larger shopping malls. Their website is also an excellent resource for what's on in Cape Town.

Supper Theaters

★ Obz Café SOUTHERN SUBURBS Popular with students, there are bands on most nights, sometimes movie nights, and occasionally standup comedy. Open from breakfast with a full range of food. *115 Lower Main Rd, Observatory.* ☎ *021-448-5555. www.obzcafe. co.za. Tickets R25–40. Map p 107.*

★★ On Broadway CITY CENTER Musical tribute bands, comedy, and brilliant drag acts perform here. Look out for the Mince Girls, who have been entertaining Cape Town for 13 years. Good range of food and drinks and open late. *88 Shortmarket St.* ☎ *021-418-8338. www.onbroadway. co.za. Tickets R90–120. Map p 108.*

Spectator Sports

★★★ Kenilworth Race Course SOUTHERN SUBURBS Although there's horse racing here throughout the year, don't miss the **J&B Met** on the last Saturday of January when the cream of Cape Town's elite gathers for a party. Each year dress is by theme; glitz and glam, and black, white, and bling are past themes. *Rosemead Av, Kenilworth.* ☎ *021-700-1600. www.jbmet.co.za. Tickets start at R60; R150 for the J&B Met. Map p 107.*

★★ Newlands Cricket Ground SOUTHERN SUBURBS Few can deny that Newlands is one of the best cricket grounds in the world, and a day here under blue skies with the mountain rising behind is a relaxing and enjoyable experience. And of course South Africa is one of the best teams in the world. Local team Cape Cobras also pack in a good crowd. *146 Campground Rd, Newlands.* ☎ *021-657-3300. www. wpcc.co.za. Tickets start at R30. Map p 107.*

★★ Newlands Rugby Stadium SOUTHERN SUBURBS Cheer on the Stormers (wear black) or the Springboks (green). South Africans are rugby freaks, so you'll be guaranteed a lively atmosphere. The Wallabies (Australia) and the All Blacks (New Zealand) are regular visitors. *8 Boundary Rd, Newlands.* ☎ *021-659-4600. www.wprugby.co.za. Tickets start at R50. Map p 107.* ●

Sign for cabaret club On Broadway.

Southern Suburbs & Cape Peninsula Lodging

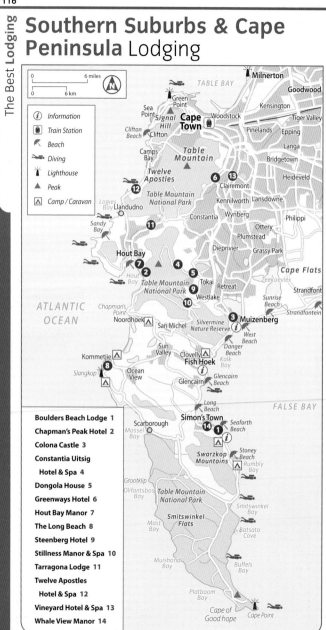

Legend:
- (i) Information
- 🚉 Train Station
- 🏖 Beach
- 🤿 Diving
- 🗼 Lighthouse
- ▲ Peak
- ⛺ Camp / Caravan

Boulders Beach Lodge 1
Chapman's Peak Hotel 2
Colona Castle 3
Constantia Uitsig Hotel & Spa 4
Dongola House 5
Greenways Hotel 6
Hout Bay Manor 7
The Long Beach 8
Steenberg Hotel 9
Stillness Manor & Spa 10
Tarragona Lodge 11
Twelve Apostles Hotel & Spa 12
Vineyard Hotel & Spa 13
Whale View Manor 14

V&A Waterfront & Atlantic Seaboard Lodging

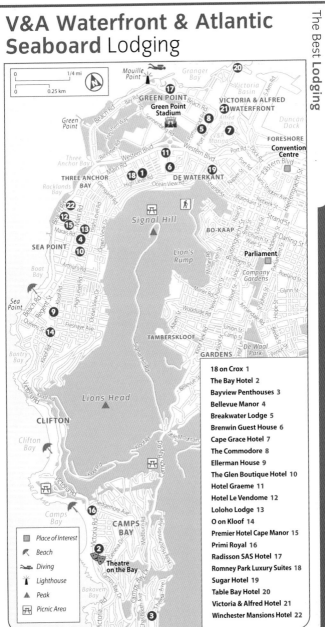

Legend
- ■ Place of Interest
- ⌅ Beach
- ⇌ Diving
- ⚲ Lighthouse
- ▲ Peak
- ⊞ Picnic Area

18 on Crox 1
The Bay Hotel 2
Bayview Penthouses 3
Bellevue Manor 4
Breakwater Lodge 5
Brenwin Guest House 6
Cape Grace Hotel 7
The Commodore 8
Ellerman House 9
The Glen Boutique Hotel 10
Hotel Graeme 11
Hotel Le Vendome 12
Loloho Lodge 13
O on Kloof 14
Premier Hotel Cape Manor 15
Primi Royal 16
Radisson SAS Hotel 17
Romney Park Luxury Suites 18
Sugar Hotel 19
Table Bay Hotel 20
Victoria & Alfred Hotel 21
Winchester Mansions Hotel 22

The Best Lodging

City Center & City Bowl
Lodging

1 On Queens 1

Adderley Hotel 2

Alta Bay 3

Ashanti Lodge 4

The Backpack 5

Cape Cadogan Hotel 6

Cape Diamond Hotel 7

Cape Heritage Hotel 8

Cape Hollow Hotel 9

Cape Milner Hotel 10

Cat and Moose 11

Daddy Long Legs 12

De Waterkant Village 13

Extreme, Fire & Ice Hotel 14

Fountains Hotel 15

Four Rosemead 16

The Grand Daddy 17

Kensington Place 18

Lions Kloof Lodge 19

Mount Nelson Hotel 20

Table Mountain Lodge 21

Townhouse Hotel 22

Tudor Hotel 23

Urban Chic 24

Villa Lutzi 25

Westin Grand Arabella
Quays Hotel 26

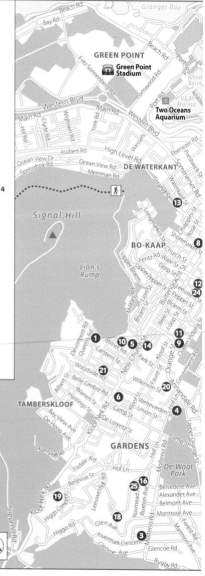

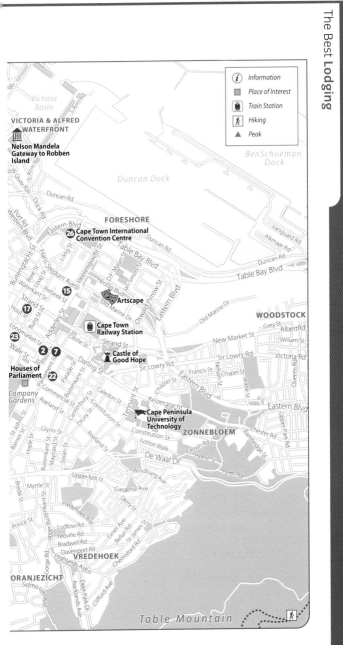

Information
Place of Interest
Train Station
Hiking
Peak

Victoria Basin

VICTORIA & ALFRED WATERFRONT

Nelson Mandela Gateway to Robben Island

Duncan Dock

BenSchoeman Dock

FORESHORE

26 Cape Town International Convention Centre

Table Bay Blvd

Table Bay Blvd

WOODSTOCK

15

Artscape

Cape Town Railway Station

Castle of Good Hope

17

23

2 7

Houses of Parliament

22

Company Gardens

Cape Peninsula University of Technology

ZONNEBLOEM

De Waal Dr

VREDEHOEK

ORANJEZICHT

Table Mountain

Lodging Best Bets

Best **Art Hotel**
★ Daddy Long Legs $$ *134 Long St (p 124)*

Best **Backpackers**
The Backpack $ *74 New Church St (p 121)*

Best **Ocean & Mountain Views**
★★★ Twelve Apostles Hotel and Spa $$$$$ *Victoria Rd, Camps Bay (p 129)*

Best **at the V&A Waterfront**
★★★ Cape Grace $$$$$ *West Quay, V&A Waterfront (p 123)*

Best **City Center Budget Hotel**
★ Cape Diamond Hotel $$ *c/ Parliament and Longmarket Sts (p 122)*

Best for **Green Point Stadium**
★★ Radisson SAS Hotel $$$$ *Beach Rd, Granger Bay (p 127)*

Best for **Fine Dining & Pampering**
★★★ Constantia Uitsig Hotel and Spa $$$$$ *Spaanschemat River Rd, Constantia (p 124)*

Best **Quirky Hotel**
★ The Grand Daddy $$$ *38 Long St (p 125)*

Best **Luxury Splurge**
★★★ Mount Nelson Hotel $$$$$ *76 Orange St (p 127)*

Best **Gay Hotel**
The Glen $$$ *3 The Glen, Sea Point (p 125)*

Best **Boutique Hotel**
★★ Sugar Hotel $$$$ *1 Main Rd, Green Point (p 128)*

Best for **Rubbing Shoulders with Models**
★★★ Urban Chic $$$ *172 Long St (p 129)*

The boutique Sugar Hotel.

Best **City Views**
★★★ Westin Grand Arabella Quays Hotel $$$$$ *Convention Sq, Lower Long St (p 129)*

Best **Sleeping in an Historical Building**
★★ Cape Heritage Hotel $$$$ *90 Bree St (p 123)*

Best for **The Beach**
★★ The Bay Hotel $$$ *69 Victoria Rd, Camps Bay (p 122)*

Best **Hotel Without Children**
★★ 18 on Crox $$ *18 Croxteth Rd, Green Point (p 121)*

Best for **Whale Watching**
★★ Whale View Manor $$ *401 Main Rd, Simon's Town (p 130)*

Cape Town Lodging **A to Z**

★ **1 On Queens** CITY BOWL This is a bright, sunny German-run guesthouse set in a mock Tuscan villa with established gardens and a pool. Rooms are compact but comfortable and have good mountain and city views. Within an easy stroll of the restaurants on Kloof Street. *1 Queens Rd, Tamboerskloof.* ☎ *021-422-0004. www.1onqueens.co.za. 9 units. R820–1220. MC, V. Map p 118.*

★★ **18 on Crox** ATLANTIC SEABOARD This intimate guesthouse is set in restored 1840s stables with just four luxury rooms decorated with a mix of contemporary furnishings and antiques. There's a tranquil courtyard and small plunge pool. No children under 16. *18 Croxteth Rd, Green Point.* ☎ *021-439-3871. www. 18oncrox.com. 4 units. R1150–1700. MC, V. Map p 117.*

★ **Adderley Hotel** CITY CENTER This modern, bright hotel has a rooftop pool and the sophisticated Bowl Restaurant, and is set behind the façades of some older buildings on Adderley Street. The stylish rooms have beech-wood furniture and kitchenettes. *31 Adderley St.* ☎ *021-469-1900. www.relaishotels.com. 27 units. R790–1850. AE, DC, MC, V. Map p 118.*

Alta Bay CITY BOWL Perched on the lower slopes of Table Mountain, this hotel has great city views from the pleasant outdoor deck and plunge pool. The comfortable rooms have crisply modern interiors with flat-screen TVs and air-conditioning. No children under 12. *12 Invermark Crescent, Higgovale.* ☎ *021-487-8800. www.altabay.com. 7 units. R1300–2700. MC, V. Map p 118.*

Ashanti Lodge CITY BOWL This is a popular backpackers' hostel in a funky bright yellow house within walking distance of the city center. There are spacious dorms or doubles, with or without bathrooms, and there's a lively bar/café and helpful travel center. *11 Hof St, Gardens.* ☎ *021-423-8721. www.ashanti. co.za. 60+ beds. Dorms R130. Doubles R370–520. MC, V. Map p 118.*

The Backpack CITY CENTER This upmarket backpackers' hostel

Ashanti Lodge has great mountain views.

is located in two adjoining Victorian houses painted in a sunny yellow with wooden floors and high ceilings. The very helpful travel center can organize tours all over Africa. *74 New Church St.* ☎ *021-423-4530. www.backpackers.co.za. 60+ beds. Dorms R145, doubles R450–750. AE, MC, V. Map p 118.*

★★ kids **The Bay Hotel** CAPE PENINSULA This occupies a fine position in Camps Bay, and all rooms are sea-facing. There's a lovely pool deck or you can trip across the crossing to the beach. If you feel like a 'lift', the wellness center offers minor medical cosmetic procedures. *69 Victoria Rd, Camps Bay.* ☎ *021-438-4444. www.thebay. co.za. 78 units. R1500–6000. AE, DC, MC, V. Map p 117.*

★ kids **Bayview Penthouses** CAPE PENINSULA This is good value considering the location in Camps Bay, and the views are unbeatable. On offer are fully equipped self-catering luxury apartments sleeping up to 4, with Wi-Fi, TV, and DVD, and a heated swimming pool. Ideal for families. *40 Teresa Ave, Camps Bay.* ☎ *021-438-2530. www.bayviewpenthouses. co.za. 5 units. R600–1050. AE, MC, V. Map p 117.*

Bellevue Manor ATLANTIC SEABOARD This affordable guest house in a restored 1895 Victorian home has been declared a National Monument. There's a fine wrought iron balcony and plunge pool in the garden. Also rents out self-catering apartments in the area. *5 Bellevue Rd, Sea Point.* ☎ *021-434-0375. www.bellevuemanor.co.za. 5 units. R625–695. MC, V. Map p 117.*

★ kids **Boulders Beach Lodge** CAPE PENINSULA The location is wonderful—it's right next to the penguin colony, and if you walk down to the little beach you may be able to swim with them. Rooms are small but tastefully decorated and the two family suites have kitchens. The popular restaurant serves seafood. *Boulders Beach, Simons Town.* ☎ *021-786-1758. www.boulders beachlodge.com. 9 units. R1150– 2200. MC, V. Map p 116.*

kids **Breakwater Lodge** V&A WATERFRONT The V&A Waterfront is a great location but isn't really affordable for the budget traveler. However, this place is the exception, and simple rooms are in either a modern block or converted 19th-century prison (complete with slit windows). *Portswood Rd.* ☎ *021-406-1911. www.breakwaterlodge. co.za. 192 units. R845–1095. AE, MC, V. Map p 117.*

Brenwin Guest House ATLANTIC SEABOARD This is an affordable guest house in a 19th-century house with pine floors and bright white bedding. There's a small pool and wooden deck in the pretty garden full of banana and palm trees. *1 Thornhill Rd, Green Point.* ☎ *021-434-0220. www.brenwin.co.za. 13 units. R640–960. MC, V. Map p 117.*

★★ **Cape Cadogan Hotel** CITY BOWL This gorgeous double-storey Victorian building is a National Monument, and there's a lounge with a warming fire in winter and a pool in the garden for summer. The impressive interiors have a mix of antiques and contemporary furnishings. Fashionable Kloof Street is just a few steps away. *5 Upper Union St, Tamboerskloof.* ☎ *021-480-8080. www.capecadogan.com. 12 units. R1140–2350. AE, MC, V. Map p 118.*

★ **Cape Diamond Hotel** CITY CENTER This good, centrally-located option is set in a restored Art Deco office block that used to be a diamond dealership—many of the original safes can be seen in the corridors. Rooms are small,

View of Table Mountain behind the Cape Grace.

comfortable, and affordable with sleek modern furnishings. The restaurant has floor-to-ceiling windows and serves buffets and daily specials. *C/ Parliament and Longmarket Sts.* ☎ *021-461-2519. www.cape diamondhotel.co.za. 60 units. R820–920. AE, MC, V. Map p 118.*

★★★ **Cape Grace Hotel** V&A WATERFRONT   Here you'll find superb luxury in an unbeatable location at the V&A's landmark hotel. Spacious and elegant rooms have views of the quays or Table Mountain; there's a large pool with deck and a rooftop spa. If you're in this league, you can also rent out the hotel's yacht. *West Quay.* ☎ *021-410-7100. www.capegrace.com. 121 units. R4180–6970. AE, DC, MC, V. Map p 117.*

★★ **Cape Heritage Hotel** CITY CENTER   Set in a building dating to 1771 in historical Heritage Square, this atmospheric hotel has recently been given a makeover. It now boasts stylish contemporary interiors, themed rooms, and locally made art

and sculpture, although it retains the original yellowwood floors and teak ceilings. *90 Bree St.* ☎ *021-424-4646. www.capeheritage.co.za. 17 units. R2520–4080. AE, MC, V. Map p 118.*

★ **Cape Hollow Hotel** CITY CENTER   This good mid-range boutique hotel is painted in creams and is within a squirrel's scurry of Company's Garden and the museums. Pay a higher rate for the fantastic mountain view rooms. There's an affordable ground floor Italian restaurant, Amici, and a relaxing spa with sauna and pool. *88 Queen Victoria St.* ☎ *021-423-1260. www.capetown hollow.co.za. 56 units. R850–1100. AE, MC, V. Map p 118.*

★ **Cape Milner Hotel** CITY BOWL   Chic and sophisticated, this hotel has rooms with modern minimalist décor, plasma flat screen TVs, and 24-hour room service. There's a good restaurant, terrace cocktail bar, and pool. *2a Milner Rd, Tamboerskloof.* ☎ *021-426-1101. www. capemilner.com. 57 units. R1420–2600. AE, MC, V. Map p 118.*

Cat and Moose CITY CENTER Party animals will love the location of this friendly backpackers' hostel—it's at the top of Long Street. Although it's a little grungy, it's one of the cheapest places to stay in the city center. *305 Long St.* ☎ *021-423-7638. www.catandmoose.co.za. 17 units. Dorms R90, doubles R280. MC, V. Map p 118.*

★★ Chapman's Peak Hotel CAPE PENINSULA The spacious penthouse suites are the draw here—with huge terraces, fireplaces, and plunge pools. Other rooms are in the original 19th-century building, and 24 sea-facing rooms with balconies are in a newly built block. *Chapmans Peak Rd, Hout Bay.* ☎ *021-790-1036. www.chapmanspeakhotel.co.za. 34 units. R880–2400. AE, MC, V. Map p 116.*

★★★ Colona Castle CAPE PENINSULA Rooms are beautifully decorated, with four-poster beds and original art, and this upmarket guesthouse has a good restaurant, large pool, and sweeping views of False Bay. A good venue for golfers, with four courses nearby. *1 Verwood St, Lakeside.* ☎ *021-788-8235.*

www.conolacastle.co.za. 8 units. R1860–4390. AE, MC, V. Map p 116.

The Commodore V&A WATERFRONT In a great location at the V&A Waterfront, this hotel has a full range of facilities including pool, gym, spa, restaurant, 24-hr cocktail bar, and spacious lounge areas. It's large though and may feel impersonal to some. *Portswood Rd.* ☎ *021-415-1000. www.legacyhotels.co.za. 236 units. R3340–3500. AE, DC, MC, V. Map p 117.*

★★★ Constantia Uitsig Hotel & Spa CAPE PENINSULA Set in a beautiful location in the Constantia Valley, and surrounded by vineyards, this is a highly acclaimed luxury hotel. Rooms have four-poster beds and marble bathrooms and there's a luxury spa rated as one of the best in the world by *Tatler* magazine. *Spaanschemat River Rd, Constantia.* ☎ *021-794-6500. www.constantia-uitsig.com. 16 units. R3100–3800. AE, DC, MC, V. Map p 116.*

★★★ Daddy Long Legs CITY CENTER This is a fabulously quirky art hotel; each themed room has

Artist designed room at Daddy Long Legs.

been designed by a local artist. There's even a glass bathroom in reception—no one can see in, but the occupant has a clear view out. *263 Long St.* ☎ *021-422-3074. www. daddylonglegs.co.za. 14 units. R650–860. AE, MC, V. Map p 118.*

★ kids **De Waterkant Village** CITY CENTER The tiny, stylish De Waterkant district has atmospheric cobbled streets. Choose from 40 self-catering properties; most are located in restored cottages dating from the 18th century. *1 Loader St, De Waterkant.* ☎ *021-437-9706. www.dewaterkant.com. 40 units. R950–2300. AE, MC, V. Map p 118.*

Dongola House CAPE PENINSULA This is located in the Constantia Valley and the rooms have contemporary décor, private entrances, and patios. The swimming pool is set on spacious lawns where guinea fowl and wild ducks wander. *30 Airlie Place, Constantia.* ☎ *021-794-8283. www.dongola house.co.za. 7 units. R590–850. AE, MC, V. Map p 116.*

★★ **Ellerman House** ATLANTIC SEABOARD The elegant suites have excellent ocean views, marble bathrooms with gold taps, and a mix of antique furniture and cutting-edge, modern décor. There's a swimming pool, spa, and gourmet food, too. Also has a gorgeous 3-bed luxury villa with a chef and butler. *180 Kloof Rd, Bantry Bay.* ☎ *021-430-3200. www.ellerman. co.za. 11 units. R5500–8900. MC, V. Map p 117.*

★★ **Extreme, Fire & Ice Hotel** CITY BOWL This arty and affordable hotel has some unique features and is a fun place to stay. The remarkable swimming pool has glass walls that wrap around the restaurant, and the reception area doubles up as a popular cocktail bar. Seats in the smokers lounge are shaped as coffins, and the public bathrooms are individually decorated in themes. Rooms are small but more than adequate. *New Church and Victoria Sts, Tamboerskloof.* ☎ *021-488-2555. www. proteahotels.com/protea-hotel-fire-and-ice.html. 130 units. R800–1250. AE, MC, V. Map p 118.*

★ **Fountains Hotel** CITY CENTER A perfect base for exploring central Cape Town; ask for a room on the top floor, where there are good views of the harbor. Facilities include Wi-Fi, a narrow pool, sauna, gym, and buffet restaurant. An easy walk to shops in St George's Mall. *1 St George's Mall.* ☎ *021-443-1100. www.fountains hotel.co.za. 160 units. R1130–1250. AE, DC, MC, V. Map p 118.*

★ **Four Rosemead** CITY BOWL This is a peaceful boutique guesthouse with tremendous city and mountain views, large beds, crisp white linen, and South African art on display. Extra touches in the rooms include snack baskets and iPod docking stations. There's a pool in the landscaped gardens and off-street parking. French speaking. *4 Rosemead Rd, Oranjezicht.* ☎ *021-480-3810. www.fourrosemead.com. 8 units. R1750–2550. AE, MC, V. Map p 118.*

The Glen Boutique Hotel ATLANTIC SEABOARD A gay-friendly guesthouse decorated with imported Italian furnishings and stone bathrooms with double showers. The friendly owners are on hand to advise on Cape Town's gay nightlife. *3 The Glen, Sea Point.* ☎ *021-439-0086. www.glenhotel. co.za. 11 units. R875–2300. AE, MC, V. Map p 117.*

★★★ **The Grand Daddy** CITY CENTER Artists, designers, and photographers have been let loose on the décor, resulting in uniquely glamorous rooms. You'll find seven Airstream trailers on the roof—

perfect for a trailer park sleeping experience, although they have been quirkily kitted out by top designers. *38 Long St.* ☎ *021-424-7247. www.daddy longlegs.co.za. 27 units. R945–1075. AE, MC, V. Map p 118.*

★★ **Greenways Hotel** CAPE PENINSULA   This is a neat option in the quiet suburb of Claremont, set in expansive manicured grounds and handy for watching sport at Newlands (see p 114). Rooms are in a Cape Dutch manor house built in the 1920s, and are sumptuously decorated with fine art and chandeliers. Enjoy a game of croquet on the lawns. *1 Torquay Ave, Bishopscourt.* ☎ *021-761-1792. www.green ways.co.za. 15 units. R1840–3580. AE, MC, V. Map p 116.*

★ kids **Hotel Graeme** ATLANTIC SEABOARD   This is a simple, mid-range hotel slap bang in front of the new soccer stadium. The rooms are on the small side but comfortable and there's a pool and jacuzzi. On the downside, it's often overrun with tour groups. Do visit their lovely Italian ice cream shop. *107 Main Rd, Green Point.* ☎ *021-434-9282. www. hotelgraeme.co.za. 38 units. R795–1250. AE, MC, V. Map p 117.*

Swimming pool at Hout Bay Manor.

★★★ **Hotel Le Vendome**
ATLANTIC SEABOARD   This hotel has super luxurious rooms with French-style décor, a pool, restaurant, boutique, and a short walk to Sea Point Promenade. Take high tea or have an after-dinner brandy in the lovely lounge. It's large, and some may find it a little impersonal. *London Rd, Sea Point.* ☎ *021-430-1200. www.le-vendome.co.za. 143 units. R4100–6500. AE, DC, MC, V. Map p 117.*

★★ **Hout Bay Manor** CAPE PENINSULA   An attractive white-washed Cape Dutch manor house built in 1871 with luxury rooms, polished wooden floors, and chandeliers. There's a gourmet restaurant and swimming pool. Admire the magnificent old oak trees in the garden. *Baviaanskloof, off Main Rd, Hout Bay.* ☎ *021-790-0116. www.hout baymanor.com. 21 units. R2340–3700. AE, MC, V. Map p 116.*

★★★ **Kensington Place** CITY BOWL   Each suite has its own laptop with Skype phone, iPod docking station, and mood-enhancing lighting at this stylish boutique guesthouse with mountain views. Every piece of furniture has been hand-picked and it's like living in a décor magazine. Breakfast is served until a decadent 1pm. *38 Kensington Crescent, Higgovale.* ☎ *021-424-4744. www.kensingtonplace.co.za. 8 units. R1760–3400. AE, MC, V. Map p 118.*

Lions Kloof Lodge CITY BOWL
This lodge will appeal to those who like the small guesthouse experience. This German-run establishment has just five individually decorated rooms with patios or balconies. There is a large swimming pool in peaceful gardens and generous healthy or cooked breakfasts are on offer. *26 Higgo Crescent, Higgovale.* ☎ *021-426-5515. www.lions kloof.co.za. 5 units. R800–1100. MC, V. Map p 118.*

Loloho Lodge ATLANTIC SEA-BOARD   This features comfortable rooms with bright white bedding, wooden floors, flat screen TVs, and DVD and CD players. There's also off-road parking and generous buffet breakfasts are taken outside on sunny days. Swimming pool; no children under 16. *13 Bickley Rd, Sea Point.* ☎ *021-434-1566. www.loloho lodge.com. 7 units. R590–1090. MC, V. Map p 117.*

★★ **The Long Beach** CAPE PENIN-SULA   You can step off the pool deck straight on to the dunes of Kommetjie's white-sand beach. Each of the six lavish suites have ocean views. They also rent out a family villa. *1 Kirsten Ave, Kommetjie.* ☎ *021-783-4183. www.thelongbeach.com. 6 units. R3250–4950. MC, V. Map p 116.*

★★★ **Mount Nelson Hotel** CITY BOWL   Presidents and rock stars stay at this iconic Cape Town institution, and the elegant rooms are spread over six wings. The manicured grounds have a pool and tennis courts and the restaurants and bars are top-class. *76 Orange St, Gardens.* ☎ *021-483-1000. www.mount nelson.co.za. 201 units. R6100–14300. AE, DC, MC, V. Map p 118.*

★★★ **O on Kloof** ATLANTIC SEA-BOARD   Contemporary décor at this gay-friendly boutique hotel means sleek mahogany fittings and splashes of color—bright red walls and purple fabrics are just some examples. Rooms have picture windows with great sea views and the opulent spa has an indoor heated pool. *92 Kloof Rd, Bantry Bay.* ☎ *021-439-2081. www.oonkloof.co.za. 8 units. R1900–3500. AE, DC, MC, V. Map p 117.*

kids Premier Hotel Cape Manor ATLANTIC SEABOARD   This is a good bet for those with children because the rooms and apartments are suitable for families. Babysitting can be arranged and youngsters can fill up for the day at the generous breakfast buffet. There's also an outdoor pool, room service, a restaurant, and cocktail bar. *1 Marias Rd, Sea Point.* ☎ *021-430-3400. www.premierhotels.co.za. 108 units. R790–1900. AE, MC, V. Map p 117.*

★ **Primi Royal** CAPE PENINSULA   This chic little hotel is conveniently located near Camps Bay beach and restaurants. The stylish rooms have floor-to-ceiling windows, balconies, air-conditioning, TVs, CD players, and mini-bars. *23 Camps Bay Dr, Camps Bay.* ☎ *021-438-2741. www. primi-royal.com. 10 units. R750–3000. AE, MC, V. Map p 117.*

★ **Radisson SAS Hotel** ATLAN-TIC SEABOARD   This hotel occupies a stunning ocean location with views of Robben Island, and within walking distance to the V&A Waterfront. Rooms are designed in a charming nautical style. Facilities include a stunning infinity pool and luxurious spa with heated indoor pool and sauna. *Beach Rd, Granger Bay.* ☎ *021-441-3000. www. radissonsas.com. 177 units. R2915–4110. AE, DC, MC, V. Map p 117.*

★★ **kids Romney Park Luxury Suites** ATLANTIC SEABOARD   These one- and two-bedroom sea-facing suites have kitchenettes. There's a great combination of five-star luxury with the convenience of being able to self-cater—or a chef will cook for you in your suite. The wellness spa is lovely and calming and there's a swimming pool. *Hill and Romney Rds, Green Point.* ☎ *021-439-4555. www.romneypark. co.za. 18 units. R1490–3660. AE, MC, V. Map p 117.*

★★★ **Steenberg Hotel** CAPE PEN-INSULA   Golfers will have a wonderful stay here, because there's an 18-hole championship golf course. Set on an historic wine estate, some of

Steenberg Hotel and golf course.

the gabled Cape Dutch buildings date back to the 17th century. There's a spa, attractive pool, and restaurants. *Tokai Rd, Constantia.* ☎ *021-713-2222. www.steenberg-vineyards. co.za. 24 units. R1935–3910. AE, DC, MC, V. Map p 116.*

★★★ **Stillness Manor & Spa** CAPE PENINSULA A perfect country retreat with elegant rooms in peaceful garden cottages or in an attractive white-washed Cape Dutch manor house. There are fine views over the Constantia vineyards, Tokai Forest, and the mountains beyond. Spend time in the relaxing spa or state-of-the-art gym. *16 Debaren Cl, Tokai.* ☎ *021-713-8826. www. stillnessmanor.com. 10 units. R1520–3260. AE, MC, V. Map p 116.*

★★ **Sugar Hotel** ATLANTIC SEA-BOARD In a great location near the new stadium this cute boutique hotel has just seven state-of-the-art rooms. You'll find plasma TVs, DVD/ CD sound systems, Wi-Fi, and iPod docking stations. There's modern décor throughout, a chic little bar, and a pool. *1 Main Rd, Green Point.* ☎ *021-430-3780. www.sugarhotel. co.za. 7 units. R1300–1995. AE, MC, V. Map p 117.*

★★★ **Table Bay Hotel** V&A WATERFRONT With its position on the headland of the V&A Waterfront, location is what it's all about here. You will get a full range of facilities but, although in the luxury bracket, the hundreds of rooms are rather uniformly decorated and it's popular with tour groups. You can also get here from the airport by helicopter if you wish. *Quay 6.* ☎ *021-406-5000. www.suninternational.com. 329 units. R5250–6690. AE, DC, MC, V. Map p 117.*

★ **Table Mountain Lodge** CITY BOWL This smart, homely, and friendly B&B in a powder-blue-and-white building was originally a farm and dates back to 1885. Attention to detail includes fresh flower arrangements and there are outstanding views directly to the top cableway station on Table Mountain. *10 Tamboerskloof Rd,*

Tamboerskloof. ☎ 021-423-0042. www-za.tablemountainlodge.co.za. 9 units. R930–1440. MC, V. Map p 118.

★★ **Tarragona Lodge** CAPE PEN-INSULA With wonderful views of the Hout Bay Valley and just a short drive to the beach, the spacious rooms in this peaceful hotel have either a balcony or terrace and there's a sunny breakfast room. *Valley Rd, Hout Bay.* ☎ 021-790-5080. www.tarragona.co.za. 10 units. R1250–1800. AE, MC, V. Map p 116.

★ **Townhouse Hotel** CITY CENTER This is a good value hotel with modern décor, Wi-Fi throughout, a restaurant, and a heated indoor pool. It's close to Company's Garden; ask for a walking tour map. *60 Corporation St.* ☎ 021-465-7050. www.townhouse.co.za. 106 units. R1250–1560. AE, MC, V. Map p 118.

Tudor Hotel CITY CENTER One of the city's oldest hotels but with a thoroughly modern interior in a great location right on Greenmarket Square. Excellent value, but parking costs extra. *153 Longmarket St.* ☎ 021-424-1335. www.tudorhotel. co.za. 26 units. R695–820. AE, DC, MC, V. Map p 118.

★★★ **Twelve Apostles Hotel & Spa** CAPE PENINSULA This five-star hotel sits in a commanding position and has gorgeous ocean views. Décor is bright, white, and refreshing. Look out for the inviting hammocks on the mountainside. *Victoria Rd, Camps Bay.* ☎ 021-437-9000. www.12apostleshotel.com. 70 units. R4900–10,600. AE, DC, MC, V. Map p 116.

★★★ **Urban Chic** CITY CENTER This contemporary four-star hotel is in a converted Art Deco block. Rooms are small but have all mod-cons. There's a sweeping marble staircase and gorgeous stainless steel chandelier in the reception. *172 Long St.* ☎ 021-426-6119. www. urbanchic.co.za. 20 units. R1300–3000. AE, DC, MC, V. Map p 118.

★★ **kids** **Victoria & Alfred Hotel** V&A WATERFRONT In an unbeatable location in the heart of the V&A, within strolling distance of the local sights and with elegant rooms and great views, this was the first V&A hotel set in a converted warehouse and service is consistently good. It offers child-minding and there's a gym and pool. *Pier Head.* ☎ 021-419-6677. www.va hotel.co.za. 120 units. R1990–4350. AE, DC, MC, V. Map p 117.

Villa Lutzi CITY BOWL Perched on the lower slopes of Table Mountain with good views of Signal Hill, this German-run guesthouse has individually decorated rooms, with wooden floors scattered with Persian rugs. *6 Rosemead Ave, Oranjezicht.* ☎ 021-423-4614. www. villalutzi.co.za. 11 units. R1150–1350. MC, V. Map p 118.

★ **kids** **Vineyard Hotel & Spa** SOUTHERN SUBURBS This establishment is set in an historical 18th-century manor house in 6 acres (2.5 hectares) of well-kept parklands, with

Sugar Hotel

Winchester Mansions Hotel on Sea Point's beachfront.

three restaurants, a sushi bar, indoor and outdoor heated pools, a spa, gym, and yoga sessions. Families should ask about self-catering units. *Colinton Rd, Newlands.* ☎ *021-657-4500. www.vineyard.co.za. 175 units. R1660–3780. AE, DC, MC, V. Map p 116.*

★★ Westin Grand Arabella Quays Hotel CITY CENTER

A Sheraton property, this 19-story blue glass block is adjacent to the Cape Town International Convention Centre. The views from both the Tower Restaurant and the spa on the top floor are superb. *Convention Square, Lower Long St.* ☎ *021-412-9999. www.arabellacapetownhotel. com. 483 units. R3400–6000. AE, DC, MC, V. Map p 118.*

★★ Whale View Manor CAPE PENINSULAR

This is an upmarket B&B decorated with items collected from around the world; for example, the Indian and Thai rooms feature Buddha statues and soft silk furnishings. As the name suggests, you may spot whales in season. *402 Main Rd, Simon's Town.* ☎ *021-786-3291. www.whaleviewmanor.co.za. 10 units. R1200–1400. MC, V. Map p 116.*

★★ Winchester Mansions Hotel ATLANTIC SEABOARD

You'll find old-world charm in this bright white mansion opposite Sea Point's promenade. There's a spa and lovely courtyard with palms and fountains, and live jazz in the restaurant on Sunday afternoons. *221 Beach Rd, Sea Point.* ☎ *021-434-2351. www.winchester.co.za. 76 units. R790–4150. AE, DC, MC, V. Map p 117.* ●

The Whale Coast

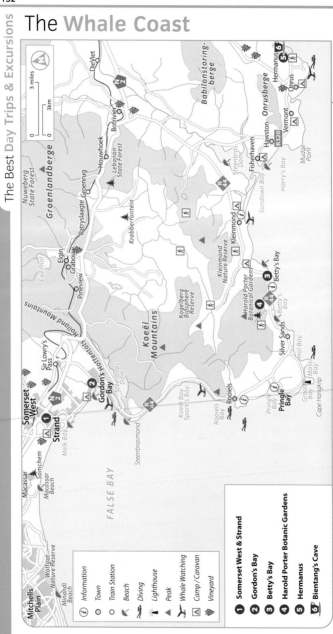

Mitchells Plain

- ⓘ Information
- ⚬ Town
- ◎ Train Station
- ⌇ Beach
- 🏊 Diving
- ⚡ Lighthouse
- ▲ Peak
- 🛬 Whale Watching
- Ⓐ Camp / Caravan
- 🌲 Vineyard

1. Somerset West & Strand
2. Gordon's Bay
3. Betty's Bay
4. Harold Porter Botanic Gardens
5. Hermanus
6. Bientang's Cave

Walker Bay in Hermanus is considered one of the world's best whale-watching destinations, and ideally from the clifftops. The whale season is from November to June, and a visit here makes a good day trip; the coastal road snakes its way around the spectacular mountains of the Overberg. START: **Take the N2, east past the airport and then turn right at Somerset West on the R44.**

① Somerset West & Strand. A commuter town, ringed by the Hottentots Holland Mountains, straddles the N2 highway. The main beach, Strand (meaning 'beach' in Afrikaans), is a pleasant wide stretch of sand lined with holiday apartments. Above the town, the N2 climbs the mountains over the spectacular Sir Lowry's Pass (see box, below). As the road starts to rise towards the pass, after Monkey World turn right to Gordon's Bay. ⏱ *1–2 hrs for the beach, otherwise drive through.*

9km (5.5 miles) from Somerset West on the R44.

② kids ★★ Gordon's Bay. The first settlement on the R44 coast road and on the eastern side of False Bay, this small resort has a main beach and the tiny arch of Bikini Beach, both of which are safe for swimming and great for kids, as there are plenty of warm shallows and rock pools to explore. The

Yachts at Gordon's Bay.

seafood restaurants along the beach road are popular with daytrippers from Cape Town. Continue

Sir Lowry's Pass

Opened in 1830, and named after the then-governor of the Cape Colony, Sir Lowry's Pass forms an alternative route from Cape Town to Hermanus (120km/75 miles) via the N2. The N2 goes through the Hottentots-Holland Mountains of the Overberg, and on through farmlands to the Garden Route. Mossel Bay, the first main town on the Garden Route, is 394km (245 miles) from Cape Town. Rising to a height of 420m (1,380ft), this is one of many impressive passes built in the 1800s to traverse the Western Cape mountain ranges. Pull over at the viewpoint for the sweeping view of the Cape Peninsula and the Cape Flats.

Harold Porter Botanic Gardens.

on the road as it winds around the headland, and on a clear day enjoy the view across to the Cape Peninsula. 🕐 *45 min.*

37km (23 miles) from Gordon's Bay on the R44.

❸ **kids** ★ **Betty's Bay.** The road passes through the villages of Rooiels and Pringle Bay, made up of mostly local holiday homes, to Betty's Bay. Apart from Boulders Beach (p 18, ❾), this is the only other

Whale Watching

Walker Bay has the advantage of low cliffs and deep water so the whales get exceptionally close to the shore—in some places only about 10m (33ft) away. The whales are Southern Rights, so called because they were considered the 'right' or easiest to catch whales during the days of whaling. In August and September the females calve in the bay and then stay another two or so months with their young in the sheltered waters before returning to the colder oceans in the south. Things to look for include: blowing—the whale exhales air through its blow-hole crating a spout of water vapor; breaching—the whale lifts its entire body out of the water in a spectacular arc; grunting—a loud noise that carries a long way over the water; lobtailing—slapping the surface of the water with its tail; sailing—lifting its tail from the water for long periods of time; spyhopping—lifting its head vertically out of the water so it has a 360° view of the ocean.

The Whale Coast: Practical Info

By far the best way to travel around the region is by car because there's no public transport. The **Greater Hermanus Tourism Bureau** is in the Old Station Building on Mitchell Street (☎ 028-312-2629, www.hermanus.co.za, Mon–Fri 8am–6pm, Sat 9am–5pm, Sun 9am–3pm). They offer an accommodation booking service, but ensure that you book well ahead in whale season. There are several good accommodation options. The **Marine** has a commanding cliff top location and luxurious rooms with four-poster beds, a spa, heated pool, and award-winning restaurant (Marine Dr, Hermanus; ☎ 028-313-1000; www.marine-hermanus.co.za; doubles R2,000–3,600). **Abalone Guest Lodge** has ocean or mountain views, and bright, airy décor with some artistic touches (306 Main Rd, Hermanus; ☎ 044-533-1345; www.abalone lodge.co.za; doubles R760–1430). **Hermanus Backpackers** is a friendly hostel with good facilities, and nightly *braais* or barbecues (26 Flower St, Hermanus; ☎ 028-312-4293; www.hermanus backpackers.co.za; dorms from R90, doubles from R260).

colony of African penguins to be found on the mainland. It's worth stopping if passing but Boulders is better. As at Boulders there's a boardwalk along the beach to view them. 🕐 *30 min. Stoney Point. Admission R5. Daily 9am–5pm.*

④ ★ Harold Porter Botanic Gardens. This attractively laid out formal garden leads to an area higher up of wild vegetation where there are hiking paths with good ocean views. Look out for the protea—South Africa's national flower. 🕐 *1–2 hrs. R44, Betty's Bay.* ☎ *028-272-9311. www.sanbi.org. Admission R15 adults, R5 kids (under-16s). Mon–Fri 8am–4.30pm, Sat–Sun 8am–5pm.*

29km (18 miles) from Betty's Bay on the R44.

⑤ kids ★★★ Hermanus. This town lives and breathes whales and can get very busy during season

(June to November), when the sandstone cliff paths of Walker Bay are populated with groups of binocular-wielding visitors hoping to catch sight of some breaching or blowing. **Hermanus Whale Festival** is held in September (www.whalefestivalco.za). Listen and look out for the Whale Crier—he blows a horn when he spots a whale from his position at the top of the cliffs. 🕐 *2–3 hrs.*

⑥ kids Bientang's Cave. In a cave right on the water's edge, with a wooden deck over the crashing waves, this is a perfect vantage point for whale-watching. Stop here for a seafood lunch served on sociable long wooden tables. The steps down are steep and are not suitable for the frail or buggies. *Marine Dr, Hermanus.* ☎ *028-312-3454. $$.*

The Winelands

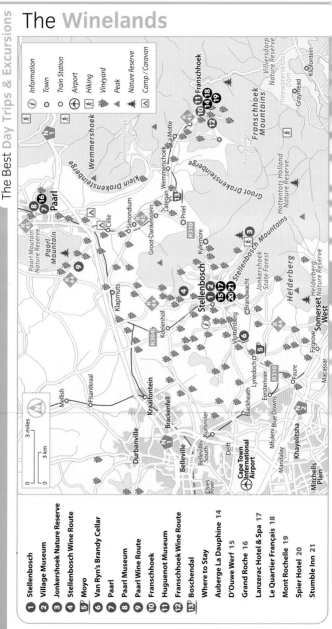

The Best Day Trips & Excursions

1 Stellenbosch
2 Village Museum
3 Jonkershoek Nature Reserve
4 Stellenbosch Wine Route
5 Moyo
6 Van Ryn's Brandy Cellar
7 Paarl
8 Paarl Museum
9 Paarl Wine Route
10 Franschhoek
11 Huguenot Museum
12 Franschhoek Wine Route
13 Boschendal

Where to Stay

Auberge La Dauphine 14
D'Ouwe Werf 15
Grand Roche 16
Lanzerac Hotel & Spa 17
Le Quartier Français 18
Mont Rochelle 19
Spier Hotel 20
Stumble Inn 21

The Cape Winelands are set in beautiful valleys and warrant at least a day's exploration. Tour operators can take you to visit a number of vineyards, or elect a designated driver and take a leisurely drive yourself. Estates are clearly signposted, and many have gourmet restaurants and/or luxury accommodation. START: N2/R310 46km (29 miles) east of Cape Town.

1 ★★ **Stellenbosch.** Established in 1680, this is South Africa's oldest town after Cape Town and has a pleasing blend of Cape Dutch, Regency, and Victorian architecture, and an attractive central square—all best appreciated on foot. Look out for the magnificent oak trees, some of which were planted in the 1600s by early farmers and are national monuments. Despite its historical nature, the town has a youthful atmosphere thanks to the large Stellenbosch University. *1–2 hrs.*

2 ★ **Village Museum.** Four 18th- and 19th-century houses have been restored and furnished with period furniture and household objects, and the gardens have been planted with popular plants of the era. Guides dressed in period clothes are on hand to show visitors around. *1 hr. Ryneveld St, Stellenbosch.* ☎ *021-887-2902. Admission R20 adults, R5 kids (under-14s). Mon–Sat 9.30am–5pm, Sun 2pm–5pm.*

9km (5.5 miles) from Stellenbosch in the Jonkershoek Valley.

3 **Jonkershoek Nature Reserve.** Near Stellenbosch, this reserve encompasses the Jonkershoek Mountains with their high peaks and deep ravines, and the Eerste River runs through it. The vegetation is mostly mountain *fynbos* and pine plantations, and there are hiking trails from 6km (4 miles) to 18km (11 miles) long. *2–3 hrs if you want to hike.* ☎ *021-866-1560. www.capenature.co.za. Admission R24 adults, R12 kids (under-16s). Daily 7.30am–6pm.*

From Stellenbosch, whichever direction you go the estates are well signposted off the R44, R310, and R304 and the other minor roads.

4 ★★★ **Stellenbosch Wine Route.** The country's oldest wine route represents more than 200 vineyards around Stellenbosch. Pick up a free map at the tourist office. Recommended is **Delheim**, which produces a good range of wine including the Grand Reserve flagship red; **Lanzerac** with its beautiful manor house

The beautiful manor house at Lanzerac.

Neethlingshof Wine Estate.

that is now a five-star hotel; **Spier** for its wine and range of other attractions including cheetahs and birds of prey; **Neethlingshof** for lovely Cape Dutch buildings and avenues of pine trees; **Simonsig** for very drinkable wines and good views of the valley; and **Vergelegen** for beautiful grounds and gracious manor house. ⏱ *Allow 30–45 min per estate. 36 Market St, Stellenbosch.* ☎ *021-886-4310. www.wineroute.co.za. Mon–Fri 8.30am–5pm.*

5 **kids** **Moyo.** Don't miss this imaginative restaurant with tables and couches in Bedouin tents or tree houses, and live entertainment in the way of music and dancing. Food is buffet style and features African dishes and seafood. *Spier Estate, R44, Stellenbosch.* ☎ *021-809-1133. $$$$.*

6 **Van Ryn's Brandy Cellar.** If brandy's your tipple, stop here for the informative guided tour to see how brandy is made, and admire the huge copper distilling vats and the fine oak barrels. ⏱ *45 min. Van Ryn Rd, off R310.* ☎ *021-881-3875. www.vanryn.co.za. Admission R30. Tours Mon–Fri 10am, 11.30am, 3pm; Sat 10am and 11.30am.*

60km (37 miles) from Cape Town on the N1/R45, or 30km (19 miles) from Stellenbosch via R310/R45.

7 ★ **Paarl.** This is another historical Winelands town with tree-lined streets of beautifully preserved Cape Dutch and Victorian architecture, overshadowed by the giant boulder of Paarl Rock. Meaning 'pearl' in English, the rock is said to shine like a pearl in the morning dew. To the west of town look up the hill to see the imposing three concrete columns of the **Afrikaanse Taalmonument** (Afrikaans

Red grapes on the vine.

South African Wine

Wine was first produced in 1659 by the first Commander of the Cape, Jan van Riebeeck, who wrote in his diary that year, 'Today, so praise be to God, wine was pressed from Cape grapes for the first time'. It was needed for the sailors on passing ships from Europe to the East Indies—red wine kept better than water and helped fight off scurvy. Early wines were also sent to Europe, and Napoleon and Fredrick of Prussia were known to enjoy a Cape Winelands tipple. Today the South African wine industry produces around a billion liters (22 million gallons) of wine each year and there are more than 4,000 wine farms in the country. Grape varieties include Chenin Blanc, Chardonnay, Sauvignon Blanc, Shiraz, Merlot, and Pinotage. Unlike other wine producers, such as in France, wine in South Africa isn't labeled by region, but by grape variety and the reputation of the vineyard.

Language Monument); considered the world's only monument dedicated to a language. ⏲ *1 hr.*

⑧ Paarl Museum. The building itself is more interesting than the assortment of Cape Dutch furniture and household objects inside. The U-shaped thatched building dates to 1767 and was a parsonage. ⏲ *20 min. 303 Main Rd, Paarl.* ☎ *021-872-2651. Admission R5. Mon–Fri 9am–5pm, Sat 9am–1pm.*

The estates are clustered around the R45 and R310 and off the N1.

⑨ ★★ Paarl Wine Route. Again, pick up a map at the Paarl tourist office of the 35 estates around the town. If you have kids in tow go to **Fairview,** where they'll love the goat tower, a spiral structure that the goats like to climb, and there's yummy goat's cheese to sample and buy. Fairview also does quite a take on French wine and labels include *Goats do Roam* and *Bored Doe*! Also visit **Laborie** and taste wine overlooking the vineyards; **Nederburg** for their quaffable award-winning wines; **KWV** Cellars, the largest wine cellar in South Africa, which holds the five largest oak vats in the world; or **Nelson's Creek,** which runs informative cellar tours. ⏲ *Allow 30–45 min per estate. 86 Main Rd, Paarl.* ☎ *021-863-4886. www.wine country.co.za. Mon–Fri 9am–5pm.*

78km (49 miles) from Cape Town via N1/R45, or 28 km (17 miles) from Paarl on R45.

⑩ ★★★ Franschhoek. This very attractive village is the self-proclaimed gastronomic capital of South Africa—and for good reason. The main street is lined with some fine award-winning restaurants and it makes a perfect place to stop for lunch. Meaning 'French corner' in Afrikaans, the name originates from a group of French Huguenots who settled here in the 17th century and developed the wine estates. ⏲ *10 min, longer for lunch.*

⑪ Huguenot Museum. The Huguenots (French Protestants) escaped persecution by Catholics in France and came to southern Africa in search of religious liberty in the late 1600s. This interesting little

Four Passes Route

As the name suggests, this scenic route goes over four mountain passes and is a recommended day trip from Cape Town, especially when combined with lunch in a fine Franschhoek restaurant or on a wine estate. Once in Stellenbosch take the R310 to Franschhoek over the Helshoogte **Pass**. After 17km (11 miles) turn right on to the R45 to Franschhoek and then over the **Franschhoek Pass**. This is some 500m (1,600ft) above Franschhoek; notice the change of vegetation from fertile vineyards to scrub vegetation and *fynbos* surrounding the Theewaterskloof Dam. Turn right across the top of the dam on the R321, and climb **Viljoens Pass**. The countryside around here is used for apple growing. At the N2 turn right and head back to Cape Town over **Sir Lowry's Pass** (p 133) where you'll be rewarded with a fine view of the Cape Flats and False Bay.

museum tells their story, and outside look out for the Huguenot Memorial of a woman on a globe holding a bible and a broken chain (representing a break from repression). ⏱ *20 min. Lambrecht St, Franschhoek.* ☎ *021-876-2532. www.museum.co.za. Admission R10 adults, R2 (under-16s). Mon–Sat 9am–5pm, Sun 2pm–5pm.*

The following estates are off the R45.

⑫ ★★★ Franschhoek Wine Route. Pick up a map at the tourist office, although all the 43 vineyards are signposted along the R45 in the Franschhoek Valley. **Boschendal** is a must for its tree-lined avenue, gracious H-shaped manor house, and wine-tasting area underneath the arms of a giant oak; **Mount Rochelle** has beautiful views of the valley and tasty wines; **La Motte** has some interesting and grand old

The Boschendal wine estate.

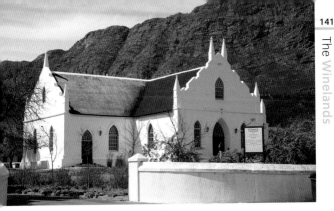

Typical Cape Dutch architecture in Franschhoek.

cellars; **Cape Chamonix** has wine tasting in the old blacksmith's cottage on the estate; and **Cabriére** is famous for its sparkling wines, which are still opened here by popping the cork with a sword. 🕐 *Allow 30–45 min per estate. Tourist Office, 70 Huguenot Rd, Franschhoek.* ☎ *021-876-3603. www.franschhoek. org.za. Mon–Fri 9am–6pm, Sat 10am–5pm, Sun 10am–4pm.*

13 Boschendal. Order a bottle of chilled Sauvignon Blanc and enjoy the daily lunchtime buffet here on this beautiful wine estate— soups, pâtés, homemade bread, roasts, succulent veggies, and decadent desserts. Reservations are essential. *R45, midway between Paarl and Franschhoek.* ☎ *021-870-4272. www.boschendalwines.com. $$$$.*

Winelands: Practical Info

No public transport adequately covers the Winelands, and so you either need to have your own car or take a day tour from Cape Town, which costs in the region of R500. Operators include **Cape Rainbow**, (☎ 021-448-3117; www.tourcapers.co.za), **Hylton Ross** (☎ 021-511-1784; www.hyltonross.com), **Springbok Atlas** (☎ 021-460-4700; www.springbokatlas.com) or **Ferdinand's Tours** (☎ 021-987-8888; www.fgroup.co.za). **Daytrippers** (☎ 021-5114766; www.daytrippers.co.za) also take mountain bikes for a couple of hours cycling. Most of the wine estates are open from Monday to Saturday from 9am until 4 or 5pm (very few open on Sundays) and the restaurants are open for lunch. Some also offer picnic baskets to enjoy among the vines. It costs R10–20 to taste about six wines and some places let you keep the glass. There's a fine selection of luxury accommodation in the Winelands and Stellenbosch has a very good backpackers' hostel for budget travelers, the Stumble Inn (see p 151).

West Coast

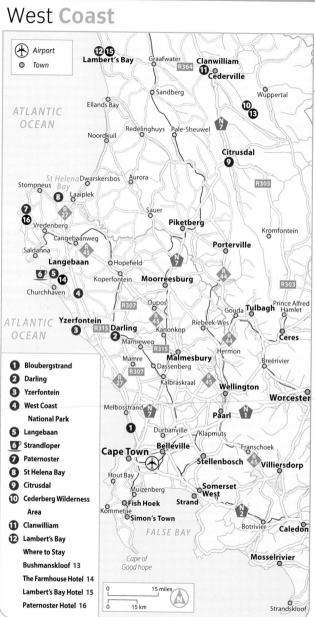

- ✈ Airport
- ○ Town

ATLANTIC OCEAN

Graafwater
R364
Clanwilliam
12 15 Lambert's Bay
11 Cederville
Sandberg
Wuppertal
Ellands Bay
10
13
Noordkuil
Redelinghuys
Pale-Sheuwel
N7
St Helena Bay
Dwarskersbos
Aurora
Citrusdal
9
Stompneus
8 Laaiplek
R303
7
Sauer
16
Vredenberg
Piketberg
Langebaanweg
Kromfontein
R27
Porterville
Saldanna
R45
Langebaan
○ Hopefield
6 5
14
Koperfontein
Moorreesburg
R44
Churchhaven
4
R303
Oupos
ATLANTIC OCEAN
Yzerfontein
R307
R45
Gouda
Tulbagh
Prince Alfred Hamlet
3
R315
Darling
Kanonkop
Riebeek-Wes
2 Mamreweg
Ceres
Mamre
R315
Malmesbury
Hermon
Breërivier
R307
Dassenberg
R44
R27
Kalbraskraal
R45
Wellington
Melbosstrand
N7
Worcester
1
Paarl
N1
Durbanville
Klapmuts
Belleville
Franschoek
Cape Town
R45
Villiersdorp
Stellenbosch
Hout Bay
Muizenberg
Somerset West
○ Fish Hoek
Strand
Kommetjie ○ Simon's Town
N2
Botrivier
Caledon
FALSE BAY
Cape of Good hope
Mosselrivier
Strandskloof

1 Bloubergstrand
2 Darling
3 Yzerfontein
4 West Coast National Park
5 Langebaan
6 Strandloper
7 Paternoster
8 St Helena Bay
9 Citrusdal
10 Cederberg Wilderness Area
11 Clanwilliam
12 Lambert's Bay

Where to Stay

Bushmanskloof 13
The Farmhouse Hotel 14
Lambert's Bay Hotel 15
Paternoster Hotel 16

0   15 miles
0   15 km
N

The West Coast north of Cape Town offers picturesque fishing villages and a sun-bleached coast backed by dunes and *fynbos* scrub. In spring, fields are blanketed with wild flowers best seen in the West Coast National Park. Inland, the N7 runs through the Swartland, a wheat and wine farming region, while the R27 hugs the coast. START: **Take the R27 north for 20km (12 miles).**

1 ★★★ **Bloubergstrand.** This suburb offers a picture-postcard view of the city and Table Mountain. Stroll barefoot on the glorious beach with the dog walkers and kite flyers. It's also a hotspot for kiteboarding (p 74). ⏱ *20 min.*

Continue north on the R27 and after 17km (10.5 miles) turn right. Darling is 35km (22 miles) from this junction on the R307.

2 ★★ **Darling.** A little inland, this pretty village is best known as the home of Evita Bezuidenhout, a South African drag artiste similar to Australia's Dame Edna Everage, who runs a charming café/theater/shop in the old railway station. In flower season (August and September) staff here will point you in the direction of local farms, which open to visitors to see the blooms. ⏱ *30 min.* *Evita se Perron, Railway Station,* ☎ *022-492-2831. Tues–Sun 10am–4pm.*

Take the R315 for 24km (15 miles).

3 ★ **Yzerfontein.** This unspoilt fishing village has a wide expanse of sandy beach and the sea has a strong swell, making it a popular surfing spot. Boats in the little harbor go out daily to fish for *snoek*, a popular fish on the West Coast traditionally eaten with bread and apricot jam. ⏱ *30 min.*

Take the R27, north for about 20km (12 miles).

4 ★★ **West Coast National Park.** In flower season (August to September) this is the best place to see the profusion of lilies, daisies, and other wild flowers. The lagoon and coastal flats are home to thousands of sea birds and waders and some 250 species have been recorded. Look out for the rare black oystercatcher. There are a number of walking trails and bird hides. ⏱ *1–2 hrs in flower season.* ☎ *022-772-2144. www.sanparks. org. Admission R20; R60 in flower season. June–Sep 7am–6.30pm, Oct–Apr 6am–8pm.*

On the opposite side of the West Coast National Park from the R27.

5 **Langebaan.** This resort town is rather overshadowed by the enormous and ugly Club Mykonos time share complex, but nevertheless the Langebaan Lagoon is very scenic and there's a good stretch of sheltered beach. ⏱ *30 min.*

Look out for wild flowers in the West Coast National Park.

6 Strandloper. This is the best eating experience on the West Coast. Kick your shoes off on the beach for a long lazy lunch of about 10 courses of fish and seafood eaten at shaded wooden tables and accompanied by a guitar player. *Langebaan Beach.* ☎ *022-772-2490. www.strandloper. com. $$$.*

Head back to the Langebaan junction on the R27, and then continue 33km (21 miles) north to R45. Drive through Vredenburg and drive 16km (10 miles) down a dirt road.

7 ★★ Paternoster. A pretty fishing village with a cluster of whitewashed houses with brightly colored tin roofs gleaming in the sun. The mainstay of the local economy here is crayfish fishing. It's a peaceful place to walk along the beach or between the distinctive white boulders. Look out for the lighthouse guarding the treacherous Cape Columbine, which has wrecked many ships in the past. It emits a flashing light that carries 50km (32 miles) out to sea. ⏱ *1–2 hrs.*

Fishing boats on the beach at Paternoster.

16km (10 miles) northeast of Paternoster.

8 ★ St Helena Bay This is another attractive fishing village with a large fleet of boats, and is the spot where Vasco da Gama first set foot on what is now South Africa on his epic voyage around the Cape, on 7th November 1497; St Helena Day. A granite monument on the shore marks the occasion. ⏱ *30 min.*

Go cross country on the R399 for about 80km (50 miles) and join the N7 at Piketberg. Citrusdal is 45km (28 miles) north.

9 Citrusdal. Away from the coast, and back on the N7, cross the impressive Piekenierskloof Pass and drive down to Citrusdal. This town is surrounded by orange groves and as the name suggests is a center for the citrus industry. ⏱ *10 min to drive through.*

Take the N7 for 27km (17 miles), and then turn right and continue for 18km (11 miles).

10 ★★ Cederberg Wilderness Area. Here you can pick up permits and maps for hikes in the dramatic and rugged Cederberg Mountains. The vegetation is mostly *fynbos* with clutches of yellowwoods and Cape beech and cedar trees, and has plenty of overhangs, mountain streams, and rocky pools to explore. If you're lucky you might spot a shy antelope such as duiker or klipspringer. ⏱ *Hikes from 1hr–1 day. Cape Nature, Algeria.* ☎ *027-482-2403. www.capenature.org.za. Day walks R36 adults, R22 kids (under-12s). Daily 8am–6pm.*

Continue 54km (34 miles) north on the N7.

11 Clanwilliam. Back on the N7, this is a quiet agricultural town

Fishermen at St Helena Bay.

famous for growing South African's favorite tea—*rooibos*; caffeine-free and more scented than regular tea. A garrison was built by the British here in 1808 and the town was named in 1814 after the father-in-law of the Cape Governor, Sir John Cradock—the Earl of Clanwilliam. The museum in the old fort is mildly interesting. ⏱ *1 hr. Museum, Main St. Admission R5 adults, R2 kids (under-16s). Mon–Fri 8am–12.30am.*

Take the R364 to Lambert's Bay, 69km (43 miles) west.

⓬ **Lambert's Bay.** A fairly remote and unattractive fish-processing town on a windswept stretch of coast 70km (44 miles) west of Clanwilliam, birdwatchers should head here to see the offshore colony of thousands of Cape gannets and, to a lesser extent, the cormorants on Bird Island. You can walk across to the island via a causeway past fishing boats. There's a bird hide to watch from. ⏱ *1 hr.*

West Coast: Practical Info

There's no public transport up the West Coast, but in flower season (August to September) coach tours are on offer from Cape Town. A leisurely self-drive tour is the best option and if you have more time you can return to Cape Town via Route 62 (see p 146) or the winelands (p 136). For recommended hotels in the West Coast region, see p 152.

Route 62

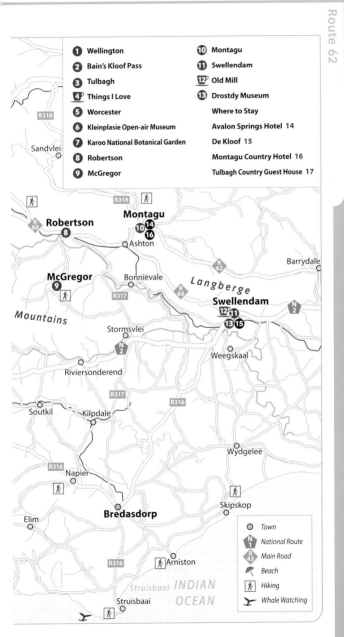

1 Wellington
2 Bain's Kloof Pass
3 Tulbagh
4 Things I Love
5 Worcester
6 Kleinplasie Open-air Museum
7 Karoo National Botanical Garden
8 Robertson
9 McGregor
10 Montagu
11 Swellendam
12 Old Mill
13 Drostdy Museum

Where to Stay

Avalon Springs Hotel 14
De Kloof 15
Montagu Country Hotel 16
Tulbagh Country Guest House 17

○ Town
N2 National Route
R43 Main Road
Beach
Hiking
Whale Watching

Like Route 66 in the USA, Route 62 is a successful tourism initiative (based around the R62 road) running from Cape Town to Port Elizabeth in the Eastern Cape on the back roads. Over a couple of days you can explore the western end—a pretty region of vineyards, orchards, and wheat fields. START: **Take the N1 50km (30 miles) to Paarl and then the R303 9km (6 miles) to Wellington.**

1 Wellington. Like the other winelands towns, this has a fine collection of historical buildings and is surrounded by vineyards. A number of estates are open to the public for wine tasting, though most grapes grown in this region are used for dried fruit. ⏱ *Allow 30–45 min per wine estate in and around Wellington.*

Follow the R301 over the spectacular Bain's Kloof Pass.

2 ★★★ Bain's Kloof Pass. One of the most scenic of the many passes in the Western Cape, this series of dramatic switchbacks was considered a huge engineering feat when it opened in 1853. It is named after Andrew Bain, who built eight passes in the Cape and whose son Thomas Bain went on to build another 24 in the late 1800s. ⏱ *1 hr, allowing time to stop and admire the views.*

Once over the pass 29km (18 miles) from Wellington, turn left on the R43 42km (26 miles).

3 ★★★ Tulbagh. Almost too pretty and perfect, this beautiful town features some fine Cape Dutch white-washed architecture and it's all false. The original village of 18th-century buildings was all but destroyed in an earthquake in 1966, but the village underwent a massive restoration and became the fine settlement you see today. Park the car and walk up and down Church Street and drop into the museum, which has information about the earthquake and a collection of Victorian furniture. ⏱ *1–2 hrs. Oude Kerk Volksmuseum.*

Dutch white-washed house in Tulbagh.

2 Church St. ☎ *023-230-1041. Admission R10 adults, kids R5 (under-16s). Mon–Fri 9am–5pm, Sat 9am–4pm, Sun 11am–4pm.*

4 Things I Love. On a sunny day build your own picnics at the deli here and chill out with a bottle of wine in the gardens or terrace. In winter enjoy light lunches next to the cozy fire. *61 Van der Stel St, Tulbah.* ☎ *023-230-1742. $-$$.*

Retrace the R27 for 17km (10.5 miles) and take the R301/R43 for 40km (25 miles).

5 ★ Worcester. This medium-sized farming town lies in the picturesque Breede River Valley and is

surrounded by orchards and vineyards. It was first settled in 1820
and named after the Marquess of
Worcester. The **Worcester Wine
Route** is worth exploring and you
can pick up maps at the Kleinplasie
museum (see **6**). *Allow 30–45
min per estate. www.worcesterwine
route.co.za.*

6 kids **★★★ Kleinplasie Open-
air Museum. This is** a fairly
absorbing museum depicting life in
the region from 1700 to 1900. It's
made up of about two dozen recon-
structed buildings such as a blacksmiths, cartwrights, post office, and
bakers. Several rural skills are dem-
onstrated by people in period costume and the geese and pigs
wandering around create a real
farmyard atmosphere. Make time
for the tearoom and shop, which
sells local wines and homemade
jam. *90 min. Robertson Rd,
Worcester. ☎ 023-342-2226. www.
kleinplasie.co.za. Admission R12
adults, R5 kids (of school age). Mon–
Sat 9am–4.30pm.*

On the opposite side of the N1
from Worcester.

7 kids **★ Karoo National
Botanical Garden.** This fine collection of indigenous semi-desert
plants is at its best in flower season
(August to October) although it's a
peaceful spot to visit at any time of
year. Kids will enjoy the hedged
maze. *1 hr. Roux Rd, Worcester.
☎ 023-342-2226. www.sanbi.org.
Admission free except in flower season (Aug–Oct) R14 adults, R6 kids
(under-16s). Daily 7am–6pm.*

Follow the R60 for 53km (33
miles) from Worcester.

8 **★★★ Robertson.** The drive
from Worcester to Robertson is
quite beautiful, as the Breede River
Valley widens out in a patchwork of
crops in contrasting colors and the

Langeberg Mountains rise up to the
north. Robertson is a sleepy farming
center featuring neat rose gardens
and orderly squares and is surrounded by vineyards. These produce excellent Chardonnays plus
dessert wines and liqueurs. Pick up
a map for the **Robertson Valley
Wine Route** at the office. *Allow
30–45 min per estate. Robertson
Wine Valley, Voortrekker St. ☎ 023-
626-4437. www.robertsonwineval-
ley.co.za. Mon–Fri 9am–5pm,
Sat–Sun 9am–1pm.*

Take a minor road, signposted to
McGregor 25km (16 miles) south.

9 **★ McGregor.** This is a picture-
perfect rural village with a clutch of
thatched whitewashed houses
gleaming in the sun, and the occasional sound of a tractor chugging
in the olive groves. *30 min.*

From Robertson the R60 continues 25km (16 miles) to Montagu.

10 kids **★★ Montagu.** The main-
stay of the economy in this region is
apples, pears, peaches, and apri-
cots as well as the inevitable wine,
and the valley here is ringed by
soaring mountains. Most people
come to visit the **Avalon Springs
Hotel** (see p 152), which has a series
of pools and facilities centered on
some hot springs. The waters are
considered therapeutic and are a
steady 48°C (118°F). *30 min.*

Continue on the R60 for 56km
(35 miles) southeast of Montagu.

11 **★★★ Swellendam.** Established as a trading post by the Dutch
East India Company in 1745, this is
South Africa's third oldest town
after Cape Town and Stellenbosch.
It also has the country's best preserved 18th- and 19th-century Cape
Dutch architecture, and many buildings have been turned into cafés
and craft shops. *1–2 hrs.*

Mountains surrounding Montagu.

12 Old Mill. Stop for afternoon tea in the pretty gardens in the sun or come by later and eat by candlelight inside the historical building in the evening, when traditional South African cuisine is on offer. *241 Voortrek St, Swellendam.* ☎ *028-514-2790. $$.*

13 ★★★ Drostdy Museum. Built in 1747 and lovingly restored, this was the house of the town's first magistrate and features include a cow-dung kitchen floor, shuttered windows, and thatched roof. Furnishings are of 19th-century vintage and in the garden are a gazebo and rose garden. ⏱ *45 min. 18 Swellengrebel St, Swellendam.* ☎ *023-514-1138. www.drostdymuseum.co.za. Admission R10 adults, kids R5 (under 16). Mon–Fri 9am–4.45pm, Sat–Sun 10am–3.45pm.*

Route 62: Practical Info

Car is by far the best way to travel around the region. Swellendam is on the N2, exactly half way between Cape Town and George at the beginning of the Garden Route, which are both about 280km (175 miles) in either direction. Your options are to return to Cape Town or go to George on the N2, or to rejoin Route 62 and follow it to Oudtshoorn and beyond (www.route62.co.za).

Where to Stay—Winelands

Auberge La Dauphine FRAN-SCHHOEK This auberge is an intimate guesthouse on a peaceful wine farm, with just six spacious rooms. *Excelsior Rd, Franschhoek.* ☎ 021-876-2606. www.ladauphine. co.za. Doubles R1,000–1,100 w/ breakfast. MC, V. Map p 136.

D'Ouwe Werf STELLENBOSCH Built in 1802, the D'Ouwe Werf is South Africa's oldest hotel and features polished wooden floors, antique furniture, a swimming pool, and vine-shaded terrace. *30 Church St, Stellenbosch.* ☎ 021-887-4608. www.ouwewerf.com. Doubles R990–1,990 w/breakfast. AE, DC, MC, V. Map p 136.

Grand Roche PAARL *Grand Roche* is one of the Wineland's finest hotels with sweeping views over the vines, and the manor house is home to the acclaimed **Boseman's Restaurant**. *Plantasie St, Paarl.* ☎ 021-863-5100. www.granderoche. co.za. Doubles R1,980–4,300 w/ breakfast. AE, DC, MC, V. Map p 136.

Lanzerac Hotel & Spa STELLEN-BOSCH The five-star Lanzerac is set on a beautiful 300-year-old wine estate, with gracious white-washed Cape Dutch architecture and superb facilities including a luxury spa and fine restaurants. *Jonkershoek Rd, Stellenbosch.* ☎ 021-887-1132. www. lanzerac.co.za. Doubles R1,980–3,520 w/breakfast. AE, DC, MC, V. Map p 136.

Le Quartier Français FRAN-SCHHOEK This is a stylish boutique hotel with courtyard and pool, and the gourmet **Tasting Room** and **Ici** are among Franschhoek's best restaurants. *16 Huguenot Rd.* ☎ 021-876-2151. www.lequartier.co.za. Doubles R3,900–6,900 w/breakfast. AE, DC, MC, V Map p 136.

Mont Rochelle FRANSCHHOEK Mont Rochelle has 24 luxurious rooms, a sparkling pool, and award-winning restaurant. *Dassenberg Rd, Franschhoek.* ☎ 021-876-2770. www.montrochelle.co.za. Doubles R1,650–5,520 w/breakfast. AE, DC, MC, V. Map p 136.

The Spier Hotel STELLENBOSCH The four-star *Spier Hotel* is set in lovely countryside on the acclaimed Spier Estate and features funky and modern décor. *5km (3 miles) off Stellenbosch on the R310.* ☎ 021-809-1100. www.spier.co.za. Doubles R1,440–1,880 w/breakfast. AE, DC, MC, V. Map p 136.

Stumble Inn STELLENBOSCH Stumble Inn offers its own wine tours, and friendly backpackers' accommodation in two adjoining houses. You can also rent bikes here. *12 Market St, Stellenbosch.* ☎ 021-887-4049. www.stumbleinn stellenbosch.hostel.com. Dorms R90, doubles R250. MC, V. Map p 136.

Where to Stay—West Coast

Bushmanskloof CEDERBERG WIL-DERNESS AREA   This is a super luxurious retreat and spa in the heart of the Cederberg Mountains. All-inclusive packages include game drives and guided tours of nearby rock art. *40km (25 miles) from Clanwilliam off the R364.* ☎ *021-685-2598. www.bushmanskloof.co.za. Doubles R4,200–8,200 w/breakfast. AE, DC, MC, V. Map p 142.*

The Farmhouse Hotel LANGE-BAAN   With gorgeous views of the Langebaan Lagoon, this quality country retreat is set in a restored Cape Dutch farmstead with thatched roof, and has a popular restaurant and pool. *5 Egret St.* ☎ *022-772-2062. www.thefarmhouselange baan.co.za. Doubles R550–1,600 w/breakfast. MC, V. Map p 142.*

Lambert's Bay Hotel LAMBERT'S BAY   The rooms here, with jaunty nautical décor, overlook the fishing boats in the harbor. The hotel's **Waves** restaurant serves excellent West Coast seafood. *Voortrekker St.* ☎ *027-432-1126. www.lamberts bayhotel.co.za. Doubles R525–1,100 w/breakfast. MC, V. Map p 142.*

Paternoster Hotel PATERNOSTER This is a charming small hotel set in historical buildings; the pub is in Paternoster's old jail. They also rent out self-catering cottages in the village, which are ideal for families. *St Augustine St.* ☎ *022-752-2703. www.paternosterhotel.co.za. Doubles R520–720 w/breakfast. MC, V. Map p 142.*

Where to Stay—Route 62

Avalon Springs Hotel MON-TAGU   Avalon Springs is famous for its complex of relaxing hot pools and has a restaurant and bar. *Uitvlucht St.* ☎ *023-614-1150. www. avalonsprings.co.za. Doubles R1,000–1,600. AE, MC, V. Map p 147.*

De Kloof SWELLENDAM   This is an elegant guest house in a Cape Dutch homestead (1801) with a swimming pool and colorful décor. *8 Weltevreden St.* ☎ *028-514-1303. www.dekloof.co.za. Doubles R650–1,250. AE, DC, MC, V. Map p 147.*

Montagu Country Hotel MON-TAGU   In a well-restored art deco

block, this hotel has a smart restaurant and wellness center with a hot mineral pool. *27 Bath St.* ☎ *023-614-3125. www.montagucountry hotel.co.za. Doubles R1,160–1,590. MC, V. Map p 147.*

Tulbagh Country Guest House TULBAGH   Here you'll find atmospheric accommodation in an immaculately restored Cape Dutch manor house with original features and decorated with art and antiques, and you can walk to the town's restaurants. *24 Church St.* ☎ *023-230-1171. www.tulbaghguesthouse. co.za. Doubles R450–700. MC, V. Map p 147.* ●

The
Savvy Traveler

Before You Go

South African Tourism Offices

In the US: 500 Fifth Ave, 20th Floor, Suite 2040, New York, NY 10110 (☎ 0212-730-2929). **In the UK:** 6 Alt Grove, London SW19 4DZ (☎ 020-8971-9350). **In Australia:** 117 York St, Sydney, New South Wales 2000 (☎ 02-9261-5000). **In Germany:** Friedensstr. 6–10, Frankfurt 60311 (☎ 069-280-950). **In France:** 61 Rue La Boetie, 75008, Paris (☎ 01-4561-0197). **In the Netherlands:** Jozef Israelskade 48A, Amsterdam (☎ 020-471-3181). The official South Africa Tourism website is www.southafrica.net.

The Best Times to Go

February to May and September to late November are the best times to visit Cape Town, with fewer crowds than in summer, which coincides with the long domestic tourism season and school holidays. Cape Town does have quite a festive atmosphere over December and January, however, and days are long, warm, and sunny. This is the best time to lie on the beach, but you'll need to book well in advance for accommodation, and flights will be at their premium. Weather-wise, almost any time of year is the right time to go, although the wet and cloudy winter months of July and August are not the best time to enjoy the outdoors and the Table Mountain Cableway closes for maintenance for two weeks in July. Nights get chilly too and given that South Africans generally don't have heating, you may have to ask for an extra blanket from your hotel. Nevertheless these months are still popular with Europeans and North Americans as they coincide with their long holidays. In short, there's always something to do in Cape Town whatever the time of year.

Festivals & Special Events

SUMMER. One of the highlights of summer in Cape Town is lying on the lawns on a picnic blanket with a good bottle of wine for the **Old Mutual Summer Sunset Concerts** at beautiful **Kirstenbosch National Botanical Garden** (p 21). Locals pounce on the program as soon as it's published (Nov–Apr; www.sanbi. org). The concerts feature anything from the Cape Town Philharmonic Orchestra to Bryan Adams and local acts such as Coda and Freshlyground. The **Spier Wine Estate** (p 151; www.spier.co.za) near Stellenbosch in the Winelands also has a summer program of performance entertainment at its open-air amphitheater. In early December the **Obz Festival** (www.obzfestival.com) in Observatory is a 3-day independent music festival and street party, especially popular with students at the University of Cape Town. The **Cape Minstrel Carnival** on 2nd January is a minstrel's parade through central Cape Town by the Cape colored community, who compete for prizes for the best turned-out and entertaining troupes. The **J&B Met** (www.jbmet.co.za) at Kenilworth Race Course (p 114) on the last Saturday of January is the highlight of the city's already very busy social calendar and is a similar event to Ascot in the UK for the hats, dresses, and bling—the horseracing seems to be secondary.

AUTUMN. **Cape Town Pride** (www. capetownpride.co.za) in March celebrates Cape Town's 'pinkness' with an elaborate street parade ending in a night-long party in the gay 'village' of De Waterkant (p 53). Over a weekend in late March, the **Cape Town Festival** (www.capetown festival.co.za) celebrates the diversity of cultures in Cape Town with bands and other acts performing on a stage in Company Gardens, and the festival ends with a street party in Long Street. The **Cape Town International Jazz Festival** (www.capetownfestival.co.za) in late March/early April attracts a huge crowd to the Cape Town International Convention Centre (CTICC) (see p 39) and draws the cream of the crop of South African and international jazz greats. Cape Town grinds to a halt for the **Cape Argus** (a newspaper) and **Pick 'n' Pay** (a grocery chain) **Cycle Tour** (www.cycletour.co.za) (p 78) in March. This is the world's largest timed cycle race and attracts some 35,000 participants. It winds its way 109km (68m) along a hilly but beautiful course around the Cape Peninsula. Cape Town literally lives and breathes cycling over this week-long chain of events, which culminates in the big race on the Sunday, when thousands of Capetonians line the route to lend their support. Also in March or April, the **Two Oceans Marathon** (www.twooceans marathon.org.za) is an equally spectacular event and runs 56 km (35 miles) around the Peninsula. Still on sports, April sees the start of the **rugby season**; details from Western Province Rugby (www.wprugby. com) or Computicket (p 114; www.computicket.co.za) for fixtures. **Taste of Cape Town** (www. tasteofcapetown.com) in early April celebrates Cape Town's love of gourmet restaurants (many of which I have listed). Buy a book of coupons and wander around the extravagant marquees, sampling mini-portions of gorgeous food and fine wines from the city's top 15 or so restaurants.

WINTER. The four-day **Stellenbosch Wine Festival** (www.wineroute.co.za), on the first weekend of August, draws wine buffs and social butterflies out to the Winelands for tastings and the quaffing of more than 500 celebrated wines. There are also fashion shows, gourmet cooking classes, and live music. Held at the Cape Town International Convention Centre (CTICC) in June, the **Cape Town Book Fair** (www.capetownbookfair) is the southern hemisphere's largest such event. Book lovers will be in heaven and famous authors from Marion Keynes to Wilbur Smith make appearances. In August, **Cape Town Fashion Week** (www. capetownfashionweek.co.za) (p 63) gets heads turned towards the catwalk at the CTICC. There are also a couple of **film festivals** on in Cape Town over winter (p 111).

SPRING. The **Cape Town International Comedy Festival** (www. comedyfestival.co.za) (p 113) in September is staged at a number of venues around the city and is always popular. Most of Cape Town gravitates to the **Hermanus Whale Festival** (www.whalefestival.co.za) over the third weekend in September for a craft market, street fair, informative environmental and marine exhibits, live music, and yummy food, but it's the whales that are the stars of the show so if you're lucky they'll put on quite a performance out in Walker Bay.

The Weather

Cape Town has a long dry summer (December to February) with long clear days and sunny skies and temperatures average around 25–35°C (77–95°F). The only downside is the persistent southeasterly wind in January and February known locally as the 'Cape Doctor'; so-called because it cleanses the city of pollution. It can also be responsible for the mountain fires that usually plague the city at this time of the year. The winter months (June to August) are

Useful Websites

- **www.tourismcapetown.co.za:** Official city tourism site with extensive cover of the Western Cape. The two tourist offices (p 42) are also a wealth of information.
- **www.southafrica.net:** South Africa Tourism's official site published in 15 languages with details of how to get to South Africa from specific countries.
- **www.cape-town.org:** Full listings for accommodation, activities, and what to see and do.
- **www.bookcapetown.com:** One stop site for accommodation, tour, and activity bookings.
- **www.tonight.co.za:** Regularly updated What's On website with listings for nightclubs, theatre, restaurants, and events.
- **www.computicket.com:** South Africa's national booking service for sporting events, concerts, theater, cinema, exhibitions, and also long distance bus tickets and domestic air tickets (p 114).
- **www.dining-out.co.za:** Useful restaurant reviews (written and audio) with photos, maps, and menus.

the coolest times, when daytime temperatures average around 18°C (64°F) but drop as low as 8°C (46°F) and even lower at night. In some years the peaks around Stellenbosch are topped with a light cover of snow and on rare occasions so is Table Mountain. This is also the wettest and cloudiest time of the year in Cape Town. Spring and autumn are warm and clear, and are when the Winelands are particularly attractive.

Cellphones

As long as you have international roaming, your cell phone will work in South Africa. Alternatively local SIM cards and pay-as-you-go top up cards are available from phone stores like MTN or Vodacom, which can be found in the shopping malls, or from grocery stores. If you would like to rent a phone, MTN has a Cell Place desk at international departures at Cape Town International Airport (☎ 021-934-3261; www.

mtnsp.co.za), and Vodacom has a Rentaphone desk at domestic arrivals (☎ 021-934-4951; www.vodacom.co.za). Both are open 6am–11pm. A phone with SIM card costs R15–22 per day and a R1000 deposit is required. You settle your bill when you return the phone. North Americans can rent a GSM phone before leaving home from InTouch USA (☎ 800/872-7626; www.intouchglobal.com) or RoadPost (☎ 888/290-1606 or 905/272-5665; www.roadpost.com).

Car Rentals

All the international car-rental companies such as Avis, Budget, and Hertz, have several offices around town and at the airport. The toll-free numbers can be phoned from within South Africa, otherwise book ahead through the websites. Avis (☎ 0861-021-111; www.avis.co.za), Hertz (☎ 0861-600-136; www.hertz.com), and Budget (☎ 0861-016622; www.budget.co.za). An excellent local agent is Aroundabout Cars (☎ 021-422-4022; www.aroundaboutcars.com). Their depot is centrally located in the city center at 20 Bloom Street; otherwise they shop around for the best deals to pick up with one of the many car hire companies at the airport.

Getting There

By Plane
There are daily direct flights to Cape Town from Europe and flying time is 11 hours from the UK. UK residents tend not to suffer jet lag because there is a minimal time difference. From North America, Delta fly in conjunction with South African Airways on a code share agreement from Atlanta to Cape Town via Johannesburg (see below), or there is the option of going via Europe or Dubai. From South America there are direct flights between Cape Town and Buenos Aires and Sao Paulo. Other international airlines touch down in Johannesburg, from where the 2 hour flight to Cape Town is offered by a number of domestic and regional carriers. Note: to not feel rushed, allow at least 2 hours transit time at Johannesburg's O.R. Tambo International Airport. For a list of some of the airlines serving Cape Town and/or Johannesburg see p 173. Cape Town International Airport is 22km (14 miles) from the city center on the N2 and, outside of rush hour, the drive takes about 20 minutes. There is no public transport (although this is set to change; see box p 159) so the two options are to take a regular metered taxi (about R200–250) or organize a shuttle bus (R150–220 per person depending on how many people), which drops off at hotels. For one or two people the shuttle bus is the better value but for three or four people a taxi is best. You can pre-book the shuttle through Magic Bus (☎ 021-505-6300; www.magicbus.co.za) or Backpacker Bus (☎ 021-439-7600; www.backpackerbus.co.za) and the driver will meet you in the arrivals hall with a sign with your name on it. All hotels and guest houses can also arrange this service when making a room reservation. If you haven't pre-booked, there are a couple of shuttle bus counters in the international arrivals hall. For both taxis and buses you'll need Rand cash to pay the drivers, and the airport has plenty of ATMs and foreign exchange bureaux.

By Car
There are three approaches to Cape Town by road. The N1 highway connects the 1,400km (875 miles) from Johannesburg to Cape Town. The N2 runs along the southern coast of South Africa from Cape Town to Durban and beyond, and the N7, which meets the N1 about 10km/6m north of Cape Town, goes all the way to the border with Namibia 714km (445 miles) away. In the city center the N1 and N2 converge on a flyover next to the Cape Town International Convention Centre (CTICC) and end at a set of traffic lights. A right turn here takes you to the V&A Waterfront, straight on goes into the city center, and a right at the next junction takes you to Green Point, Sea Point and beyond.

By Bus
Mainline coach companies link Cape Town with the other cities on various routes (www.greyhound.co.za; www.translux.co.za; www.intercape.co.za). The Baz Bus (☎ 021-439-2323; www.bazbus.co.za) is a popular hop-on and hop-off service that runs from Johannesburg/Pretoria to Durban via either the Drakensberg

Mountains or Swaziland to Durban, and then along the coast to Cape Town in both directions. It drops off at backpacker hostels along the way.

By Train

Cape Town Railway Station is on Adderley Street in the center of town. It is presently being upgraded for the 2010 soccer World Cup. The mainline coach companies also have their terminuses here. Passenger trains are run by Shosholoza Meyl (☎ 011-774-4555; www. spoornet.co.za/ShosholozaMeyl),

which is part of the national rail network Spoornet. There are daily trains between Cape Town and Johannesburg/Pretoria (29 hours) and weekly trains between Cape Town and Durban (38 hours). Accommodation is in sleeping coupés and there's a dining car available, but facilities are very basic and they are extremely slow compared to the long distance buses. The better options are the luxury services between Cape Town and Johannesburg/Pretoria: The Blue Train (www.bluetrain.co.za); Pride of Africa (www.rovos.co.za); and Premier Classe (www.premierclasse.co.za).

Getting **Around**

By Taxi

Taxis are plentiful but can't be hailed in the street. They do, however, park outside large hotels, shopping malls, and tourist sites, or they can be phoned. Any hotel or restaurant can do this for you and the taxi will appear in minutes. Rates are R9 per km (0.6m). Larger groups and wheelchair users should request a Toyota Venture, which can take up to nine passengers or accommodate a wheelchair. Rikki Taxis (☎ 0861-745-547; www.rikkis. co.za) are shared taxis, which pick up other people along the way and take them to destinations near your own. This considerably brings down the cost (R20–35 depending on your destination), but they take a little longer than regular taxis. You can flag these down if you see one—they look like London Hackney cabs painted in brightly colored advertising—or phone and tell them where you want to be picked up. Increasingly Rikki freephones can be found at backpackers' hostels, supermarkets, and petrol stations. They run

24 hours. Minibus taxis run along the main routes, though the standard of driving is notoriously bad and there is the danger of pick-pocketing because they can be very crowded. A short ride costs R3.75, and you just wave them down.

By Bus

Yellow and orange Golden Arrow buses (☎ 0800-656-463; www. gabs.co.za), whose slogan is 'the bus for us', run regularly from the central bus station on Strand Street on the main roads; bus stops are clearly marked. A short ride will cost no more than R4, but you won't have much of a chance of getting on one of these during commute times. The best way to get around the tourist sites is to go on the red hop-on, hop-off City Sightseeing open top bus (see p 12 for details).

By Car

Although it's not essential to hire a car—there are plenty of day tours available (p 25), the City Sightseeing bus (see p 12) connects all the

Integrated Rapid Transport (IRT)

In line with requirements for the 2010 FIFA World Cup South Africa, a new transport system is currently being implemented in Cape Town and is known as the Integrated Rapid Transport (IRT). The first phase is an airport-city link and a route from the West Coast suburbs into the city. Plans (at the time of writing) are well underway and should be operational by 2010. A bus service will run on both dedicated 'trunk' routes on specific traffic lanes, mostly in the middle of the road with larger vehicles (18m (60ft) articulated buses), and 'feeder' routes on normal roads with smaller (8–12m (26–40ft)) buses. This system has worked well in other international cities, and although travel is by road, it works along a similar system as a regular tram/light railway because of the dedicated routes. The scheme intends to incorporate the current minibus taxi and local bus industries and possibly offer a park-and-ride option. The dedicated routes will also be designed for use for bicycle and pedestrian access in and around the city.

tourist sites, and some of the shopping malls provide shuttle services—having your own wheels does give you the greatest flexibility and driving isn't challenging. For those who want to explore the Cape Peninsula, the Winelands, Whale Coast, and West Coast independently, it's a good idea to rent a car. See p 156 for a list of rental car companies.

By Motorbike

If you have a license, hiring a scooter is a great way to get around Cape Town in summer and there are a number of places around town. Try Cape Town Scooter (☎ 082-450-9722; www.capetownscooter.co.za) or La Dolce Vita Biking (☎ 083-528-0897; www.la-dolce-vita.co.za). Finally for the ultimate Cape Peninsula road trip, hire a Harley from Harley Davidson Cape Town (☎ 021-446-2999; www.harley-davidson-capetown.com) or a classic vintage ex-Chinese Red Army motorbike and sidecar from Cape Sidecar Adventures (☎ 021-434-9855; www.sidecars.co.za).

By Metrorail

Metrorail (☎ 0800-656-463; www.capemetrorail.co.za) operates from the central railway station on Adderley Street and most routes serve commuters to and from the suburbs. However there are problems with petty crime, as many routes go through unsavory areas, so only travel during peak commuter times. Useful (and relatively safe) for visitors is the line to Simon's Town, which offers superb views once on the coast.

On Foot

The compact city center is ideal for walking. See p 37 for walking tours.

Fast **Facts**

APARTMENT RENTALS Among the online resources www.capestay.co.za and www.cape-accommodation.co.za list contacts and descriptions of properties.

ATMS/CASHPOINTS Maestro, Cirrus, MasterCard, Diners, American Express, and Visa cards are readily accepted at all ATMs. Exchange currency either at banks or bureaux de change. The airport has both ATMs and bureaux de change, which open to meet all incoming flights. Be warned: never accept 'help' at an ATM—this is a scam to grab your money as it comes out.

BUSINESS HOURS Banks and post offices are open Monday–Friday from 8.30am to 3.30pm and on Saturday mornings until 11 or 12am. Most offices and businesses are open Monday through Friday from 9am to 5pm. At restaurants, lunch is usually from 11.30 to 2 or 3pm and dinner from 6 to 11pm, but many restaurants are open all day from breakfast. Shops are open 9am–5.30pm Monday–Friday and until 1pm on Saturday, but the shopping malls are generally open Monday–Saturday 9am–6pm and Sunday 9am–1pm, and the larger ones such as Cavendish Square (see p 32) and Victoria Wharf (see p 31) at the V&A Waterfront are open daily until 7pm and 9pm respectively.

CONSULATES & EMBASSIES The main embassies are in Tshwane (Pretoria) and the **Department of Foreign Affairs** list all contact details on their website; www.dfa.gov.co.za. In Cape Town, the consular offices are: **US Consulate**, 2 Reddam Ave, Westlake 7945, ☎ 021-702-7300, southafrica.usembassy.gov; **British Consulate**

General, 15th floor, Southern Life Centre, 8 Riebeek Street, ☎ 021-405-2400, www.fco.gov.uk; **Consulate General of Canada**: 19th floor, South African Reserve Bank Building, 60 St. George's Mall, ☎ 021-423-5240, www.canadainternational.gc.ca; **Irish Consulate**: LG Building, No. 1 Thibault Square, Long Street. ☎ 021-419-0636, www.foreignaffairs.gov.ie.

DOCTORS Pharmacies and your hotel can recommend a nearby doctor. For medical emergencies **Medi-Clinic** (www.mediclinic.co.za), is a private hospital with several branches around the city.

ELECTRICITY Most hotels operate on 220 volts AC (50 cycles). Plugs and sockets are three-point round-pin, so you will need an adaptor for appliances.

EMERGENCIES For an ambulance or medical emergencies, dial ☎ 10177; for fire ☎ 10111. For all emergencies from a cell phone, call ☎ 112.

GAY & LESBIAN TRAVELERS South Africa is very progressive, and same sex marriages were legalized in 2006. Cape Town is the undisputable Pink Capital of Africa and has a thriving gay and lesbian scene; there are many events throughout the year (p 102). Cape Town Tourism publishes the **Pink Map** of Cape Town highlighting gay friendly places. Another good resource is **www.capetown.tv**. Alternatively, contact the official gay info center **Atlantic Tourist Information at 27-21-434-2382** or www.arokan.co.za. **Wanderwomen** is a personalized women's-only travelagent; visit www.wanderwomen.co.za or call ☎ **021-788 9988.**

The International Gay and Lesbian Travel Association (IGLTA; ☎ 800/448-8550 or 954-776-2626; www.iglta.org) is the trade association for the gay and lesbian travel industry. It offers an online directory of gay- and lesbian-friendly travel business; go to their website and click on "Members."

HOLIDAYS Holidays observed include: 1st January (New Year's Day), 21st March (Human Rights Day), March/April (Good Friday and Easter Monday; the latter is also known as Family Day), 27th April (Freedom Day), 1st May (Workers Day), 16th June (Youth Day), 9th August (National Woman's Day), 24th September (Heritage Day), 16th December (Day of Reconciliation), 25th December (Christmas) and 26th December (Day of Goodwill).

INSURANCE Check your existing insurance policies before you buy travel insurance to cover trip cancellation, lost luggage, medical expenses, or car rental insurance. There are a wide variety of travel insurance policies to choose from so shop around. For South Africa, policies should cover the loss of personal effects and in the event of a medical emergency, air repatriation to your home country. Medical bills in South Africa have to be paid up-front or before you leave hospital, so ensure you keep all receipts to make a claim on your insurance when you return home. Public hospitals offer poor service and should be avoided in favor of the top class facilities and care in the private hospitals.

INTERNET Internet access is plentiful, both in Internet cafés and in most hotels, guest houses, and backpacker hostels, although it is slow and there can be download limits. The airport and many coffee shops and shopping malls now offer Wi-Fi. The densest crops of Internet cafés can be found on Long Street, Kloof Street, and Main Road in Sea Point.

LANGUAGE Although the Afrikaner and colored communities of Cape Town speak Afrikaans, everybody understands English and it is the predominant language. There are, however, a few Afrikaans words, as well as some unique South African slang, which visitors are likely to encounter. For a list, see p 168. Afrikaans may still be seen on older street signs.

LOST PROPERTY Call credit card companies the minute you discover your wallet has been lost or stolen and file a report at the nearest police precinct. Your credit card company or insurer may require a police report number or record. In South Africa, **Visa**'s emergency number is ☎ 0800-990-475; **American Express** ☎ 0800-110-929; **MasterCard** ☎ 0800-990-418; **Diners Club** ☎ 0860-346-377.

MAIL & POSTAGE South African post offices (www.spo.co.za) are identified by their blue-and-red 'Post Office' signs and banks of blue PO boxes outside. They are open Monday–Friday, 8.30–3.30pm and on Saturday mornings until 11.30. **Postnet** (www.postnet.co.za) is a private company offering postage and courier services, plus printing, copying, faxing, and Internet access: branches can be found in the shopping malls.

MONEY The currency in South Africa is the **rand.** At press time, the exchange rate was US$1 = R8.30, GBP1=R13.35). For up-to-the minute exchange rates check the currency converter website **www.xe.com**.

VAT Refunds

Visitors (i.e., non South African residents) can claim refunds for the 14% VAT (value added tax) paid on all purchases if they are taken out of the country. This is done at the airport, where you need to get receipts stamped by customs officers before you check in. Once airside, present receipts to the VAT refund desk where you'll be issued a check in rands, which you can pay into your home bank account, cash at a bureau de change at the airport, or have the amount debited to your Visa or MasterCard. There is a pre-processing VAT refund desk in the Clock Tower (p 31) at the V&A Waterfront, to get your receipts stamped, but you still have to claim the refund at the airport, and you must show your passport and air ticket. For more information, visit www.taxrefunds.co.za.

PASSPORTS No visas are required for US, Canadian, European, Australian, or New Zealand visitors to South Africa and a 90-day entry stamp is issued on arrival. You must have one empty page in your passport for this and your passport must be valid for at least 30 days after your visit to South Africa. If your passport is lost or stolen, contact your country's embassy or consulate immediately. See 'Consulates & Embassies' p 160. Make a copy of your passport's critical pages and keep it separate from your passport.

PHARMACIES Pharmacies operate during normal business hours and can be found in every neighborhood. 24-hour pharmacies can be found at the hospitals.

POLICE The national police emergency number is ☎ 10111. To locate a local police station visit www.saps.gov.za. If you need a police report for stolen items, avoid the central police station on Buitenkant Street as it's consistently busy. Instead, try one in the suburbs.

SAFETY Violent crime involving tourists is rare, but opportunistic thieves will target tourists if temptation is put in their way, so keep valuables hidden. Be wary when using ATMs. Never accept help using the machine and preferably use one inside a bank or shopping mall. Don't walk around central Cape Town after dark and always take a taxi. Muggings have occurred on the hiking routes up Table Mountain and so leave valuables in your hotel safe.

SMOKING The no smoking in public places law came into effect in South Africa in 2001 and includes the workplace and public transport. Restaurants and bars are legally allowed to have 25% of their area dedicated to smokers, which must be outside or enclosed from the non-smoking section.

TAXES Tourists can claim a 14% VAT refund on goods purchased in South Africa and taken out of the country. For details, see p 66 or visit **www.taxrefund.co.za**.

TELEPHONES For national directory enquiries, dial ☎ 1023, and for international directory enquiries ☎ 1025. To make an international call, dial 📞 00, wait for the tone, and dial the country code, area code, and number. If you're making a local call, dial the three-digit city code first (**021** in Cape Town) and then the seven-digit number. To make a long-distance call within South Africa, the procedure is exactly the same; you must dial the city prefix no matter from where you're calling. Coin and card phone boxes can be found on the street and phone cards are available from local convenience stores. Hotels mostly add a hefty surcharge on to phone calls.

Places of Worship

The right to freedom of religion was granted by the Dutch colony in 1803, and is enshrined in South Africa's constitution. Consequently one can find all of the major religions and more in Cape Town. Places of worship of historical interest include: the Evangelical Lutheran Church; the Central Methodist Mission Church; the Groote Kerk (Great Church); St Mary's Roman Catholic Cathedral; St Georges Anglican Cathedral; the Auwal Masjid and Palm Tree Mosque; and Gardens Shul (The Great Synagogue).

- **Baha'i** The Baha'i faith has been present in South Africa since 1911.For more information visit: http://www.bahai.org.za/cm/ or contact: capetown@bahai.org.za.
- **Buddhism** There are currently 5 Buddhist centres in the Western Cape. For address, tradition, and contact visit: http://buddhanet.info/wbd/province.php?province_id=497
- **Christianity** Christianity being the most widespread religion in South Africa, most of the Western mainstream denominational families are represented. To find yours try: http://www.capecodapps.com/databases/churches/search.php.
- **Hinduism** There are few public Hindu places of worship in Cape Town. For more information visit www.hinduism.co.za or contact hinduism2000@yahoo.com.
- **Islam** South Africa's first mosque Auwal Masjid was established in Cape Town circa 1804. Most of the mosques in Cape Town are located in the Bo-Kaap district. For the Bo-Kaap Mosque Information Guide visit: http://www.bokaap.co.za/attractions/mosque_info.htm. For addresses and phone numbers of Cape Town mosques visit: http://www.muslims.co.za/mosques_sa.htm.
- **Judaism** Cape Town's Jewish community was the first in South Africa, and built the first synagogue next to Parliament in 1849. In 1905 the Great Synagogue opened alongside it. For addresses and phone numbers of Cape Town synagogues visit: http://www.mavensearch.com/synagogues/C3433Y41682RX. For phone number and name of Rabbi visit: http://www.jewishweb.co.za/pages/synagogues/synagogue-Cape.htm.

The **Savvy Traveler**

TIME   South Africa is 8 hours ahead of USA Eastern Standard Time and 2 hours ahead of Greenwich Mean Time (GMT). However between March and October when the UK observes daylight saving, South Africa is GMT+1.

TIPPING   It's normal to tip waiters, taxi drivers, and tour guides about 10% for good service. For coffees and snacks most people just leave a few coins or round up to the nearest R10. Some restaurants will include a service charge for large groups (five or more) so check the bill (this word is used rather than 'check' in South Africa). If you're driving it's common practice to tip R2–5 for both gas station attendants and car guards on the street (identified by a badge or yellow work vest).

TOILETS   These are generally of a good standard, although away from the shopping malls and tourist sites there are few independent blocks. Most restaurants will allow you to use their facilities whether you're eating there or not.

TOURIST INFORMATION   **Cape Town Tourism** has two very helpful drop-in offices. See p 42.

TRAVELERS WITH DISABILITIES   Cape Town has improved considerably in recent years with regards to accessibility, and no new building is built without ramps or elevators. Most tourist sites are accommodating and some facilities, such as a Braille Trail in Kirstenbosch National Botanical Garden or the Table Mountain Cableway, have been designed with the needs of the disabled in mind. All shopping malls and public buildings have designated parking for the disabled near the entrance, and modern hotels have specially adapted rooms. **Endeavor Safaris** (☎ 021-556-6114; www.endeavor-safaris.com) can arrange specialist tours for wheelchair users, the visibility and hearing impaired, and visitors who require oxygen or regular kidney dialysis. **Flamingo Tours** (☎ 021-557-4496; www.flamingo tours.co.za) also offer tours for the disabled, including sign language tours of Cape Town, and can supply a registered nurse if needed.

Cape Town: **A Brief History**

1487 The first ship to round the Cape is captained by Bartholomeu Dias, who names it Cabo de Bõa Esperança or the Cape of Good Hope.

1497 Vasco da Gama, on a voyage from Portugal to the East Indies, sets foot on southern Africa at today's St Helena Bay.

1503 Antonio de Saldanha and his crew land in Table Bay and are the first Europeans to climb Table Mountain. They name it Taboa da Caba (Table of the Cape).

1575 The Portuguese produce the first maritime map of the southern Africa coast.

1580 English admiral Francis Drake rounds the Cape and says: 'This Cape is a most stately thing, and the fairest Cape we saw in the whole circumference of the earth'.

1595 The first Dutch ships reach the southern African coast.

1652 Van Riebeeck arrives in Table Bay to build a fort and establish a refreshment station for water, fresh produce, and meat for ships of the Dutch East India Company; in Dutch, the Ver-eenigde Oost-Indische Compag-nie (VOC).

1655 Exploration begins into the interior, and the first slaves arrive from Java and Madagascar.

1659–60 Skirmishes with the local Khoi people results in them los-ing considerable amounts of land to the Dutch.

1662 The Cape refreshment station becomes a Dutch colony.

1666 Work begins on the Castle of Good Hope, which replaces the fort.

1679 The Slave Lodge is built. Simon Van der Stel is appointed Com-mander of the Cape and further develops Cape Town.

1680 Stellenbosch is established as a vine- and wheat-growing region.

1685 The Dutch East India Company grants Van der Stel an estate at Constantia in appreciation of his achievements and he plants the first vineyards.

1688 A group of persecuted Protes-tants known as Huguenots arrive from France and Van der Stel gives them land at Franschhoek ('French corner').

1713 An outbreak of smallpox intro-duced by the Europeans virtually decimates the Khoi population.

1717 The population of the colony is now 5,400, of which 50% are slaves.

1739 Hendrik Swellengrebel becomes Governor of the Cape.

1743–45 Swellendam is established and Dutch Reformed churches are built across the Cape.

1778–81 By now the colonists have reached Plettenberg Bay, where they erect a beacon, the Xhosa region to the east, and present-day Keetmanshoop in Namibia to the north.

1780–83 War between the Nether-lands and England reduces the Dutch East India Company's eco-nomic and political power in Europe.

1795–1806 The British arrive and annex the Dutch colony after the Battle of Muizenberg. They lose it back to the Dutch but regain con-trol in 1806. The Dutch East India Company goes bankrupt.

1807 The Abolition of the Slave Trade Act is passed in Britain, though it is still legal to keep slaves.

1825 With the onset of the Industrial Revolution in Europe, the first steam ship arrives in Table Bay.

1834 The official emancipation of slaves is declared on 1st Decem-ber in Greenmarket Square, and 59,000 slaves are freed in the Cape Colony.

1836–40 Dutch farmers are not impressed by the British, who have stripped them of their cheap, slave labor. The Great Trek begins, and some 10,000 Dutch families leave the Cape with their ox-wagons to form new republics in the interior. They became known as Voortrek-kers and later Boers.

1840 The Cape Town Municipality is formed. The population is put at 20,000, half of which is white.

1870–80 The discovery of diamonds and gold in the north shifts eco-nomic importance away from Cape Town, but it remains the principal port. Alfred Basin is completed in 1870.

1901 After an outbreak of bubonic plague, native Africans are moved to Ndabeni, 6km (4 miles) east of the city, Cape Town's first black township.

1905 The docks at Victoria Basin are completed.

1910 The Union of South Africa is formed, joining the British colonies of the Cape and Natal with the Boer republics in the Transvaal and Orange Free State.

1912 Native National Congress formed; later to be renamed African National Congress (ANC).

1913 The Native's Land Act is passed, which deprives many residents of the right to own land. It is the first of many racial segregation legislations.

1914 The National Party is formed.

1918 Nelson Mandela is born in a village in the Eastern Cape.

1929 Commercial flights between London and Cape Town commence.

1936 The Representation of Natives Act is passed, which denies non-whites in the Cape the right to vote.

1943 The city begins reclaiming 1.9 km² (480 acres) of land on the foreshore in front of the Castle of Good Hope.

1948 The National Party comes into power and apartheid (meaning 'being apart' in Afrikaans) policies such as the Prohibition of Mixed Marriages Act (1949) and the Group Areas Act (1951) are passed.

1955 The Congress of the People meets in Soweto, Johannesburg, and draws up the Freedom Charter, which becomes the cornerstone of ANC policy.

1956 156 anti-apartheid activists are arrested and the Treason Trial begins.

1960 The Sharpeville Massacre. Police kill 69 people demonstrating about carrying pass books. By now all non-whites have to carry them. The government bans the ANC and other groups.

1961–63 The ANC launches its armed wing; *Umkhonto we Sizwe* (Spear of the Nation) under the leadership of Nelson Mandela, but he is arrested in 1961. Other leading ANC members including Walter Sisulu are arrested at Liliesleaf Farm near Johannesburg in 1962. Mandela and others get life sentences on Robben Island for treason.

1966 District Six is declared a white area and is razed to the ground. Its residents are forcibly moved to the Cape Flats.

1967 Professor Christiaan Barnard performs the world's first heart transplant in Cape Town.

1977 The Soweto Uprising sparks unrest throughout the country and some 600 black demonstrators are killed by police.

1980S The ANC's military wing and other terrorist groups step up activities and bomb many railways, police stations, and public buildings. The South African Defence Force reacts by killing perpetrators and attacking ANC missions overseas. The townships become war zones. The international community imposes economic sanctions on South Africa and appeals for peace and reform.

1984 Cape Town's Archbishop Desmond Tutu receives the Nobel Peace Prize for bringing the protest against apartheid to an international level.

1986 Pass books are finally abolished.

1989 President PW Botha and Nelson Mandela meet. Later in the year FW De Klerk becomes president. More than 100,000 people attend a protest march in Cape Town.

1990 The tide is turning. De Klerk unbans the ANC, scraps apartheid legislation, lifts the 10-year state of emergency on the country, and releases Mandela and other political prisoners from prison. Mandela meets exiled ANC President Oliver Tambo for the first time. The ANC suspends its armed struggle.

1991 Peace talks headed by De Klerk and Mandela begin in earnest and a new constitution is drawn up with equality for all.

1993 De Klerk and Mandela jointly win the Nobel Peace Prize.

1994 South Africa's first multi-racial democratic elections take place. The ANC win and Mandela is sworn in as President.

1995 Archbishop Desmond Tutu is appointed chairman of the Truth and Reconciliation Commission, which becomes part of the

healing process for the victims of apartheid. Reports find both the apartheid government and the ANC responsible for human rights abuses.

1999–2006 The ANC wins the next two elections and Mandela steps down as president in favor of Thabo Mbeki. Mandela continues to be an activist for HIV/Aids and other world issues.

2007 Despite facing corruption charges, Jacob Zuma is elected chairman of the ANC.

2008 Nelson Mandela retires from public life on his 90th birthday. Claiming poor performance, the ANC recalls President Mbeki, who resigns and is replaced by interim president Kgalema Motlanthe until elections in April 2009.

2009 Just two weeks before the elections, the National Prosecuting Association drops corruption charges against Zuma citing misdemeanors in the investigation process.

2009 South Africa goes to the polls. The ANC wins 65.9% of the vote and Zuma becomes president.

2010 South Africa hosts the 2010 soccer World Cup.

Tips **on Dining**

Southern Africa does not have a hugely developed cuisine that it can call its own, but there are a few dishes worth looking out for. Easiest on the newly initiated palate are the **Cape Malay dishes,** characterized by sweet aromatic **curries.** These include *bobotie,* a delicious baked meatloaf, mildly curried and served with chutney; and *bredie,* a tomato-based stew, usually with lamb.

Another Cape delicacy not to be missed is *waterblommetjie bredie,* or waterlily stew, usually cooked with lamb. Many South African menus also feature **Karoo lamb,** favored because the sweet and aromatic herbs and grasses of this arid region flavor the animals as they graze, and **ostrich,** a delicious red meat that tastes more like beef than anything else and is extremely healthy. Your dessert may be *melktert*, a cinnamon-flavored custard tart of Dutch origin; malva pudding, served with hot custard; or *koeksisters*, plaited doughnuts, deep-fried and dipped in syrup.

On the East Coast, Durban is famed for its **Indian curries,** whose burn potential is indicated by such ingenious names as Honeymooners' Delight (hot) and Mother-in-Law Exterminator (damn hot!). The coastline supplies seafood in abundance: fish, abalone, mussels, oysters, crabs, squid, langoustines, and the Cape's famous rock lobster (crayfish), but for a uniquely South African-flavored seafood feast, you'll need to head for one of the West Coast beach restaurants. Here, **snoek,** a firm white fish, is traditionally served with *konfyt* (fruits preserved in sugar syrup, from the French *confit,* a legacy of the French Huguenots).

Look for the spiraling smoke trailing over suburban fences and township yards each weekend, when throughout the country South Africans barbecue fresh meat over coals. The ubiquitous *braaivleis* **(barbecues)** or *tshisanyamas* (literally 'burn the meat') feature anything from ostrich to *boerewors;* the latter, a coriander-spiced beef-and-pork sausage, is arguably South Africa's staple meat. The most basic African foodstuff is **corn,** most popularly eaten as *pap,* a ground maize porridge, and not unlike polenta, or the rougher wholegrain *samp,* and served with a vegetable- or meat-based sauce.

If you're a serious gourmand or are going to be here for a while, there are three restaurant guides worth purchasing: *Eat Out* (www.eatout.co.za), an annual overview of restaurants throughout the country with an annual top 10, is very thorough, but its size may make it a little unwieldy; *dine,* published by *wine magazine,* also covers the country, with an annual top 100, but is a slim, pocket-size booklet. Equally so is *Rossouw's Restaurants* (www.rossouws restaurants.com), an annual guide to restaurants in Cape Town, the Winelands, and the Garden Route. The latter divides top picks according to budget, as well as useful selections under categories like 'Family' and 'Romantic'; best of all, reviews are sent in by Cape diners, so you're not being influenced by one food critic's palate.

South African **Words & Phrases**

SOUTH AFRICAN	ENGLISH
Ag man!	Oh man!
As well	Me too, also; the accent is on the 'as'
Babbelas	Hangover; originally derived from IsiZulu
Bakkie	Pick-up truck
Biltong	A snack of dried salted meat
Boer	Farmer; Afrikaans
Boerewors	Coarse spicy sausage; can be shortened to wors
Bokkie	Babe, honey, etc; bok in Afrikaans means doe

SOUTH AFRICAN	ENGLISH
Bru	Dude, mate, etc; short for brother in Afrikaans
Braai	Mainstream word for BBQ; verb and noun
Buck(s)	Rand (cash)
China	Mate; derived from British Cockney 'china plate'
Chow	To eat
Cooldrink	Cold soft drink
Dop/Doppie	An alcoholic drink; verb and noun
Dorp	Village or small town
Eish!	No way! Derived from IsiZulu
Fundi	Expert; from the Nguni language
Hard up	Cape colored expression for in lurve
Howzit?	How is it/How are you?
Indaba	Meeting/conference; from IsiZulu
Izit?	Is that so?
Ja	Yes in Afrikaans but commonly used
Ja-well-no-fine	Fine, yes, but not really
Jol	To have fun/party
Just now	To do something fairly soon
Kwaito	South African rap, hip-hop, and house music
Lighty	Refers to a son/daughter or younger sibling
Lekker	Good, great, super; Afrikaans for sweet
Muti	Medicine; derived from IsiZulu
Now now	To do something immediately
Oke	Guy, bloke
Pap	Maize porridge; an African staple similar to grits
Pasop	Danger; Afrikaans. Seen on signposts
Posie or pozzy	Home; derived from the English for position
Potjiekos	Three-legged cast iron cooking pot
Robot	Traffic light
Rooibos	Popular local tea
Scheme/scheming	Deep thought/thinking
Shebeen	Informal township pub; similar to speakeasy
Shame	Expression of sympathy; can also mean cute
Skraal	Very hungry; from the Afrikaans word for thin
Skrik	Fright; Afrikaans
Sommer	For no particular reason/because I can
Sosatie	Meat on a stick/kebab
Spaza	Informal convenience shop/stall
Stoep	Porch/veranda; like a US stoop
Tannie	Respect for an older woman; Afrikaans for aunt
Takkies	Sneakers/trainers
Tsotsi	Gangster. Also a township rap language
Tune/tuning	Have a go verbally/give lip
Vaalies	Inland people from the old Transvaal Province
Vrot	Rotten or drunk; derived from Afrikaans
Yebo	Yes in IsiZulu but commonly used

Recommended **Books**

South Africa is well known for its literary talent and has produced two Nobel literature laureates. The first, **Nadine Gordimer**, who won in 1991, has been a published author since the age of 16 and has been writing short stories for the New Yorker since the 1950s. Most of her early work dealt with racial oppression under apartheid, and she was an active member of the ANC. Consequently much of her work was banned or censored in South Africa for a long period of time. Of her many books, **The Conservationist** (Penguin, 1984) was the joint winner of the Booker Prize in 1974. It is a character study of a white industrialist in Johannesburg who takes on a small farm as a hobby, but has little emotion for the poor conditions that his black laborers endure, or affinity with or respect for the land. **Burgher's Daughter** (Penguin, 1980) was written soon after the 1976 Soweto Uprising. A young white woman's anti-apartheid activist father dies in prison, and she has to come to terms with her own political beliefs. **July's People** (Penguin, 1982) is set in a fictional civil war in South Africa when a white family has to escape to safety to the home village of their servant July.

Born in Cape Town, **JM Coetzee** has been writing novels since the 1970s and won the Nobel Prize for Literature in 2003. His best-known novel, Booker Prize winner **Disgrace** (Penguin, 1999) is a powerful and harrowing novel. A successful English professor at a Cape Town university loses everything after he seduces a student, and has to start a new life on his daughter's farm, where he and his daughter are violently attacked. **Life and Times of**

Michael K (Penguin, 1985) is another Booker Prize winner and tells the story of an impoverished Cape Town gardener who takes his ailing mother to a new life in the countryside.

André Brink is another prolific South African author and his novels are published in both Afrikaans and English. During apartheid his stories were set in that period, but he's also used the Cape's historical background as a setting. Shortlisted for the 1976 Booker Prize, **An Instant in the Wind** (Sourcebooks Landmark, 2008) is a story set in 1749 of a white woman whose husband dies while they are trekking into the interior, and she enlists the help of an escaped slave to take her back to Cape Town. **A Chain of Voices** (Sourcebooks Landmark, 2007) explores the relationship between a white settler family and their slaves over three generations on their farm near Tulbagh in the early 1800s, and is basically a study of the oppressive dynamics of slavery.

Published in 1948 in the same year the National Party came into power, Alan Paton's **Cry The Beloved Country** (Scribner, 2003) is probably the most famous novel to come out of South Africa, and is a moving story of a black Anglican priest who goes to Johannesburg to search for his son, who is later condemned to death for the murder of a white activist.

Although born in Zambia, **Wilbur Smith** has written over 30 blockbuster novels, and his first Courtney sequence follows a South African Boer family from the Zulu War period until the Union of South Africa was formed. The second sequence follows the Courtney family through the World Wars, and then Smith jumps back in the third sequence to cover the arrival of Courtney's at the Cape and their subsequent adventures from the mid-1600s to the mid 1700s.

Given its turbulent history, there's a vast range of non-fiction books about South Africa and more than 120 have been written about Nelson Mandela alone. These include the superbly illustrated *Mandela: The Authorized Portrait* by **Mac Maharaj** and **Ahmed Kathrada** (Wild Dog Press, 2006), which covers his life story and clearly demonstrates Mandela's exceptional humility. Nelson Mandela's autobiography, *Long Walk to Freedom* (Holt McDougal, 2000) is a gripping and detailed read and he wrote much of it in secret during his incarceration on Robben Island. There are also many autobiographies or biographies about most of the key anti-apartheid activists. *The*

powerful Bang Bang Club; Snapshots of a Hidden War, (Basic Books, 2001) by **Greg Marinovich** and **Joao Silva**, follows the lives of four acclaimed photo-journalists as they document the violent chaos going on in the townships during the final fight against apartheid in the 1980—90s. One of them is killed by a stray bullet and another commits suicide. Journalist and poet **Antjie Krog's** *Country of my Skull* (Three Rivers Press, 2000) tells the wrenching tales of victims of apartheid as they were told to the Truth and Reconciliation Commission. Her depth of writing gives voice to stories previously unheard. *Diamonds, Gold and War; the British, the Boers, and the making of South Africa* (Public Affairs, 2008) by **Martin Meredith** is a good account of South Africa's history and explains how the diamond and gold rushes laid down the foundations of apartheid.

Recommended **South African Wines**

South African wine is not rated by vintage or region, but rather by the grape and the reputation of the wine-maker. Look out for these labels; not all are expensive.

Reds
Shiraz Groot Constantia, Nederburg, Steenberg, Saxonburg, Stellenzicht, De Grendal, KWV, La Motte, De Meye, Yonder Hill, Eagle's Rest.

Cabernet Sauvignon Le Riche, Conradie, Klein Zalze, Nederburg, Bottelary, Guardian Peak, Fleur du Cap.

Merlot Steenberg, Bredell's, La Petite Ferme, Bain's Kloof, Yonder Hill, Saxenberg, Lanzerac, Longridge, Spier, Plaisir de Merle.

Pinotage Morkel, Simonsig, Windmeul, Kanonkop, Laroche L'Avenir, Allée Bleue, Groot Constantia, Beyerskloof, Rijk's.

Pinot Noir Hamilton Russell, Chamonix, Sumaridge.

Red Blends Ernie Els, Simonsig, Elkendal, Vergelegen, Buitenverwachtig, Spier.

Whites

Chenin Blanc Ken Forrester, Bellingham, Jean Daneel, Rudera Robusto, Spier, Villiera, Simonsig, Windmeul.

Sauvignon Blanc Steenberg, Graham Beck, Kleine Zalze, Rietvallei, Backsburg, Cape Point, Cederberg, David Nieuwoudt, Fleur du Cap, Klein Zalze, Mooiplaas, Du Preez, Nederburg, Zonnebloem.

Chardonnay Zonnebloem, Fleur du Cap, De Westhof, Groot Constantia, Van Loveren, Slanghoek.

Semillion Steenberg, Cape Point, Rijk's, Fairview, Contantia Uitsig.

Sweet/dessert wine Delheim, Weisser, Nuy, Nederburg, Neethlingshof, Klein Constantia. Sparkling Cap.

Méthode Cap Classique Graham Beck, Jacques Bruére, Simonsig, Pongrácz, Villiera.

Other

Old Brown Sherry Uitvlucht.

Port Boplass, Die Krans, Bredell's, Axe Hill.

Drinking with a Conscience

The South African wine industry is still grappling to redress the economic and social injustices resulting from apartheid-era policies, such as the lack of land ownership by black and "coloureds", the shortage of qualified black winemakers and viticulturists, widespread unemployment, and rampant alcohol abuse. Significant change is in progress, however, through macro-initiatives such as the Wine Industry Transformation Charter, being finalized under the auspices of a Black Economic Empowerment (BEE) Steering Committee. Integral to the charter will be a scorecard, in which wine industry participants will accumulate points commensurate with their performance in such key areas as equity, asset, ownership, land reform, shareholding, skills development, procurement practices, and more.

Broader developments such as these should bolster the individual transformative efforts of entities like the South African Vintners Alliance, recently established to further the interests of BEE wineries, and the encouragement provided to black oeno-entrepreneurs by the original BEE producers, like **New Beginning (☎ 021-869-8453),** the first black-owned wine farm in the country, and **Bouwland (☎ 021-852-5052), Crossroads Wines (☎ 021-461-0360),** and **African Roots (☎ 082-571-4157).**

Airline Numbers **& Websites**

BRITISH AIRWAYS
☎ 1300/767-177 in Australia
☎ 011-441-8400 in South Africa
☎ 0870/850-9850 in UK
☎ 800/247-9297 in US/Canada
www.british-airways.com

KLM
☎ 1300/392-192 in Australia
☎ 020/4-747-747 in the Netherlands
☎ 0860/247-747 in South Africa
☎ 0870/243-0541 in UK
☎ 800/374-7747 in US/Canada
www.klm.com

LUFTHANSA
☎ 1300/655-727 in Australia
☎ 01805-805-805 in Germany
☎ 0861/842-538 in South Africa
☎ 0871/945-9747 in UK
☎ 800/645-3880 in US/Canada
www.lufthansa.com

MALAYSIA AIRLINES
☎ 132 627 in Australia
☎ 01300-88-3000 in Malaysia
☎ 021-419-8010 in South Africa
☎ 0871/423-9090 UK
☎ 0800/552-9264 in US/Canada
www.maylasiaairlines.com

SINGAPORE AIRLINES
☎ 131 011 in Australia
☎ 06223-8888 in Singapore
☎ 021-674-0601 in South Africa
☎ 0844/800-2380 in UK
☎ 0800/742-3333 in U.S./Canada
www.singaporeair.com

SOUTH AFRICAN AIRWAYS
☎ 1300/435-972 in Australia
☎ 0861-808-808 in South Africa
☎ 0871/722-1111 in UK
☎ 0800/722-9675 in US/Canada
www.flysaa.com

VIRGIN ATLANTIC
☎ 1300/727-340 in Australia
☎ 011-340-3500 in South Africa
☎ 800/862-8621 in US/Canada
☎ 0870/380-2007 in UK
www.virgin-atlantic.com

Index

Index

See also Accommodations and Restaurant indexes, below.

A

Abseil Africa, 73
Adventure sports, 72–75
African National Congress (ANC), 13, 166, 167
African Roots (vineyard), 172
Afrikaanse Taalmonument (Afrikaans Language Monument), 138, 139
Air travel, 157, 173
Alba Lounge, 99
Amphitheatre, at V&A waterfront, 111, 113
ANC. See African National Congress
Antiques, 60
Apartheid, 166
Apartheid history tour, 13, 24–25
Apartment rentals, 122, 127, 129, 160
Aquariums, 12, 27
Architecture
    Gold of Africa Museum, 52–53
    on Long Street, 43
    Old Town House, 41–42
    Parliament building, 47
    Shell Building, 41
    Swellendam, 149
    Union Castle Building, 11–12
Art galleries and museums, 60, 61
    Carmel Art, 60
    Everard Road, 60, 61
    Irma Stern Museum, 21
    Johans Borman Fine Art, 61
    Michaelis Collection, 42
    South African National Gallery, 48
Artscape, 106, 111
Asoka Son of Dharma (bar), 99
Atlantic Tourist Information, 160
Atlas Trading Store, 36, 51
ATMs, 160
Authors, South African, 170–171
Auwal Masjid Mosque, 51, 163
Aviaries, 28

B

Babysitting, 29, 127
Baha'i places of worship, 163
Bain's Kloof Pass, 148
Baker, Herbert, 11, 21, 41, 46
Ballet, 112
Ballooning, 73
Barmooda (club), 101
Bars, 99–101
Bascule Bar, 98, 103
Baxter Theatre, 106, 112, 113
B&Bs, 128–129, 130
Beaches, 16, 17, 68–71
    at Bloubergstrand, 69, 143
    Boulders, 5, 18, 69, 134, 135
    Camps Bay, 16, 17, 27, 69, 75
    Cape of Good Hope, 69, 70
    Clifton, 16, 70, 74, 75
    Dungeons, 71
    Fish Hoek, 19, 70
    Glen, 69
    Hout Bay, 70, 74
    at Langebaan, 143
    Llandudno, 70–71
    Long, 71
    Muizenberg, 19, 71
    Noordhoek, 17, 71, 75
    nudist, 70–71
    Seaforth, 71
    Somerset West Strand, 133
Betty's Bay, 134, 135
Beulah Bar, 102
Bicycles
    mountain, 17, 74, 78
    races, 78, 155
    renting, 17, 74, 141, 151
Big Bay, 74
Bird Island, 145
Bird-watching, 71, 77, 143, 145
Bloubergstrand, 69, 143
Bo-Kaap Museum, 51
Bo-Kaap neighborhood, 50–53
Books, 61, 170–171
Boschendal (vineyard), 140
Botanical gardens. See Gardens
Boulders Beach, 5, 18, 69, 134, 135
Bouwland (vineyard), 172
Brandy, 138
Brink, André, 170
Bronx Action Bar, 102

Buddhist centers, 163
Buena Vista Social Café, 98, 99
Buses, 4, 157–158, 159
Business hours, 160

C

Cabriére (vineyard), 141
Cabrinha Kite-boarding, 74
Café Caprice, 98–100
Café Manhattan, 102
Camps Bay, 5, 16, 17, 27, 69, 75
Canal Walk (mall), 32
Cape Argus and Pick 'n' Pay Cycle Tour, 78, 155
Cape Chamonix (vineyard), 141
Cape Columbine, 144
Cape Flats, 5, 24, 25
Cape Malay community, 51, 52, 167
Cape Minstrel Carnival, 154
Cape of Good Hope Beach, 69, 70
Cape of Good Hope Nature Reserve, 18, 77
Cape Peninsula, 16–18, 133, 134
Cape Point, 18, 70
Cape Point Ostrich Farm, 18
Cape Quarter (mall), 32, 53
Cape to Cuba (bar), 100
Cape Town
    favorite moments in, 4–6
    history of, 164–167
    maps, 2–3
Cape Town Book Fair, 39, 155
Cape Town City Ballet, 106, 112
Cape Town Fashion Week, 39, 63, 155
Cape Town Festival, 154–155
Cape Town Holocaust Centre, 49
Cape Town International Comedy Festival, 106, 113, 155
Cape Town International Convention Centre (CTICC), 39, 63, 112, 155
Cape Town International Jazz Festival, 106, 113, 155
Cape Town Minstrel Carnival, 113
Cape Town Opera, 112
Cape Town Philharmonic Orchestra, 40

Cape Town Pride (festival), 154
Cape Town Station, 39–40
Cape Town Tourism, 42, 164
Carmel Art, 60
Caroline's Fine Wine, 36
Car rentals, 156–157
Carrol Boyes (store), 63–64
Cashpoints, 160
Casino, 101
Castle of Good Hope, 40, 54, 165
Cavendish Square (mall), 32
Cederberg Wilderness Area, 144
Cellphones, 156
Chapman's Peak Drive, 17, 70
Childcare, 29, 127
Children, activities for, 26–29, 35
    at beaches, 69–71
    in Bo-Kaap, De Water-kant and Green Point, 52–54
    along Cape Peninsula, 16–18
    in City Center, 40, 41
    on False Bay Coast, 18–19
    along Government Avenue, 46, 49
    in parks and nature reserves, 10, 21–22, 77, 78
    performing arts, 111–112
    along Route 62, 149
    shopping, 66
    on Whale Coast, 133–135
    in Winelands, 139
Christmas, 161
Chrome (club), 98, 101, 102
Churches, 45, 53, 163
Cigars, 36
Cinema Nouveau, 106, 110, 111
Cinemas, 110
Citrusdal, 144
City Center, 38–43
City Hall, 40
City Sightseeing Bus, 4, 12, 28, 158, 159
Clanwilliam, 144–145
Classical music, 40, 110
Clifton Beaches, 16, 70, 74, 75
Climate, 154, 155, 156
Clock Tower, 12
Clock Tower Centre, 12, 31
Coastal Kayaking, 74

Coetzee, JM, 170
Comedy festival, 106, 113, 155
Company Gardens, 46–47, 129, 155
Computicket, 63, 114, 155, 156
Constantia (market), 33
Constantia Uitsig, 22
Consulates, 160
Cover charges, 104
Cricket, 114
Crossroads settlement, 25
Crossroads Wines, 172
CTICC. See Cape Town International Convention Centre
Currency, 161
Curries, 167, 168

D
Da Gama, Vasco, 144, 164
Dance clubs, 101–102
Darling, 143
Darling Street, 40–41
Day of Goodwill, 161
Day of Reconciliation, 161
Day trips and excursions, 132–152
    Route 62, 146–150, 152
    West Coast, 142–145, 152
    Whale Coast, 132–135
    Winelands, 136–141, 151
Deep-sea fishing, 74
De Klerk, FW, 11, 13, 167
Delheim (vineyard), 137
De Tuynhuys, 48
Devil's Peak, 74
De Waterkant neighborhood, 16, 50, 53, 102
Dialing codes, 162–163
Diamonds, 65
Diamonds of Africa (store), 31, 56, 65
Dias, Bartolomeu, 39, 164
Dine (magazine), 168
Dining. See also Restaurant Index
    best bets, 84
    maps, 80–83
    along Route 62, 148, 150
    on West Coast, 144
    on Whale Coast, 135
    in Winelands, 138, 141, 151
Dining Out (magazine), 93, 156
Disabilities, travelers with, 164

District Six, 24, 166
District Six Museum, 24, 25, 40
Diving, 75
Doctors, 160
Downhill Adventures, 17, 71, 74
Driving, 17, 135, 141, 145, 150, 157–159
Drostdy Museum, 150
Duiker Island, 17
Dungeons Beach, 71
Dutch East India Company, 40, 47, 54, 149, 165

E
Easter Monday, 161
Eat In (magazine), 93
Eat Out (magazine), 93, 168
Electricity, 160
Embassies, 160
Emergencies, 160
Encounters South African International Documentary Festival, 106, 111
Endeavor Safaris, 164
Everard Road, 60, 61
Exchange rate, 161

F
Fairview (vineyard), 139
False Bay, 18–19, 78
Family Day, 161
Fashion designers, 62–63
Fehr Collection, 40
Ferryman's Tavern, 98, 100
Festivals, 113, 154–155
FIFA World Cup, 40, 53, 159, 167
Film festivals, 111, 155
Fireman's Arms (bar), 98, 100
First National Bank, 41
Fish Hoek Beach, 19, 70
Fishing, 74
Flamingo Tours, 164
Flea markets, 32, 33, 40, 53
Flower farms and markets, 40–41, 143
Food, gourmet, 34–36
Four Passes Route, 140
Franschhoek, 4, 139, 165
Franschhoek Pass, 140
Franschhoek Wine Route, 140–141
Freedom Day, 161
Full-day tours, 8–22
    one day, 8–13
    two day, 14–19
    three day, 20–22
Funicular rides, 18

G

Gansbaai, 75
Gardens
    Company Gardens,
      46–47, 129, 155
    Harold Porter Botanic
      Gardens, 135
    Karoo National Botani-
      cal Garden, 149
    Kirstenbosch National
      Botanical Garden,
      21–22, 77, 78, 106,
      111, 154
Gay and lesbian travelers,
  125, 127, 160–161
    clubs for, 53, 102–103
    special events for, 102,
      111, 154
Gay Pride (festival), 102
Geyser Island, 75
Giovanni's Deliworld, 35
Glen Beach, 69
Golden Acre Shopping Com-
  plex, 40
Gold of Africa Museum,
  52–53, 90
Golf, 127
Good Friday, 161
Gordimer, Nadine, 170
Gordon's Bay, 133, 134
Government Avenue, 44–49
Grand Arena, 112, 113
Grand Parade, 40, 46
GrandWest Casino, 98, 101,
  112, 113
Greater Hermanus Tourism
  Bureau, 135
Great Synagogue, 49, 163
Green Dolphin (music
  venue), 106, 110
Greenmarket Square, 32, 41
Green Point Flea Market, 33,
  53
Green Point neighborhood,
  16, 50, 53–54
Green Point Stadium, 16, 53
Groot Constantia, 22
Groote Kerk (Large Church),
  45
Group Areas Act, 25, 166
Guesthouses, 120–122, 124–
  126, 152
Guguletu township, 25

H

Harold Porter Botanic Gar-
  dens, 135
Heerengracht, 39–40
Helicopter rides, 74
Helshoogte Pass, 140

Hemisphere (club), 98, 102
Heritage Day, 161
Heritage Square, 51
Hermanus, 5–6, 135
Hermanus Whale Festival,
  135, 155
Hiking, 11, 73, 78, 137, 144
Hindu places of worship, 163
Historical attractions and
  museums
    Bo-Kaap Museum, 51
    Cape Town Holocaust
      Centre, 49
    in Clanwilliam, 145
    District Six Museum, 24,
      25, 40
    Drostdy Museum, 150
    Groot Constantia, 22
    Heritage Square, 51
    Huguenot Museum,
      139–140
    Irma Stern Museum, 21
    Kleinplasie Open-air
      Museum, 149
    Koopmans-De Wet
      House, 42, 43
    Maritime Centre
      museum, 11–12
    Paarl Museum, 139
    Robben Island, 4, 6, 12,
      13, 54, 74
    Rust en Vreugd, 48–49
    Slave Lodge Museum,
      46, 165
    in Tulbagh, 148
    Village Museum, 137
    William Fehr Collection,
      40
Holiday Nanny, 29
Holidays, 161
Homeland Tours, 71
Hooked on Africa, 74
Hopper helicopter rides, 74
Horseback riding, 71, 75
Horse races, 114, 154
Hostels, 120–122, 124, 135,
  141, 151
Hot-air ballooning, 73
Hotel bars, 103
Hotels. See Accommoda-
  tions Index
Hot springs, 149, 152
Houses of Parliament, 47
Hout Bay, 17, 33, 70, 74
Huguenot Museum,
  139–140
Human Rights Day, 161

I

Indian curries, 168
Insurance, 161

Integrated Rapid Transit
  (IRT), 159
International Gay and Les-
  bian Travel Association
  (IGLTA), 161
Internet access, 161
Irma Stern Museum, 21

J

Jazzathon, 113
Jazz music, 110, 111, 113
J&B Met, 106, 114, 154
Jewelry, 65–66
Jo'burg (muisc venue), 98,
  103
Johans Borman Fine Art, 61
Jonkershoek Nature
  Reserve, 137

K

Kalk Bay, 19
Kalk Bay Theatre, 112
Kamikaze Kanyon, 73
Karoo National Botanical
  Garden, 149
Kayaking, 74
Kenilworth Race Course,
  114, 154
Khayelitsha settlement, 25
Kirstenbosch National Botan-
  ical Garden, 21–22, 77, 78,
  106, 111, 154
Kite-boarding, 74, 143
Klein Constantia, 22
Kleinplasie Open-air
  Museum, 149
Kloofing, 73
Kloof Street, 43
Kommetjie, 71
Koopmans-De Wet House,
  42, 43
KWV Cellars, 139

L

Labia (cinema), 106, 110
Labia on Kloof (cinema), 110
Laborie (vineyard), 139
Lamb, Karoo, 167
Lambert's Bay, 145
La Med (bar), 100
La Motte (vineyard), 140
Langa township, 25
Langebaan, 143
Langeberg Mountains, 149
Lanzerac (vineyard),
  137–138
Leopard Lounge, 98, 103
Lion's Head, 16, 75
Little Theatre, 112
Llandudno Beach, 70–71

Lodging
along Route 62, 149, 152
best bets, 120. See also Accommodations Index
maps, 116–119
on West Coast, 152
on Whale Coast, 135
in Winelands, 141, 151
Loft Lounge, 98, 103
Long Beach, 71
Long Street, 6, 43
Lost property, 161
Lutheran Church, 52
Luthuli, Alfred, 11

M

Mail, 161
Malls, 6, 31–32, 40, 41, 53, 60
Mandela, Nelson, 6, 11, 13, 40, 45, 166, 167, 171
Mandela Rhodes Place, 45, 46
Manenberg's Jazz Café, 111
Marathons, 77, 155
Marimba (music venue), 104
Maritime Centre museum, 11
Markets, 4, 33, 35
Martin Melck House, 52
Masque Theatre, 113
Maynardville Open Air Theatre, 106, 111, 112
McGregor, 149
Medical emergencies, 160
Melck, Martin, 52
Mercury Live & Lounge, 98, 104
Metrorail, 159
Michaelis Collection, 42
Military Museum, 40
Minibus taxis, 158
Mini-golfing, 28
Mitchell's Brewery, 98, 100
Mobile phones, 156
Money, 161
Montagu, 149
Mosques, 163
Mossel Bay, 133
Mother City Queer Project, 102
Motorbikes, 159
Mouille Point, 4, 28, 53–54
Mountain biking, 17, 74, 78
Mount Rochelle (vineyard), 140
Mr Pickwicks (café), 43
MTN Science Centre, 29
Muizenberg Beach, 19, 71

Museums. See also Art galleries and museums; Historical attractions and museums
Gold of Africa Museum, 52–53
Military Museum, 40
Slave Church Museum, 43
South Africa Museum, 49
South African Jewish Museum, 49
Music
classical, 40, 110
at festivals, 154, 155
jazz, 110, 111, 113
shopping for, 66
venues for, 43, 103–104, 111
Mutual Heights, 40

N

National Woman's Day, 161
Nederburg (vineyard), 139
Neethlingshof (vineyard), 138
Neighborhood walks, 38–54
Bo-Kaap to Green Point, 50–54
City Center, 38–43
Government Avenue, 44–49
Neighbourgoods Market, 4, 33, 35
Neighbourhood Bar & Lounge, 100
Nelson Mandela Gateway, 12, 13
Nelson's Creek (vineyard), 139
New Beginning (vineyard), 172
Newlands Cricket Ground, 114
Newlands Rugby Stadium, 114, 125
New Year's Day, 161
Nightlife, 96–104
along Kloof Street, 43
bars and pubs, 99–101
best bets, 98
casino, 101
cover charges, 104
dance clubs, 101–102
gay and lesbian clubs, 102–103
hotel bars, 103
live music venues, 103–104
maps, 96–97, 99

Nobel Square, 11
Noon Day Gun, at Signal Hill, 78
Noordhoek Beach, 17, 71, 75
Nudist beaches, 70–71
Nu-Metro (cinema), 110, 111
Nursery Ravine, 78

O

Obz Café, 114
Obz Festival, 154
Old Biscuit Mill, 4, 35
Old Mutual Summer Sunset Concerts, 154
Old Mutual Two Oceans Marathon, 77, 155
Old Post Office, 40
Old Town House, 41–42
On Broadway (theatre), 106, 114
Open-air performance venues, 111
Opera, 112
Ostriches, 18, 167–168
Outdoor activities, 68–78
adventure sports, 72–75
beaches, 68–71
parks and nature reserves, 76–78
Out in Africa (film festival), 111

P

Paarl, 4, 73, 138–139
Paarl Museum, 139
Paarl Wine Route, 139
Pan African Market, 33
Para-Pax, 75
Paragliding, 75
Parks and nature reserves, 76–78. See also Gardens
Cape of Good Hope Nature Reserve, 18, 77
Cederberg Wilderness Area, 144
Jonkershoek Nature Reserve, 137
Rondevlei Nature Reserve, 77, 78
Signal Hill, 78
Silvermine Nature Reserve, 78
Table Mountain National Park, 10, 18, 78
Tokai Forest, 78
West Coast National Park, 143

Parliament building, 47
Passports, 162
Paternoster, 144
Penguins, 5, 18, 69, 74, 122, 135
Performing arts, 106–114
  ballet and opera, 112
  best bets, 106
  classical music, 40, 110
  film, 110
  jazz music, 110, 111
  maps, 107–109
  open-air venues, 111
  theatres, 111–114
Pharmacies, 162
Photographic supplies, 66
Piekenierskloof Pass, 144
Pink Map of Cape Town, 102, 160
Places of worship, 163
Planetarium, 27, 49
Planet Champagne Bar, 98, 103
Plattekfip Gorge, 73, 78
Police, 162
Porter Estate Produce Market, 33
Postage, 161
Postnet (company), 161
Prestwich Memorial, 53
Pubs, 11, 100

Q
Quay Four (pub), 11

R
Rafiki's (bar), 100
Rand, 161
Rappeling, 73
Ratanga Junction, 29
Red Shed, 31
Religious sites
  Auwal Masjid Mosque, 51, 163
  Bo-Kaap Museum, 51
  Great Synagogue, 49, 163
  Groote Kerk (Large Church), 45
  Lutheran Church, 52
  places of worship, 163
  St George's Cathedral, 46, 106, 110
  Slave Church Museum, 43
  South African Jewish Museum, 49
Relish (bar), 101
Restaurant reviews, 93
Restaurants. See Dining
Rhodes, Cecil John, 21, 45, 47

Rhodes Memorial, 21
Rikki Taxis, 158
Robben Island, 4, 6, 12, 13, 54, 74
Robertson, 149
Robertson Valley Wine Route, 149
Rondevlei Nature Reserve, 77, 78
Rooiels, 134
Route 62 (highway), 146–150, 152
Roxy Revue Bar, 113
Rugby, 114, 155
Rust en Vreugd, 48–49

S
Safety, 70, 162
St Andrews Square, 53
St George's Cathedral, 46, 106, 110
St George's Mall, 41
St Helena Bay, 144
St Helena Day, 144
Sandbar (bar), 101
Sand-boarding, 74
Sandy Bay, 70–71
SAN-Parks (South Africa National Parks), 42
Science center, 29
Scooters, 159
Seaforth Beach, 71
Seals, 17
Sea Point neighborhood, 16
Sea Point Promenade, 4, 28–29
Sea Point Swimming Pool, 28–29
Shark Alley, 75
Shark Diving Unlimited, 75
Sharks, 70
Shell Building, 41
Shimansky Collection (store), 31, 56, 65
Shopping, 6, 30–33, 56–66
  antiques, 60
  best bets, 56
  books, 61
  for children's clothes and toys, 66
  fashion and accessories, 62–63
  gifts and souvenirs, 63–64
  gourmet food and wine, 34–36
  health and beauty, 64
  home décor, 64–65
  jewelry, 65–66
  malls, 6, 31–32, 40, 41, 53, 60
  maps, 57–59

music, 66
  photography, 66
  souvenirs, 31
  at V&A Waterfront, 10, 11
Signal Hill, 4, 78
Signal Hill Winery, 45–46
Silvermine Nature Reserve, 78
Simonsig (vineyard), 138
Simon's Town, 18–19
Sir Lowry's Pass, 133, 140
Sisulu, Walter, 166
Sitter 4 U, 29
Skeleton Gorge, 78
Slave Church Museum, 43
Slave Lodge Museum, 46, 165
Sleepy Hollow Horse Riding, 75
Smith, Wilbur, 170–171
Smoking, 162
Soccer, 40, 53, 159, 167
Somerset West, 133
Somerset West Strand, 133
South Africa
  cuisine of, 167–168
  language of, 161, 168–169
South Africa Museum, 49
South Africa National Parks (SAN-Parks), 42
South African Council of Churches, 45
South African Jewish Museum, 49
South African National Gallery, 48
South African National Library, 47
South African National Parks (SAN-Parks), 42
South African Vintners Alliance, 172
Souvenirs, 31, 63–64
Spas, 123–125, 127–130, 151
Special events, 154–155
Special interest tours, 24–36
  apartheid history, 24–25
  for children, 26–29
  gourmet food and wine, 34–36
  shopping, 30–33
Spier Wine Estate, 138, 151, 154
Sports
  adventure, 72–75
  bicycling. See Bicycles
  cricket, 114
  fishing, 74
  horseback riding, 71, 75
  rugby, 114, 125

soccer, 40, 53, 159, 167
spectator, 114
surfing, 19, 69, 71, 74, 143
Springbok Atlas, 141
Standard Bank, 40
Stellenbosch, 4, 137, 165
Stellenbosch Wine Festival, 155
Stellenbosch Wine Route, 137–138
Ster-Kinekor (cinema), 110
Stern, Irma, 21
Summer concerts, 106, 111, 154
Supper theaters, 114
Surfing, 19, 69, 71, 74, 143
Swellendam, 149
Swimming pools, 28–29
Synagogues, 163

T
Table Bay Diving, 75
Table Mountain, 4, 21, 69, 73, 143, 164
Table Mountain Cableway, 5, 10, 11, 69, 78, 154
Table Mountain National Park, 10, 18, 78
Table View, 74
Taste of Cape Town, 155
Taxes, 66, 162
Taxis, 158
Tea, 5, 36
Telephones, 156, 162–163
Theatre On the Bay, 106, 113
Theater, 111–114
Theatre @ The Pavilion, 113
Theewaterskloof Dam, 140
Theme parks, 29
Three Anchor Bay, 74
Three Continents Film Festival, 111
Tickets, concert, 114
Tiger Tiger (club), 102
TimeOut for Visitors (magazine), 93
Time zone, 164
Tipping, 164
Tobago's (bar), 98, 103
Toilets, 164
Tokai Forest, 78
Tourism offices, 154
Tourist information, 42, 164
Tour operators, 17, 25, 141
Tours, guided, 164
of Cape Peninsula, 17
of Castle of Good Hope, 40
of Groot Constantia, 22
of Robben Island, 13

Slave Lodge Museum, 46
of townships, 5
of West Coast, 145
Townships, 5, 25
Trafalgar Place, 40
Trains, 158
Travel agents, 160
Truth and Reconciliation Commission, 45, 167
Tulbagh, 148
Tutu, Desmond, 11, 45, 46, 166, 167
Twelve Apostles (mountains), 17, 69, 74
Two Oceans Aquarium, 12, 27
Two Oceans Aquarium Diving, 75

U
Union Castle Building, 11–12

V
Van der Stehl, Simon, 165
Van Riebeeck, Jan, 39, 54, 139, 164
Van Ryn's Brandy Cellar, 138
VAT refunds, 66, 162
Vaughn Johnson Wine and Cigar Shop, 36
Vergelegen (vineyard), 138
Vertigo (club), 102
Victoria Wharf (mall), 31
Viljoens Pass, 140
Village Museum, 137
Vineyards, 137–141, 172
Visas, 162

W
Walker Bay, 5–6, 134, 135, 155
Walking around, 28, 54, 159
Wanderwoman, 160
Waterfront Craft Market, 31
Weather, 154, 155, 156
Websites, useful, 156, 173
Wellington, 148
Wellness Market, 31
West Coast, 142–145, 152
West Coast National Park, 143
Western Province Rugby, 155
Whale Coast, 132–135
Whale watching, 5–6, 134, 155
Wi-Fi access, 161
Wildflowers, 143
William Fehr Collection, 40

Winchester Mansions Hotel, 111
Wine, 21, 34–36, 139, 171–172
Wine estates, 22
Wine Industry Transformation Charter, 172
Winelands, 4, 73, 136–141, 151
Winesense (bar), 46
Woolworths, 61
Worcester, 148–149
Worcester Wine Route, 149
Workers Day, 161
World Heritage Site, 4, 6, 12, 13, 54, 74
World of Birds, 28

Y
Youth Day, 161
Yzerfontein, 143

Z
Zula Sound Bar, 104

Accommodations Index
1 on Queens, 121
18 on Crox, 120, 121
Abalone Guest House (Hermanus), 135
Adderley Hotel, 121
Alta Bay, 121
Ashanti Lodge, 121
Auberge La Dauphine (Franschhoek), 151
Avalon Springs Hotel (Montagu), 149, 152
Backpack, 120–122
Bay Hotel, 120, 122
Bayview Penthouses, 122
Bellevue Manor, 122
Boulders Beach Lodge, 122
Breakwater Lodge, 122
Brenwin Guest House, 122
Bushmanskloof (Cederberg Wilderness Area), 152
Cape Cadogan Hotel, 122
Cape Diamond Hotel, 120, 122–123
Cape Grace Hotel, 120, 123
Cape Heritage Hotel, 51, 120, 123
Cape Hollow Hotel, 123
Cape Milner Hotel, 123
Cat and Moose, 124
Chapman's Peak Hotel, 88–89, 124
Colona Castle, 124
Commodore, 124
Constantia Uitsig, 22

Constantia Uitsig Hotel, 120, 124
Daddy Long Legs, 120, 124–125
De Kloof (Swellendam), 152
De Waterkant Village, 125
Dongola House, 125
D'Ouwe Werf (Stellenbosch), 151
Ellerman House, 125
Extreme, Fire & Ice Hotel, 125
Farmhouse Hotel (Langebaan), 152
Fountains Hotel, 125
Four Rosemead, 125
Glen Boutique Hotel, 120, 125
Grand Daddy, 120, 126
Grand Roche (Paarl), 151
Greenways Hotel, 125–126
Hermanus Backpackers, 135
Hotel Graeme, 126
Hotel Le Vendome, 126
Hout Bay Manor, 126
Kensington Place, 126
Lambert's Bay Hotel, 152
Lanzerac Hotel & Spa (Stellenbosch), 151
Le Quartier Français (Franschhoek), 151
Lions Kloof Lodge, 126
Loloho Lodge, 127
Long Beach, 127
Marine (Hermanus), 135
Montagu Country Hotel, 152
Mont Rochelle (Franschhoek), 151
Mount Nelson Hotel, 5, 36, 120, 127
O on Kloof, 127
Paternoster Hotel, 152
Premier Hotel Cape Manor, 127
Primi Royal, 127
Radisson SAS Hotel, 120, 127
Romney Park Luxury Suites, 127
Spier Hotel (Stellenbosch), 151
Steenberg Hotel, 127–128
Stillness Manor & Spa, 128
Stumble Inn (Stellenbosch), 141, 151
Sugar Hotel, 120, 128
Table Bay Hotel, 128
Table Mountain Lodge, 128–129
Tarragona Lodge, 129
Townhouse Hotel, 129
Tudor Hotel, 129

Tulbagh Country Guest House, 152
Twelve Apostles Hotel & Spa, 120, 129
Urban Chic, 120, 129
Victoria & Alfred Hotel, 129
Villa Lutzi, 129
Vineyard Hotel and Spa, 129–130
Westin Grand Arabella Quays Hotel, 120, 130
Whale View Manor, 120, 130
Winchester Mansions Hotel, 111, 130

Restaurant Index
95 Keerom, 85
221 Waterfront, 85
Addis in Cape, 85
Africa Café, 51, 84, 85
Anatoli, 85
Andiamo, 53
Arnold's, 85–86
Asoka, 86
Aubergine, 86
Azure, 84, 86
Baia, 84, 86
Balducci's, 86
Belthazar, 84, 86–87
Beluga, 87
Benkei, 87
Bientang's Cave (Hermanus), 135
Black Marlin, 18
Blues, 84, 87
Blue Water Café, 87
Bohemian Yard, 87
Bon Appétit, 87
Boschendal, 141
Boseman's Restaurant (Paarl), 151
Brass Bell, 87
Bravo, 54
Bukhara, 84, 87
Café Maxim, 87
Café Paradiso, 87–88
Cape Colony, 84, 88
Cape Town Fish Market, 88
Catharina's, 84, 88
Caveau, 52, 88
Chapman's Peak Hotel, 88–89
Chef Pon's Asian Kitchen, 84, 89
Codfather, 84, 89
Company Gardens Tea Room, 47
Daawat, 89
De Goewerneur Restaurant, 40
Dias Tavern, 89

District Six Museum Café, 25
Dunes, 84, 89
Emily's, 84, 89
Empire Café, 89
Fiesta Tapas Café Bar, 89
Fish On the Rocks, 70
Five Flies, 89–90
Fork, 84, 90
Fynbos Deli, 22
Giovanni's Deliworld, 35
Gold Restaurant, 90
Greens on Park, 27
Harbour House, 90
Hildebrand, 90
Ici (Franschhoek), 151
Josephine's, 33
Kalky's, 90
La Colombe, 22, 84, 90
Long Street Café, 43
Mama Africa, 90–91
Manos, 91
Melissa's, 36
Miller's Thumb, 91
Miss K Food Café, 91
Mount Nelson Hotel, 5, 36
Moyo (Stellenbosch), 138
Newport, 29
Nose Restaurant & Wine Bar, 98, 100
Nyoni's Kraal, 91
Old Mill (Swellendam), 150
Paranga, 91–92
Paulaner Bräuhaus, 13, 92
Pepenero, 92
Pigalle, 84, 92
Posticino, 92
Pure, 84, 92
Quay Four, 11
Rhodes Memorial Restaurant, 21
Salt, 92–93
Salty Sea Dog, 93
Savoy Cabbage, 84, 93
Shelley's, 93
Signal, 93
Simply Asia, 93
Societi Bistro, 93, 94
Strandloper (Langebaan Beach), 144
Tank, 84, 94
Tasting Room (Franschhoek), 151
Theo's, 84, 94
Things I Love (Tulbagh), 148
Tom Yum, 94
Two Oceans, 18
Victoria Wharf Food Court, 32
Wakame, 84, 94
Waves (Lambert's Bay), 152
Wharfside Grill, 94
Winesense, 46
Yindee's, 94

Photo **Credits**

Notes

Explore over 3,500 destinations.

Frommers.com makes it easy.

Find a destination. ✓ Book a trip. ✓ Get hot travel deals.
Buy a guidebook. ✓ Enter to win vacations. ✓ Listen to podcasts.
Check out the latest travel news. ✓ Share trip photos and memories.
And much more.

day BY day

Get the best of a city in 1,2 or 3 days

Day by Day Destinations

Frommer's®
A Branded Imprint of **WILEY**

Available wherever books are sold